COMPETENCE IN ENGLISH

A FRESH LOOK AT THE BASICS

SECOND EDITION

Competence in English

A FRESH LOOK AT THE BASICS

— SECOND EDITION

WITH DIAGNOSTIC AND MASTERY TESTS

J. N. Hook

University of Illinois at Urbana

 Harcourt Brace Jovanovich, Inc.

New York   Chicago   San Francisco   Atlanta

ISBN: 0-15-512426-9

Library of Congress Catalog Card Number: 77-71157

Printed in the United States of America

TO THE INSTRUCTOR

Competence in English: A Fresh Look at the Basics, Second Edition, is intended to help students who have not yet mastered the essentials of syntax, diction, mechanics, and usage, as well as other fundamentals that are discussed in a new section, "Gaining Respect for Your Ideas." Presented here, in a straightforward manner and with an attempt to avoid both a martinet's insistence on debatable rules and a permissivist's assumption that anything goes, are those basics I consider essential for the student who may never be a master writer but who will need to write in order to conduct his or her own affairs and perhaps those of an employer.

Competence in English makes students largely responsible for their own learning. Each unit opens with a concise explanation of a principle or of closely related principles, continues with modified programed material intended to illustrate the principles and to provide drill on them, and concludes with a set of sentences or other items that may be written out or, if the instructor prefers, used for class practice or discussion.

The exercises in Section B of each unit require students to read actively; they cannot simply let their eyes drift idly down the page. They must make a written response in each exercise (an average of a dozen responses per unit). The required answers are obvious enough so that students will seldom make mistakes: when they do respond improperly, they are expected to go back and reread to determine the reasons for their errors and to see why a different answer is preferable. This modified programing helps students to understand the reasons behind most of the principles. Instead of being presented as a dictum from higher authority, the principles are shown to be based on the inherent characteristics and rationale of the English language. Finally, the programing saves the instructor precious time from paper grading. Students in effect grade their own work as they proceed, checking immediately the correctness of each response.

The terminology used in *Competence in English* is generally traditional, but frequently includes insights provided by structural and transformational grammarians and by scholars of English usage. The indebtedness shows up particularly in Part 2, "The Sentence," where I have made considerable use of what transformational grammarians have taught concerning long sentences as combinations of basic or "kernel" sentences.

Competence in English may be used in any one of these ways:

1. An instructor who does not want to devote class time to syntax, usage, and the like may merely ask students to do their exercises on their own to overcome whatever difficulties they are having.

2. Another instructor may require each student to work specific exercises or groups of exercises in accordance with individual needs. For instance, a student with punctuation troubles may be advised to work the entire series on punctuation independently.

3. Individualization may be carried further by use of the self-scoring diagnostic test, which can show students which units they should study. Students are told that they are responsible for their own improvement in the areas where they missed one or more items. Throughout the term they work independently on the units assigned them by the test. (Instructors may, if they wish, check periodically to make sure that the work is being done; an end-of-term flurry of activity by a student would be unrewarding, even counterproductive.) By the end of the term students are expected to have overcome the weaknesses revealed by the diagnostic test. A mastery test, similar in form and difficulty, is included for use as a final check. Users of the first edition, however, have preferred to stress not test scores but the quality of the student's writing at the end of the term; the mastery test, which ordinarily reveals considerable improvement, then serves to strengthen student self-confidence.

4. Another method of individualization involves marking of compositions. When the instructor finds, say, an *either . . . or* fallacy, he or she makes a marginal note (CIE *either . . . or*, or just *Unit 5* if a numerical system seems preferable) that tells the student to do Unit 5. Another student may be sent to the unit on figures of speech, another to the unit on apostrophes in contractions, and so on. Thus students are given the specific help that they need *when they need it*, without wasting the class time of others who do not share this particular deficiency. (Ordinarily no more than three or four units should be assigned to a student in connection with a single composition, for little is learned or retained if too many units are assigned at once.)

5. Still another instructor may wish to discuss in class the units that a number of students need. If, for example, half or more of the students are having trouble with misplaced modifiers, a few minutes or even an hour may be rewardingly spent on Units 18 and 19.

6. It is also possible to use this book for more extensive class discussion. The instructor assigns two or three units, has the students work out the exercises at home, and discusses with them in class the commentary and exercises.

This second edition differs in a number of ways from the first. The following fifteen units are totally new:

Unit 1: The Unwise Generalization
Unit 2: Qualifying
Unit 3: Separating Opinions and Facts
Unit 4: Avoiding Stereotypes
Unit 5: Avoiding the *either . . . or* Fallacy
Unit 6: Logical Relationships
Unit 8: Editing and Proofreading
Unit 9: The Basic Sentences of English
Unit 14: Other Ways to Combine Sentences
Unit 25: Some Nonstandard Expressions
Unit 27: Words Often Confused (I)

In addition, all the other units have been reorganized, many examples have been changed, and a number of explanations have been simplified. Some units have been combined, and two or three of the more esoteric have been eliminated.

The general goal has been to make the book even more useful than before for students whose previous preparation has not brought them up to a satisfactory level of competence. I have especially kept in mind remedial English classes, classes in adult education, and classes in institutions that admit students of widely varying backgrounds.

J. N. H.

TO THE STUDENT

Competence in English is designed to help you master the basic principles of writing you have not yet learned to apply satisfactorily. A diagnostic test is included to help you discover your individual needs, and a mastery test will enable you later on to determine how well you have succeeded.

The major part of each of the seventy-five units in the book is self-instructional. Each unit consists of three parts:

Section A summarizes the principle and provides any other needed explanation. Study it carefully.

Section B is modified programed material, requiring you to write an answer for each exercise.

Section C consists of supplementary exercises, which your instructor may want you to do only for your own enlightenment, may use for class discussion, or may have you write and hand in. It gives added practice to reinforce what you have learned in Sections A and B.

In doing Section B, you may find it helpful to follow these suggestions:

1. *Work slowly and thoughtfully*. It is possible to rush through an exercise in a few minutes and perhaps even to get all the answers right. But doing so may not improve your writing, because you may not thoroughly understand what you are doing. It is much better to ponder each exercise, trying to understand exactly what is being presented and why, and what its significance is for your own writing.

2. *Check each of your answers as soon as you have written it*. The answers to the exercises are at the end of each unit. Unless answers are labeled MODEL, yours should be exactly like the printed ones. When model answers are given, yours should be basically similar but may not use the exact words. This immediate check is to show whether or not you are on the right track and helps you to correct any misunderstanding.

3. *Reread as much as necessary*. The exercises in this book are intended to be reread. If, for instance, in exercise 7 you discover that you need something from exercises 1 and 2 that you have not completely grasped, reread exercises 1 and 2. Or if at any time you answer incorrectly, go back and reread as much as necessary to understand why the correct response is correct.

4. *Don't cheat yourself*. It's easy to cheat with Competence in English, but you alone will lose if you do so. To cheat, all you need to do is look at an answer before writing your own. Cheating will give you a perfect score, but it won't help you to learn. The profit from Competence in English comes less from

having correct answers than from writing well in your next composition and from writing well throughout your life. The answers, then, aren't really important. What is important is your understanding of principles and the ability to apply those principles.

Your instructor may use *Competence in English* in any of a number of ways, perhaps including some class discussion. It is possible that on the basis of either the diagnostic test or the marginal marks on your compositions he or she will use it to individualize instruction. When you take the diagnostic test, which is self-scoring, its results will show you which of the seventy-five units you especially need to study during the term; your classmates may need to study either fewer or more units than you need. Similarly, if your instructor decides to individualize by means of his or her marks on your compositions, your classmates may be assigned different exercises because their problems are not necessarily the same as yours.

If you repeat an error, you may be assigned the same exercise more than once. If so, erase your answers in Section B, restudy Section A, and rewrite your answers to Section B.

Competence in English lets you assume major responsibility for mastering the fundamentals. It provides information and help, but the success of your learning depends on you.

J. N. H.

CONTENTS

CONTENTS

COMPETENCE IN ENGLISH

A FRESH LOOK AT THE BASICS

SECOND EDITION

DIAGNOSTIC TEST

Instructions for Taking the Diagnostic Test

The purpose of this self-scoring test is to discover the extent of your knowledge and also your specific weaknesses in sentence structure, certain matters of diction and usage, punctuation, and other mechanics of writing, as well as your knowledge of certain means of gaining respect for your ideas expressed in writing. The results may be used as a guide to what you particularly need to study.

The test consists of seventy-five groups of four sentences each. You are to select the sentence or sentences in each group that are well constructed and that conform to presently accepted standards of usage, punctuation, and the like. You are to do nothing with the poor sentences.

Insert a carbon paper (shiny side up) behind each page in turn. (Do not look at the backs of the pages, for the test results may be invalidated. The diagnosis, not the score on the test, is what is important.) As a basic procedure you should encircle the number corresponding to each sentence that you consider *acceptable in modern standard and reasonably formal writing*. For some groups you will be given special instructions; a few others are obviously intended to represent a conversational situation in which a high degree of formality would not be appropriate. In some groups you may not find it necessary to encircle any number. In others you may need to encircle one, two, three, or even all four numbers. Think before you draw your circles. Do not black out the numbers and *do not erase*. If you want to change an answer, mark an **X** through the undesired answer, and then indicate in the usual way the answer you believe to be correct.

Tabulating Test Results

When you encircle the numbers, your answers are recorded on the back of the test page. You will find the correct answers there, alongside your own encircled answers. After you have completed the entire test, make a check mark on the line provided with each group if you missed one or more items in the group.

On the Record Sheets following the test enter a check mark for any group in which you made one or more errors.

Your total score on the diagnostic test is not especially significant, but if you want to determine it for any reason, count the number of your correct responses. The possible total is 117 items correctly encircled.

After you have completed your study of any unit in the book, you may want to look again at the group of test sentences for that unit. Do not look at the Mastery Test, however, until you have completed all assigned units.

Be sure to insert a carbon (shiny side up) behind this page.

Part One—Gaining Respect for Your Ideas

In groups 1 and 2 some statements should be qualified in order to be really believable. Choose those that seem satisfactory as they are.

1

Our system for choosing Presidents should be abolished.	1–1
Every community ought to have a museum.	1–2
Our community should have a music museum to honor the ten famous composers and performers who were born here.	1–3
Study of foreign languages improves the mind.	1–4

2

"Good fences make good neighbors."	2–1
Some women are physically stronger than some men.	2–2
After the Industrial Revolution everybody had to work for slave wages in grimy factories.	2–3
Women are more emotional than men.	2–4

In this group choose any statements that are factual or at least possible to check.

3

The French are the most intellectual people in the modern world.	3–1
The discoverer of hydrogen was Henry Cavendish.	3–2
The first state to ratify the Constitution of the United States was Delaware.	3–3
Our football team this year was better than any other team in our school's long history.	3–4

In groups 4 and 5 select any statements that you believe most thoughtful persons would be willing to accept as true.

4

Officers of corporations are greedy.	4–1
Professional athletes have little formal education	4–2
Many towns have historically interesting names.	4–3
Sometimes athletics do the participants more harm than good.	4–4

1–1

1–2

1–3

1–4

This group tests your ability to distinguish between unwise generalizations and statements that are sufficiently specific. You should have encircled 1–3 but no other number.

_____ Check here if you missed any item.

2–1

2–2

2–3

2–4

This group tests your ability to distinguish satisfactory statements from those that need some qualifying. You should have encircled 2–2 but no other number.

_____ Check here if you missed any item.

3–1

3–2

3–3

3–4

This group tests your ability to distinguish factual or checkable statements from those that represent only opinion. You should have encircled 3–2 and 3–3 but no other number.

_____ Check here if you missed any item.

4–1

4–2

4–3

4–4

This group tests your ability to distinguish stereotypes from statements that are more defensible. You should have encircled 4–3 and 4–4 but no other number.

_____ Check here if you missed any item.

Be sure to insert a carbon (shiny side up) behind this page.

5

Either a team must win most of its games or the coach gets fired.	5–1
Unless postal rates come down, magazines will be out of business.	5–2
If the rain pours down all day, the St. Louis Cardinals' home baseball game this afternoon will be postponed.	5–3
Either we'll have to avoid "dust bowls" or Americans will starve to death.	5–4

In this group select any statements that seem logical in their wording.

6

Her ambition at that time was a teacher.	6–1
In home economics we are taught how to buy food, how to prepare it, and how to serve it attractively.	6–2
Blood is the most terrifying movie that anyone perhaps ever saw.	6–3
While in Alaska he obtained seven Kodiak bears to be mounted and graduated from the University of Alaska.	6–4

In this group choose the two sentences that would be appropriate in a formal piece of writing.

7

Early flags were often pictorial.	7–1
People in those days went for pictures of rattlesnakes and pine trees and a lot of things like that on their banners.	7–2
Also, they tended to inscribe on their flags mottos such as "Appeal to Heaven" or "Don't Tread on Me."	7–3
Quite a few of the new countries in this day and age haven't yet gone conservative, and they stick pictures on their flags, too.	7–4

5–1
5–2

This group tests your ability to distinguish incorrect *either . . . or* statements from those that admit other possibilities. You should have encircled 5–3 but no other number.

5–3

_____ Check here if you missed any item.

5–4

6–1

This group tests your ability to select statements that are worded in a logical way. You should have encircled 6–2 but no other number.

6–2

6–3

_____ Check here if you missed any item.

6–4

7–1

This group tests your ability to select sentences that are written in relatively formal language. You should have encircled 7–1 and 7–3 but no other number.

7–2

_____ Check here if you missed any item.

7–3

7–4

Be sure to insert a carbon (shiny side up) behind this page.

In this group select any statements that have no editorial slip-ups or misprints.

8

With only two minutes to go, Frank Miller scored a touchdow and Larry Grimes kicked the extra point.   8–1

Among the fabrics especially popular that year were gingham, muslim, and voile.   8–2

A special program on Dante (who wrote the *Inferno*) was presented by the daughter of the author in celebration of the 700th anniversary of his birth.   8–3

Professional Peter Brown and amateur William McCormick were declared the winners yesterday in the Valley open tournament which was canceled because of rain.   8–4

Part Two—The Sentence

In groups 9–15 choose all the sentences that you consider well constructed.

9

Hiram Ulysses Grant changed his name.   9–1

His initials, *H.U.G.*, sometimes embarrassing to him and possibly interfering with his career.   9–2

The West Point registrar mistakenly wrote his name as Ulysses S. Grant.   9–3

Grant liked this name because the initials *U.S.* looked patriotic.   9–4

10

The boys and girls playing near the water.   10–1

The boys and girls near the water.   10–2

The boys and girls are playing near the water.   10–3

The boys and girls played near the water.   10–4

11

It was an hour after lunch. We went swimming. The water was very cold.   11–1

After we had swum for an hour, we lay on the grassy shore until the mosquitoes found us.   11–2

The mosquitoes were ferocious. They were unusually large. They were hungry.   11–3

To escape them, we hurried to the cottage and sprayed ourselves with Bug-off.   11–4

8–1

This group tests your ability to spot careless editing or misprints. You should have encircled no number at all.

8–2

_____ Check here if you missed any item.

8–3

8–4

9–1

This group tests your ability to distinguish a sentence from a fragment. You should have encircled 9–1, 9–3, and 9–4 but not 9–2.

9–2

_____ Check here if you missed any item.

9–3

9–4

10–1

This group tests your ability to recognize sentences containing complete verbs. You should have encircled 10–3 and 10–4 but no other number.

10–2

10–3

_____ Check here if you missed any item.

10–4

11–1

This group tests your ability to recognize undesirably short sentences. You should have encircled 11–2 and 11–4 but no other number.

11–2

_____ Check here if you missed any item.

11–3

11–4

Be sure to insert a carbon (shiny side up) behind this page.

12

Sarah got out of bed, and she stepped on the empty coffee cup beside it, but it was empty, so she swore only mildly.   12–1

She turned on the shower, but there was no hot water.   12–2

Next she was going to brush her teeth, and the toothpaste tube was empty.   12–3

She was disgusted and she was still sleepy and so she went back to bed.   12–4

13

The earthquake occurred late at night, and it killed eight hundred people.   13–1

Because our bus broke down, our team was almost late for the tournament.   13–2

Three of our planes were shot down because I saw the headline in the paper.   13–3

I heard on the news broadcast where stock prices have gone up again.   13–4

14

James Monroe was born on April 28, 1758. This was in Westmoreland County, Virginia. He eventually became our fourth President.   14–1

Monroe, who feared a strong central government, opposed adoption of the Constitution.   14–2

His chief opponent, Alexander Hamilton, was of course in disagreement.   14–3

Today Monroe is best remembered for the Monroe Doctrine, which warned foreign powers to stay out of the Americas.   14–4

15

The farmers in our area still plow their corn frequently, harvest good crops, and plant good seed.   15–1

Careful writers gather their material, choose a point of view, decide on a pattern of organization, write, and revise.   15–2

The members of the orchestra tuned their instruments, the conductor mounted the podium, and the concert began.   15–3

Near the creek I found myself face to face with a half-grown bear, but I had seen its tracks earlier.   15–4

12–1

12–2

12–3

12–4

This group tests your ability to recognize good compound sentences. You should have encircled 12–2 but no other number.

_____ Check here if you missed any item.

13–1

13–2

13–3

13–4

This group tests your recognition of effective subordination. You should have encircled 13–2 but no other number.

_____ Check here if you missed any item.

14–1

14–2

14–3

14–4

This group tests your ability to recognize other effective methods of subordination. You should have encircled 14–2, 14–3, and 14–4 but not 14–1.

_____ Check here if you missed any item.

15–1

15–2

15–3

15–4

This group tests your knowledge of effective arrangement of sentence parts. You should have encircled 15–2 and 15–3 but no other number.

_____ Check here if you missed any item.

Be sure to insert a carbon (shiny side up) behind this page.

In groups 16 and 17 choose the two most emphatic sentences in each group.

16

The sound of a flute, on the other hand, soars effortlessly through the higher ranges.	16–1
The sound of a flute soars effortlessly through the higher ranges, on the other hand.	16–2
Down the home stretch roared car number 13.	16–3
Car number 13 roared down the home stretch.	16–4

17

Van Cliburn performed with his usual brilliance at the piano.	17–1
The piano was played with his usual brilliance by Van Cliburn.	17–2
My grandfather erected a sturdy bridge across the narrow stream.	17–3
A sturdy bridge was erected by my grandfather across the narrow stream.	17–4

Resume choosing all the sentences that you consider well constructed.

18

One cat in our house, which has yellow fur, is the favorite of all of us.	18–1
The man with the big nose that was running down the street is said to be a gangster.	18–2
The room next to the one with the red sofa on which we sat last night is my bedroom.	18–3
The covered bridge across Sugar Creek, which flows through the lovely Indiana countryside, is over one hundred years old.	18–4

19

After seeing *The Sound of Music* three times, its melodies were firmly fixed in my mind.	19–1
Facing toward the north, we could see the dim outlines of the mountains.	19–2
Talking to friends now and then he seems very sad.	19–3
To construct the factory, a bridge first had to be built across the creek.	19–4

16–1

16–2

16–3

16–4

This group tests your understanding of word order as a factor in emphasis. You should have encircled 16–1 and 16–3 but no other number.

_____ Check here if you missed any item.

17–1

17–2

17–3

17–4

This group tests your knowledge of the relative merits of the active and the passive voice as contributors to emphasis. You should have encircled 17–1 and 17–3 but no other number.

_____ Check here if you missed any item.

18–1

18–2

18–3

18–4

This group tests your recognition of logical placement of adjective clauses to prevent ambiguity. You should have encircled 18–3 and 18–4 but no other number.

_____ Check here if you missed any item.

19–1

19–2

19–3

19–4

This group tests your recognition of logical placement of adverbial modifiers, in contrast to "dangling" or "squinting" modifiers. You should have encircled 19–2 but no other number.

_____ Check here if you missed any item.

20

She is always serene, pleasant, and people like to have her around.	20–1
Either he is a fake or a cheat.	20–2
He is either a fake or unreliable.	20–3
A student in good health, willing to work hard, and who has at least average intelligence can succeed in college.	20–4

21

Mike likes the dog more than his sister.	21–1
I enjoyed *Macbeth* better than any of Shakespeare's plays.	21–2
Moses is as strong politically, if not stronger, than Watkins.	21–3
Linda plays better than anyone her age.	21–4

Part Three—Diction

In this group choose the sentences that are most concrete.

22

Any alteration in the status quo is likely to be fraught with risk.	22–1
If the workers go out on strike, the stockholders are likely to lose money.	22–2
The candles were burning low in their holders, and some of the guests were yawning openly.	22–3
Time was moving on with its usual degree of inexorability.	22–4

In this group choose the two sentences that are least slanted for or against the students.

23

Student demonstrators yesterday marched in protest against the government's foreign policy.	23–1
Yelling uproariously, a large gang of students yesterday staged an hour-long march apparently in vague protest against our government's foreign policy.	23–2
A group of students yesterday conducted a carefully planned march to protest some of the debatable parts of the government's foreign policy.	23–3
Yesterday approximately two hundred students marched down Main Street, handing out leaflets protesting the foreign policy of the federal government.	23–4

20–1

20–2

20–3

20–4

This group tests your recognition of parallel structure. You should not have encircled any number.

_____ Check here if you missed any item.

21–1

21–2

21–3

21–4

This group tests your knowledge of accuracy and completeness in the statement of comparisons. You should not have encircled any number.

_____ Check here if you missed any item.

22–1

22–2

22–3

22–4

This group tests your recognition of concrete and abstract words. You should have encircled 22–2 and 22–3 but no other number.

_____ Check here if you missed any item.

23–1

23–2

23–3

23–4

This group tests your knowledge of connotations. You should have encircled 23–1 and 23–4 but no other number.

_____ Check here if you missed any item.

Be sure to insert a carbon (shiny side up) behind this page.

In this group choose the two sentences that make the best use of figurative language.

24

The refrigerator developed a noise like that of an automobile engine idling too rapidly.	24–1
Her hands were as cold as ice, but her face was as red as a beet.	24–2
The old man's harsh voice cawed a warning: "Naw! Naw!"	24–3
The mathematics instructor assigns us oceans of problems, each one as hard to crack as a black walnut.	24–4

In groups 25–31 choose the sentences that you believe use all words correctly.

25

If Grayson would of been elected, our representation would be stronger than it is.	25–1
Workers oughtn't expect to be given raises unless they are willing to work.	25–2
Irregardless of the consequences, the two motorcyclists roared ahead.	25–3
She had left her keys somewheres in the house.	25–4

26

The sergeant looked at me contemptibly, as if I were an insect.	26–1
Widow Perkins must have loved her diseased husband very much.	26–2
She is indeed a progeny of learning.	26–3
I like to wander through old graveyards, reading the epithets on the tombstones.	26–4

27

The effect of the strike was already being felt.	27–1
Most fathers are not averse to giving advise.	27–2
A large amount of accident-caused injuries occur on this site.	27–3
Beside being censured by his employer, he lost two days of his vacation.	27–4

24-1

24-2

24-3

24-4

This group tests your sensitivity to figures of speech. You should have encircled 24–1 and 24–3 but no other number.

_____ Check here if you missed any item.

25-1

25-2

25-3

25-4

This group tests your recognition of certain nonstandard expressions. You should have encircled 25–2 but no other number.

_____ Check here if you missed any item.

26-1

26-2

26-3

26-4

This group tests your knowledge of certain words sometimes confused with other words. You should not have encircled any number.

_____ Check here if you missed any item.

27-1

27-2

27-3

27-4

This group tests your knowledge of certain words sometimes confused with other words. You should have encircled 27–1 but no other number.

_____ Check here if you missed any item.

28

My conscience hurt me because I had devised an ingenious but slightly illicit scheme.

28—1

Hearing such counsel from an eminent lawyer like Judge Corso left me incredulous.

28—2

I would not want to imply that duels are healthy.

28—3

We had less problems than before, but some stupid mistakes continued to detract from our chances.

28—4

29

It's important to build up the morale of the personnel.

29—1

The luxurious growth of the vines is liable to cause troubles with the air conditioners.

29—2

There was a close contest in which Dexter defeated Marsh 2382 to 2370 —a majority of only 12 votes.

29—3

This noted surgeon says that the Golden Rule is the guiding principle of her life.

29—4

30

The coach of the team he wanted a time out.

30—1

We had not sent enough money neither.

30—2

Instances of attempted extortion by employees of the firm are not unknown.

30—3

As the only unelected President, he occupied a unique spot in American history.

30—4

31

All the necessary information that you will need to make your reservation will be sent to you.

31—1

I did not hear the first time and asked the teacher to repeat the question again.

31—2

Crime stories on television are often monotonously alike.

31—3

Far off on the horizon to the north, as far as the eye could see, a tiny black cloud appeared.

31—4

28–1

28–2

28–3

28–4

This group tests your knowledge of certain words sometimes confused with other words. You should have encircled 28–1 and 28–2 but no other number.

_____ Check here if you missed any item.

29–1

29–2

29–3

29–4

This group tests your knowledge of certain words sometimes confused with other words. You should have encircled 29–1 and 29–4 but no other number.

_____ Check here if you missed any item.

30–1

30–2

30–3

30–4

This group tests your recognition of double subjects and double negatives. You should have encircled 30–3 and 30–4 but no other number.

_____ Check here if you missed any item.

31–1

31–2

31–3

31–4

This group tests your alertness to concise expression and your awareness of its opposite—wordiness or redundancy. You should have encircled 31–3 but no other number.

_____ Check here if you missed any item.

Be sure to insert a carbon (shiny side up) behind this page.

In this group choose the two sentences that provide the most specific information.

32

My father is an employee of the executive branch of the federal government.   32–1

My father is a crop inspector for the United States Department of Agriculture.   32–2

Wrens have been known to nest in old hats, bushel baskets, and even rubber boots, all of which they cram full of sticks.   32–3

The nesting habits of birds vary considerably from species to species and are sometimes remarkably idiosyncratic.   32–4

Part Four—Punctuation and Other Mechanics

In groups 33–56, as you choose the best sentences, pay particular attention to punctuation and other mechanical matters.

33

I wonder whether a hacksaw will cut through it.   33–1

Dr. Landers and Mr. J. P. Witham, Sr, both testified for the defense.   33–2

Did you ask, "What is fennel?"?   33–3

Yes!! The tire tracks match exactly!!!   33–4

34

Although Fred favored Jack Marvin was elected.   34–1

Once inside the dog became calm again.   34–2

Even with his gloves on his hands were still cold.   34–3

The battle over the painful mopping-up procedures were still left.   34–4

35

The flag has red yellow and green stripes.   35–1

Wilson opened the top drawer of a large, gray, filing cabinet.   35–2

A wide-eyed, frightened-looking child came to the door.   35–3

Pewter-making in Norwich began in 1730, and metal-manufacturing is still a leading industry.   35–4

32–1

32–2

32–3

32–4

This group tests your ability to distinguish between specific and general statements. You should have encircled 32–2 and 32–3 but no other number.

_____ Check here if you missed any item.

33–1

33–2

33–3

33–4

This group tests your knowledge of terminal punctuation (periods, question marks, and exclamation marks). You should have encircled 33–1 but no other number.

_____ Check here if you missed any item.

34–1

34–2

34–3

34–4

This group tests your knowledge of the use of commas to prevent momentary misreading. You should not have encircled any number.

_____ Check here if you missed any item.

35–1

35–2

35–3

35–4

This group tests your knowledge of the use of commas with coordinate elements (similar types of words, phrases, or clauses). You should have encircled 35–3 and 35–4 but no other number.

_____ Check here if you missed any item.

36

"Sir Edward Lutjens," he explained, "was the English architect who planned New Delhi."   36–1

The roof in contrast has a steep pitch.   36–2

My grandparents first settled in Lincoln Nebraska.   36–3

His first major work, "Symphony in Scarlet," was performed on March 18, 1949.   36–4

37

My mother who grew up in Idaho still loves the mountains.   37–1

A person who has grown up in the mountains usually retains his or her affection for mountainous country.   37–2

The Magna Carta which is one of the most important documents in British history was signed in 1215.   37–3

When he was running down the hill at top speed the boy fell.   37–4

38

The reason is, that the dress is too elegant to wear.   38–1

Their armed forces excelled, on the ground, and in the air, but not on the sea.   38–2

We brought our own light furniture, such as, tables, chairs, and a bedroom suite.   38–3

We brought with us, our own light furniture.   38–4

39

A protractor is semicircular in shape, it is used to measure angles.   39–1

A rhizome is an underground rootlike stem; from it, roots go down and leafy shoots go up.   39–2

The ricer squeezed out long white strings of mashed potatoes; which curled enticingly in the bowl.   39–3

Homonyms are pronounced alike, but they differ from each other in meaning, in origin, and generally in spelling; so, sow, and sew are examples.   39–4

36–1
36–2
36–3

36–4

This group tests your knowledge of the use of commas with interpolated elements such as dates, places, transitions, appositives, and expressions such as *she said*. You should have encircled 36–1 and 36–4 but no other number.

_____ Check here if you missed any item.

37–1

37–2

37–3
37–4

This group tests your knowledge of the use of commas with nonessential (nonrestrictive) clauses and phrases. You should have encircled 37–2 but no other number.

_____ Check here if you missed any item.

38–1

38–2

38–3
38–4

This group tests your understanding of the need to avoid unnecessary commas. Since one or more commas should have been left out of each sentence, you should not have encircled any number.

_____ Check here if you missed any item.

39–1

39–2

39–3

39–4

This group tests your knowledge of the use of semicolons in compound sentences. You should have encircled 39–2 and 39–4 but no other number.

_____ Check here if you missed any item.

Be sure to insert a carbon (shiny side up) behind this page.

40

Charles said: "Why don't we offer to pay for the damages?" 40–1

The declaration begins in this way: "Because the elected officials of this assemblage have grievously neglected their stipulated duties, we, the undersigned, are officially submitting this protest." 40–2

The following states did not vote in favor of the amendment: Alabama, Georgia, Maine, Minnesota, and Wyoming. 40–3

Dear Sir,
    I am writing to inquire about my order of May 9, 1976. 40–4

41

The Evans'es dogs ruined our flowerbeds. 41–1

Ladies' clothing, but not much men's clothing, was strewn all about. 41–2

That dog's bark sounds familiar. Could the dog be your's? 41–3

Two butterfly's were hovering on the thistle's. 41–4

42

Can't you convince her that she's too thin? 42–1

Does'nt the store have the sweater that you're looking for? 42–2

I'd rather not go, but I'll not insist. 42–3

Theyre still in the attic, arent they? 42–4

43

Your 3s and your 5s look oddly alike. 43–1

I seldom use the #s' and the *s' on my typewriter. 43–2

How many *t*'s should there be in *benefited*? 43–3

You use too many *and*'s and *so*'s. 43–4

44

He always was looking for easy money, for an opportunity to strike it rich. 44–1

Getting easy money was less simple than he thought it would be. 44–2

One of the sergeants came running to the captain with a message. 44–3

The first detour that we encountered was one a-
long Route 32. 44–4

40–1

This group tests your knowledge of certain uses of colons. You should have encircled 40–2 and 40–3 but no other number.

_____ Check here if you missed any item.

40–2

40–3

40–4

41–1

41–2

This group tests your knowledge of the use of apostrophes with possessives. You should have encircled 41–2 but no other number.

_____ Check here if you missed any item.

41–3

41–4

42–1

42–2

This group tests your knowledge of the use of apostrophes in contractions. You should have encircled 42–1 and 42–3 but no other number.

_____ Check here if you missed any item.

42–3

42–4

43–1

43–2

This group tests your knowledge of the use of apostrophes in certain rather unusual plurals. You should have encircled 43–3 and 43–4 but no other numbers.

_____ Check here if you missed any item.

43–3

43–4

44–1

This group tests your knowledge of the use of hyphens in dividing words at the ends of lines. You should have encircled 44–3 but no other number.

_____ Check here if you missed any item.

44–2

44–3

44–4

Be sure to insert a carbon (shiny side up) behind this page.

45

I have thirty-eight arrowheads in my collection, but my friend has over one hundred.

45–1

My mother-in-law and her stepdaughter both were interested in the estate left by my great-grandfather.

45–2

About one third of the questionnaires were not returned, and one-seventh of the replies were unusable.

45–3

The well-liked professor was an authority on the H-bomb.

45–4

46

While we were eating—no, I think it happened before we started to eat.

46–1

"What does he," I started to say.
"I'll ask the questions!" the detective interrupted.

46–2

The cornetist—a balding man with a huge belly—was constantly hitting sour notes.

46–3

We ate some of my favorite foods, steak, deviled eggs, bean salad, and cherry shortcake.

46–4

47

The cornerstone (it was made of gray marble) was laid with much ceremony.

47–1

The cornerstone [it was made of gray marble] was laid with much ceremony.

47–2

"When Roosevelt was elected in 1933 [actually 1932], the country was deep in the Depression," the speaker reminded us.

47–3

The Mollusks (see Plate VII) are popularly called *shellfish*.

47–4

48

Irene said "that she had found the ring in an old cupboard."

48–1

"I especially enjoy Steele's short stories," Sally told us.

48–2

"Who first said, "To err is human"? Glenn asked.

48–3

The witness said that Spartle had addressed him "in a loud and raucous voice."

48–4

45–1   This group tests your knowledge of miscellaneous uses of hyphens. You should have encircled all four numbers.

45–2   _____ Check here if you missed any item.

45–3

45–4

46–1   This group tests your knowledge of some of the uses of dashes. You should have encircled 46–1 and 46–3 but no other number.

46–2   _____ Check here if you missed any item.

46–3

46–4

47–1   This group tests your knowledge of the use of parentheses and brackets. You should have encircled 47–1, 47–3, and 47–4 but not 47–2.

47–2

          _____ Check here if you missed any item.

47–3

47–4

48–1   This group tests your knowledge of the use of quotation marks with direct quotations. You should have encircled 48–2 and 48–4 but no other number.

48–2

48–3   _____ Check here if you missed any item.

48–4

Be sure to insert a carbon (shiny side up) behind this page.

49

"After that," Randolph said, "the mongoose trotted down the path."   49-1

"Run"! they screamed.   49-2

Did Professor Gray say, "Tiger beetles are carnivorous?"   49-3

He told us that his short story was called "Shastri;" it dealt with the
India of long ago.   49-4

50

Chapter VII is entitled *Terra Cotta*.   50-1

The article, which he called "The Dances of Ancient Egypt," appeared
in *The Terpsichorean Review*.   50-2

My favorite poem is Henley's Invictus.   50-3

I began reading a short story called *Mrs. Bradley's Temptation*.   50-4

51

"What now?" she asked. "We'll need to get down into the valley,"
Dean told her.   51-1

"The first reason is simple. The scouts will already have reported
our presence.
"The second reason," he went on, "is less obvious. I am talking
about their leader's known aversion to the unusual."   51-2

"Aren't you interested in anything besides surfing?" Clayton asked.
"Is there something else?" she retorted.   51-3

The crowd began shouting. "Foul!" "Throw him out!" "Are you
blind?" "He fouled him!"   51-4

52

His first book, *Adam's Sons*, went almost unnoticed.   52-1

I consider "Harper's" and "Saturday Review" almost indispensable.   52-2

"I am yours," he whispered, "tout à vous."   52-3

The *Times* and the *Tribune* took opposite points of view.   52-4

49–1

49–2

49–3

49–4

This group tests your knowledge of the placement of other punctuation marks with quotation marks. You should have encircled 49–1 but no other number.

_____ Check here if you missed any item.

50–1

50–2

50–3

50–4

This group tests your knowledge of the use of quotation marks with certain kinds of titles. You should have encircled 50–2 but no other number.

_____ Check here if you missed any item.

51–1

51–2

51–3

51–4

This group tests your knowledge of paragraphing of conversation. You should have encircled 51–2, 51–3, and 51–4 but not 51–1.

_____ Check here if you missed any item.

52–1

52–2

52–3

52–4

This group tests your knowledge of the use of italics. You should have encircled 52–1 and 52–4 but no other number.

_____ Check here if you missed any item.

53

Jennifer commented, "he certainly speaks German well."   53–1

"Mr. Dugan paints portraits," Nancy told me, "And he also sculpts—if there is such a word."   53–2

Mrs. Green said that her late husband's hobby had been "whittle art."   53–3

Dear Mr. Brill:

_____

_____

Yours truly,   53–4

54

My Uncle urged me to take Spanish and History.   54–1

My Aunt Agatha wanted me to take Russian and chemistry.   54–2

My own preferences, as I told my mother, were French and geology.   54–3

I said to the professor who was my adviser, "I'm thoroughly confused, professor Egbert. What should I take, professor?"   54–4

55

In English we read the play *Death Of A Salesman*.   55–1

The period of history that fascinates me most is the middle ages.   55–2

Each Spring my thoughts turn again to the West, where I grew up.   55–3

The pagan Gods could be thoroughly confused by a modern Main street.   55–4

56

We delivered one hundred eleven boxes of supplies to Room two thirty-one.   56–1

The Maroons won the game, 64 to 63.   56–2

1917 was the year when the United States entered the war.   56–3

The address is 4116 South Walden Street, Chicago, Illinois 60608.   56–4

53–1

53–2

53–3

This group tests your knowledge of capitalization in sentences and in formal parts of letters. You should have encircled 53–3 and 53–4 but no other number.

_____ Check here if you missed any item.

53–4

54–1

54–2

54–3

This group tests your knowledge of capitalization of school subjects, titles of relatives, and other titles. You should have encircled 54–2 and 54–3 but no other number.

_____ Check here if you missed any item.

54–4

55–1

55–2

55–3

This group tests your knowledge of capitalization of proper names and miscellaneous items. You should not have encircled any number.

_____ Check here if you missed any item.

55–4

56–1

56–2

56–3

56–4

This group tests your knowledge of conventional ways of indicating numbers. You should have encircled 56–2 and 56–4 but no other number.

_____ Check here if you missed any item.

Be sure to insert a carbon (shiny side up) behind this page.

Part Five—Usage

In groups 57–75 be sure that the sentences you select have all their words in the proper forms.

57

Uncle George always brought presents for my sister and I.	57–1
Braden and him were waiting at the top of the stairs.	57–2
They and we were sent in opposite directions.	57–3
Between you and me, I suspect that he drinks too much.	57–4

58

(*On the telephone*) Yes, this is she.	58–1
Two soldiers, the sergeant and him, escaped through the enemy's lines.	58–2
John waited for us girls.	58–3
I enjoy him impersonating politicians.	58–4

59

Alice told her sister that she would have to leave immediately.	59–1
I enjoyed *Moby Dick*. He certainly knows a lot about whaling and even more about human nature.	59–2
I'd like to drive through the South. They say that many highways there are better than in the North.	59–3
The word *philosophy* interests me. Perhaps I would like to become one.	59–4

60

Sometimes a person is inclined to neglect the easiest subject entirely, but this is something you should not do.	60–1
After you have seen the Taj Mahal, no other architectural triumph is likely to impress one so much.	60–2
When a person plays football for a while, other games seem mild to them.	60–3
Somebody has lost their gloves.	60–4

57–1
57–2
57–3
57–4

This group tests your knowledge of the cases of personal pronouns to be used as subjects and objects. You should have encircled 57–3 and 57–4 but no other number.

_____ Check here if you missed any item.

58–1
58–2
58–3
58–4

This group tests your knowledge of the cases of pronouns in predicate nominatives, in appositives, and before gerunds. You should have encircled 58–1 and 58–3 but no other number.

_____ Check here if you missed any item.

59–1

59–2

59–3
59–4

This group tests your knowledge of pronoun reference. You should not have encircled any number.

_____ Check here if you missed any item.

60–1

60–2

60–3
60–4

This group tests your knowledge of consistency in pronoun person and case. You should not have encircled any number.

_____ Check here if you missed any item.

Be sure to insert a carbon (shiny side up) behind this page.

61

Ancient armies and navies had no complex weapons.	61–1
Volleys of shots burst out across the once-peaceful valleys.	61–2
This phenomena is so rare that you may never witness it again.	61–3
The brother-in-laws of two of the alumnus were already candidates.	61–4

62

The French-fried shrimp tasted unusually well.	62–1
The woodwinds section sounds very good this evening.	62–2
His scoring is excellent, but he doesn't play defense very good.	62–3
The workmanship is good. Note how well the joints fit together.	62–4

63

Of the two theories, Jackson's seems more probable.	63–1
This line is more horizontal than that one.	63–2
As for Raymond and McLean, I believe that Raymond speaks most forcefully.	63–3
The Senator tonight was candider than usual.	63–4

64

The players were dressed in shorts or slacks.	64–1
George Anderson is the man from whom I bought my car from.	64–2
Be careful when you step off of the curb.	64–3
Did you see that in the newspaper or television?	64–4

65

The President was awfully eager to have the pact signed.	65–1
It sure was an exciting evening.	65–2
Millicent seemed kind of unhappy.	65–3
The boys were unhurt but somewhat bedraggled.	65–4

61–1
61–2
61–3
61–4

This group tests your knowledge of certain plural forms. You should have encircled 61–1 and 61–2 but no other number.

———— Check here if you missed any item.

62–1
62–2
62–3
62–4

This group tests your knowledge of the use of *good* and *well* and thus indirectly your knowledge of other adjectives and adverbs. You should have encircled 62–2 and 62–4 but no other number.

———— Check here if you missed any item.

63–1
63–2
63–3
63–4

This group tests your knowledge of comparative and superlative uses of adjectives and adverbs. You should have encircled 63–1 but no other number.

———— Check here if you missed any item.

64–1
64–2
64–3
64–4

This group tests your awareness of both omitted prepositions and unnecessary prepositions. You should have encircled 64–1 but no other number.

———— Check here if you missed any item.

65–1
65–2
65–3
65–4

This group tests your knowledge of the use of intensifiers (words such as *very, rather,* and *somewhat*) in formal writing. You should have encircled 65–4 but no other number.

———— Check here if you missed any item.

66

The explanation for the postponements and the delays were hard to believe.   66–1

The bushes, but surprisingly not the tree, was damaged by the storm.   66–2

Each of the three peaks were covered with snow.   66–3

Is either of the typewriters in good working order?   66–4

67

There was no simple explanation for the defeat.   67–1

There was several simple explanations for the defeat.   67–2

Among the trees stand a deserted house.   67–3

Here is some apples from the Jonathan tree.   67–4

68

The children and their mother were safe.   68–1

The mother and her children were safe.   68–2

Either the children or their mother is sure to be safe.   68–3

Either the mother or her children is sure to be safe.   68–4

69

A flock of blackbirds was jabbering in the trees.   69–1

A flock of blackbirds were pursuing insects, swooping through the air, sitting in the treetops, or just making noisy nuisances of themselves.   69–2

The audience is applauding vigorously.   69–3

The team is happily dressing, posing for pictures, and accepting congratulations on the last-minute victory.   69–4

70

We had not yet eaten breakfast, although we had drove almost two hundred miles.   70–1

She hasn't spoke a word, and I'm sure that she hasn't written to anyone.   70–2

You should have taken Route 234. I've ridden on it many times.   70–3

I shook the hand that had shook the hand of Tom Seaver.   70–4

66–1
66–2
66–3
66–4

This group tests your knowledge of the use of singular and plural verbs when words intervene between subject and verb. You should have encircled 66–4 but no other number.

_____ Check here if you missed any item.

67–1
67–2
67–3
67–4

This group tests your knowledge of the use of singular and plural verbs in sentences where the subject follows the verb. You should have encircled 67–1 but no other number.

_____ Check here if you missed any item.

68–1
68–2
68–3
68–4

This group tests your knowledge of the use of singular and plural verbs with compound subjects. You should have encircled 68–1, 68–2, and 68–3 but not 68–4.

_____ Check here if you missed any item.

69–1
69–2
69–3
69–4

This group tests your knowledge of the use of singular and plural verbs with collective nouns as subjects. You should have encircled 69–1, 69–2, and 69–3 but not 69–4.

_____ Check here if you missed any item.

70–1
70–2
70–3
70–4

This group tests your knowledge of the use of the troublesome verbs *drive, eat, ride, shake, speak, take,* and *write.* You should have encircled 70–3 but no other number.

_____ Check here if you missed any item.

71

The choir begun the program. It sung first "Ave Maria."	71–1
Have you swum in Lake Moreau? Have you drunk from the spring at the north end?	71–2
The alarm rang, it seemed to me, just after I had sank into a heavy sleep.	71–3
Clay has always drank too much.	71–4

72

I had done well in the first inning, having thrown the third strike past two of the batters.	72–1
They had seen that his shirtsleeve was tore, and they had told him to mend it.	72–2
I drew a picture of the way the valley had looked after the dam burst.	72–3
My father had not known that Mr. Atkins had once run for political office.	72–4

73

Lie down, Rover, and then lay still.	73–1
The package was still laying where I had laid it.	73–2
After she had lain in the sun for a few minutes, she decided to lie in the shade.	73–3
She laid the baby in his crib, and he lay there smiling up at her.	73–4

74

Set the goblet on the mantel, and make sure that it will sit there without falling.	74–1
He raised up too soon and bumped his head sharply.	74–2
Grandpa has set in that chair every day for the past decade.	74–3
The sun had set and the moon had risen.	74–4

75

Mr. and Mrs. Wallace and Dr. Welch returned early in the A.M.	75–1
Roy Harris, Jr., lives in Washington, D.C.	75–2
Be sure to bring sheets, pillowcases, silverware, etc.	75–3
On Sat., Dec. 1, the Dr. and his family moved to Salem, Ore.	75–4

71–1

71–2

71–3

71–4

This group tests your knowledge of the use of the troublesome verbs *begin, drink, ring, sing, sink,* and *swim.* You should have encircled 71–2 but no other number.

_____ Check here if you missed any item.

72–1

72–2

72–3

72–4

This group tests your knowledge of the use of a number of other troublesome verbs. You should have encircled 72–1, 72–3, and 72–4 but not 72–2.

_____ Check here if you missed any item.

73–1

73–2

73–3

73–4

This group tests your knowledge of the use of *lie* and *lay.* You should have encircled 73–3 and 73–4 but no other number.

_____ Check here if you missed any item.

74–1

74–2

74–3

74–4

This group tests your knowledge of the use of *set, sit, raise,* and *rise.* You should have encircled 74–1 and 74–4 but no other number.

_____ Check here if you missed any item.

75–1

75–2

75–3

75–4

This group tests your knowledge of the correct use of abbreviations. You should have encircled 75–2 but no other number.

_____ Check here if you missed any item.

RECORD SHEET

In each space in the "Error" column place a check if you missed one or more items in a group. The second column is to indicate what you need to study if there is a check mark in the first column. (The numbers in the margin correspond to the numbers of the units in *Competence in English*.) The "Mastered" column may be checked when you have studied the indicated material and believe that you have mastered it.

ERROR	UNITS TO STUDY	MASTERED
1		
2		
3		
4		
5		
6		
7		
8		
9		
10		
11		
12		
13		
14		
15		
16		
17		
18		
19		
20		
21		
22		

ERROR	UNITS TO STUDY	MASTERED
23		
24		
25		
26		
27		
28		
29		
30		
31		
32		
33		
34		
35		
36		
37		
38		
39		
40		
41		
42		
43		
44		
45		
46		
47		
48		
49		
50		

ERROR	UNITS TO STUDY	MASTERED
51		
52		
53		
54		
55		
56		
57		
58		
59		
60		
61		
62		
63		
64		
65		
66		
67		
68		
69		
70		
71		
72		
73		
74		
75		

PART ONE

GAINING RESPECT
FOR YOUR IDEAS

You have probably heard or made remarks like these:

"That person makes sense."

"I try never to miss any of her columns."

"Every time he opens his mouth, I listen."

Some people have a knack for making others listen to them; their opinions command respect. Yet other people, whose opinions may be much the same, are ignored or even laughed at.

Why the difference? That is what we will try to find out in Part One. Obviously the quality of ideas must be good to start with, and information must be accurate. We will see what can be done to present good ideas and accurate information so that people will respect and often accept them.

Unit 1—The Unwise Generalization

A: COMMENTARY

Joe, a recent high school graduate, said, "I know all about electricity. I studied it in physics."

What Joe didn't think about, or didn't know, was that colleges and technical schools offer scores of courses in electricity, electronics, and electrical engineering, that new electrical instruments are patented almost every day, that some researchers are still trying to find out exactly what electricity is, and that others are studying relationships between electricity and other physical and biological phenomena—for instance, just how electrical charges enable us to think. Joe obviously didn't know *all* about electricity; a single physics course can touch only a few superficial points. To gain respect for our ideas, we must try to avoid unwise generalizations like Joe's.

B: EXERCISES

1 It has been said that no one can possibly write *everything* about a single drop of water.

Explain why you agree or disagree with that statement. _____

_____

_____

_____

2 Joe's father said to him the day after high school graduation, "Now that you have finished your education, it's time to get a job."

Has Joe finished his education? _____ Explain your answer. _____

_____

_____

3 An acquaintance of mine had two unsuccessful marriages. His son was in prison for forgery, and his daughter was a high-school dropout. He himself had lost most of his money because of dishonest or inept business associates.

My acquaintance used to say, "People are just no good."

From your own experience relate briefly one or two incidents which show that there are exceptions to my friend's generalization.

_____

_____

_____

_____

_____

_____

4 **"You're the greatest person in the world."**

Explain why no one can honestly make that statement. _____

_____

_____

5 A. **"He's an incompetent teacher."**
  B. **"He's an incompetent teacher in these ways: First, . . . Second, . . . Third, . . ."**

Are you more likely to respect the ideas of A or B? _____ Why?

_____

_____

C: ASSIGNMENTS

• Discuss (or explain in writing) the weaknesses in each of the generalizations below. Look for exceptions to the statement and try to find alternative possibilities.

1. Intelligence tests don't really measure anything.
2. Mercy killings are never justifiable.
3. Mercy killings are justifiable.
4. Without war, the human race will perish because of overcrowding.
5. George is the biggest liar in the country.
6. Medical doctors are the most important members of society.
7. If there were no books, civilization would perish.
8. The best way to find out whether students are successful is to look at their grades.
9. There are so many abuses in school and college athletics that all competitive events should be banned.
10. Who loses anything if whales and dolphins are killed? What has a whale done for you lately?

ANSWERS TO SECTION B

1. MODEL   I agree, for in order to write *everything* about a drop of water one would have to know and write much about chemistry, physics, geology, geography, hydrology, meteorology, and other sciences, and perhaps even to discuss literature and religion.
2. No MODEL   As long as he is conscious, his education continues.
3. Give yourself credit if you wrote an answer based on your own experience.
4. MODEL   Greatness of this sort cannot be measured. Even if it could, one would have to measure the greatness of all the people in the world to make the statement honestly.
5. B MODEL   B supports opinion with reasons.

Unit 2—Qualifying

A: COMMENTARY

Marty had been reading about recent increases in armed robberies and about the large number of murders committed by people using handguns. Then, on the way to a party, he and his wife had been held up and robbed by someone with a gun.

At the party Marty was understandably upset and angry. He recounted their experience, cited some general crime statistics, and concluded, "More than ever I am convinced that guns should be banned."

The other guests were sympathetic, but one said, "Marty, do you mean *all* guns?"

"I do. Every gun."

"Don't policemen need guns?"

"Oh, yes, policemen have to have them for protection against criminals," Marty conceded.

"And game wardens and night watchmen?"

"Some of them may need them."

"Would you prohibit hunting?"

"Probably—I'm not sure. People don't often use little handguns for hunting."

"Oh. You want to ban just little handguns?"

"Well, mainly. But crimes are sometimes committed with other guns."

"Should you yourself be allowed to keep a gun in your home to protect your family?"

"That's debatable. If the crooks didn't have guns, I wouldn't need any."

As the conversation shows, Marty had to back down somewhat from his original assertion that *all* guns should be banned. Finally he said, "Well, yes, some responsible people like policemen and watchmen and maybe some others should be permitted to have guns. But I think that much stricter control of guns is imperative, so that hoodlums like the one that robbed us can't keep on stealing and killing the way they do."

Marty's original statement was too extreme to support strongly. But when he toned it down by adding some qualifications, many listeners agreed with him and respected what he said.

B: EXERCISES

Each of the generalizations given below may be defensible if it is qualified in some way. Think about what changes would make the generalization acceptable to you, and rewrite it with those modifications included.

1 **Women are more observant than men.** _____

_____

_____

_____

2 **Birds are a farmer's main allies. Without them crops wouldn't grow, and we'd all starve.** _____

_____

_____

_____

3 **Final exams are unnecessary.** _____

_____

_____

_____

4 **Adults get more out of education than young people do.**

_____

_____

_____

5 **Adults don't learn as fast as young people do.**

_____

_____

_____

6 *All Things Bright and Beautiful* is a great book. (Clarify what you mean by *great*.) _____

_____

_____

_____

7 Jack will steal anything that isn't nailed down.

_____

_____

_____

8 This school is ideal. _____

_____

_____

_____

9 Everyone should exercise for an hour each day.

_____

_____

_____

10 The greatest American was Benjamin Franklin.

_____

_____

_____

C: ASSIGNMENTS

• As in Section B, decide what qualifications you would like to have in order to make each generalization acceptable. (Some of the changes may have to be quite drastic!)

1. Football is now America's major pastime.
2. The date of Easter keeps jumping around unpredictably.
3. Modern music is ugly.
4. Modern painting is a ripoff of a gullible public.
5. The best World Series was played in 1975. (On what grounds would you decide that a World Series was "best"?)

6. The rose is the prettiest flower.
7. Architecture isn't what it used to be.
8. The Spanish language is easy.
9. The Olympic games are a complete disaster and should never be held again—just look at the hard feelings they arouse between countries.
10. Presidential nominating conventions are the only possible way to select candidates.

ANSWERS TO SECTION B

1. MODEL   Some women are more observant than some men, especially with regard to people or things related to people.
2. MODEL   Birds are among a farmer's main allies because they eat harmful insects. Crops would almost certainly be smaller without them, and the world's food supply would diminish greatly.
3. MODEL   Final exams are unnecessary if the instructor has other adequate ways to measure students' accomplishments.
4. MODEL   Some adults get more out of education than some young people do, particularly if the adults have strong motivation.
5. MODEL   Some adults don't learn as fast as some young people do, although motivation and health may be important factors in learning speed, regardless of age.
6. MODEL   Realism, truth, compassion, and an enjoyable style are among my criteria for literary greatness, and *All Things Bright and Beautiful* ranks high in all these.
7. MODEL   Jack has been convicted of theft seven times.
8. MODEL   This school has teachers who exceed the state-required qualifications. It has attractive physical facilities, including a fine library. Its students are cooperative and well motivated.
9. MODEL   Everyone whose health will permit it should exercise appropriately for about an hour each day.
10. MODEL   Among the greatest Americans, at least as far as versatility is concerned, was Benjamin Franklin.

Unit 3—Separating Opinions and Facts

A: COMMENTARY

Two nine-year-old boys were talking:
"Cherry pie is the best there is."
"No! Chocolate is best!"
"Cherry!"

"Chocolate!"

Soon they were wrestling on the sidewalk. They had not learned that some disagreements concern only matters of opinion and cannot be decided by evidence—and certainly not by fighting.

Now listen to three adults:

"It's hot in here."

"I think it's just right."

"It feels a little chilly to me."

A look at a thermometer showed them that the temperature was 70°F. They might still disagree about whether that temperature was satisfactory, but at least they now had some factual evidence and not just opinion.

Your ideas will gain respect if you do not insist on arguing about opinions that cannot be supported by facts. And you will strengthen your arguments whenever you can bring in facts to bolster them.

B: EXERCISES

1 Do you believe that cherry pie is better than chocolate? _____

Would you argue or fight with someone who disagreed with you? _____

Why or why not? _____

_____

Could you prove that the other person was wrong? _____

2 Some beliefs, such as what kind of pie is best, are really not arguable, for they are only matters of opinion or personal preference. Which two of

these sentences represent mere opinion? _____ and _____

A. Canada is a better country than the United States.
B. Canadian winters are colder than those in the United States.
C. Canadian people are more friendly than those in the United States.

3 Many a barroom (or other) topic is not arguable for a different reason.

First patron: Catfish Hunter had the best earned-run average in the American League in 1975.
Second patron: No, he didn't. It was some other guy.

Baseball statistics are available, perhaps within the bartender's reach. It is pointless to argue about something for which there is a definite answer. Don't argue; just look up the answer.

Is the following proposition arguable? _____ **Ohio's population is greater than that of Illinois.** Why or why not? _____

_____

4 The sort of topic that *is* arguable is one that has some evidence on each side. The point of the argument, then, is to determine which side has more and stronger evidence.

In the remainder of this unit we'll look at points advanced by supporters and opponents of ex-Governor Milledge, now a candidate for nomination for the Presidency. You will be asked to evaluate a number of statements.

"At the end of Milledge's term as Governor, the state treasury was $300 million richer than at the beginning."

A. Does this statement appear to be factual? _____

B. Would it be fair to ask the source of the statistic? _____

C. If the statistic proves to be true, does the statement appear helpful to

Milledge's candidacy? _____ Why or why not? _____

_____

_____

5 **"Milledge makes an excellent impression on television."**

A. Is this statement factual? _____

B. How could a research organization prove or disprove the statement?

_____

C. If the statement is proved true, is it a good argument in favor of Milledge? _____ Why or why not? _____

_____

6 **"No former governor has ever been elected president."**

A. Does this statement appear factual? _____

B. Can the statement be proved or disproved? _____

C. If the statement were true, would it provide a good reason for voting against Milledge? _____ Why or why not? _____

_____

7 **"Milledge was the worst governor this state ever had."**

A. Is this statement factual or a matter of opinion? _____

B. Can the statement be proved or disproved? _____

Why or why not? _____

_____.

8 **"Milledge has an attractive family."**

    A. Is this statement factual or a matter of opinion? _____

    B. Assuming that most people will agree with the statement, does it pro-

        vide a good reason for voting for Milledge? _____

        Why or why not? _____

9 **"Milledge has little experience in foreign affairs."**

    A. Is this statement factual or a matter of opinion? _____

    B. Explain your answer to A. _____

    C. Is the statement arguable? (Assume that Milledge is a veteran of a
        foreign war, has traveled extensively, and has met socially several heads

        of foreign countries.) _____ Why or why not? _____

10 **"I am proud to introduce Clifton Milledge, the next President of the
United States."**

    A. During a campaign, is this statement arguable? _____

    B. Why or why not? _____

C: ASSIGNMENTS

• Decide whether each of the following statements is (a) arguable, (b) not
arguable because it is just a matter of opinion, (c) not arguable because a
simple factual answer can be found.

1. The northernmost point in the United States, with the exception of
   Alaska, is in Minnesota.
2. The French Revolution was less successful than the American Revolution.
3. The poetry of Robert Frost is technically superior to that of Robert
   Browning.
4. A sulphate is a salt.
5. It's harder to make a living now than it was a hundred years ago.
6. South America is the continent of the future.
7. South Dakota was admitted to the Union in 1889.
8. Leather goods should be outlawed, because they necessitate the killing of
   animals.

9. Of the two Roosevelts, Teddy was the better President.
10. In camp, the smell of frying bacon is even better than that of boiling coffee.

• Write two original statements that are arguable, two others that represent just matters of opinion, and two others that can be proved or disproved by available statistics.

ANSWERS TO SECTION B

1. The first two answers are matters of personal opinion. MODEL Yes No I would not fight because tastes are matters of opinion, not absolute qualities. No
2. A C
3. No MODEL The answer can be found in reference books.
4. A. Yes B. Yes C. Yes MODEL It shows that he was more conservative in spending than most politicians are.
5. A. No B. It could conduct a poll. C. No MODEL Some people look good on television but are not effective administrators.
6. A. Yes B. Yes (The statement is untrue.) C. No MODEL Even if the statement were true, there is no reason why a governor could not make a good president.
7. A. Opinion B. No MODEL An acceptable measure would have to be applied to all the state's governors, but there is no such measure.
8. A. Opinion B. No MODEL A politician's family provides no measure of his or her ability as an administrator.
9. A. Opinion B. MODEL *Little* needs definition. C. Yes MODEL We need to decide whether these qualifications give him more than "little" experience.
10. A. Yes B. MODEL Until Milledge has actually been elected and sworn in, the statement has not been proved.

Unit 4—Avoiding Stereotypes

A: COMMENTARY

The members of a family may resemble each other in some ways, but they aren't all alike in every way. Some are older, shorter, darker, braver, more intelligent, less emotional, or more impulsive than others. So we have to be very careful when we are inclined to make a statement like "All Joneses are crooks (religious, handsome, reckless, and so on)." Not all members of any group are exactly alike; in fact, the differences among them are often greater than the similarities. It is commonly thought, for instance, that poets and musicians are impractical people. Some of them, like some of the rest of us, are indeed impractical, but others have combined their poetry or music with successful careers in science, medicine, law, or other fields. Others simply define practicality in their own way, which may differ from ours.

When we say or imply that all members of a group are alike, we have to be sure that there are no exceptions. Otherwise we are guilty of using a stereotype—a false generalization—and our intelligent listeners or readers will be quite justified in saying, "That is not true. I know several poets (musicians, members of the Jones family, professors, or what have you) who aren't like that at all."

B: EXERCISES

1 A definition of *stereotype* in the *American Heritage Dictionary* is as follows: "A person, group, event, or issue considered to typify or conform to an unvarying pattern or manner, lacking any individuality: *the very stereotype of a college sophomore.*"

Keeping that definition in mind, put a check after each item that represents a stereotype:

A. **As silly as a sophomore** _____

B. **A stupid football player** _____

C. **Children don't like vegetables.** _____

D. **Take lots of vitamin pills. They make you strong.** _____

E. **Red-heads are hot-tempered.** _____

F. **Bacteria are harmful.** _____

2 Do you believe that it is true that *some* sophomores are silly? _____ that *some* football players (English majors, painters, plumbers, and so on) are

stupid? _____
that each of the other items in exercise 1 may apply to *some* members of

the group? _____

3 Do you believe that *all* sophomores are silly? _____
that *all* football players (architects, Congress members, tree surgeons, and

so on) are stupid? _____
that each of the other items in exercise 1 may apply to *all* members of the

group? _____

4 Let's turn around the items in exercise 1.

    A. **Sophomores are sober and serious.**
    B. **Football players are intelligent.**
    C. **Children like vegetables.**
    D. **Don't take vitamin pills. They don't help you.**
    E. **Red-heads are calm and unemotional.**
    F. **Bacteria are harmless.**

Choose one of those statements and write what you would say to someone who said it during a discussion. _____

_____

_____

5 The trouble with stereotypes, which are often like the items in exercises 1 and 4, is that they seem to say that something is true of *all* members of a group. Actually, *some* sophomores are silly, but not all; *some* sophomores are sober and serious, but not all. Finish each of these statements:

    A. **Some teachers are unfair,** _____.

    B. **Some teachers are helpful,** _____.

    C. **Some teachers are wise,** _____.

    D. **Some students cheat,** _____.

    E. **Some students work hard,** _____.

    F. **Some students are highly intelligent,** _____.

6 We can have negative stereotypes, too. These use words like *no, none,* or *never.* What is wrong with each of these statements?

    A. **Referees never favor either team.** _____

_____

    B. **No politicians are worth their salt.** _____

_____

    C. **No marriage is happy for very long.** _____

_____

7 Someone once wisecracked, "Always remember never to say *always* and *never.*" Another wisecrack is "All generalizations are false, including this one."

    Under one condition it makes sense to use *never, always, none,* or *all.*

What is that condition? _____

_____

8 Fill in each of these blanks with the name of a group of people.

A. _____ are lazy.

B. _____ are happy-go-lucky.

C. _____ are good to their pets.

9 Explain what is probably wrong with the three statements you completed

for exercise 8. _____

_____

_____

C: ASSIGNMENTS

• Write a paragraph (or perhaps several paragraphs) concerning a personal experience of yours that caused you to disbelieve one of the following familiar stereotypes.

Fat people are jolly.	You can't believe anything you read.
Women make bad drivers.	Advertising is a pack of lies.
All men are fickle.	Drunks never get hurt.
You can't teach an old dog new tricks.	God protects fools and little children.
	Barbers talk too much.
Poetry is dull.	Americans worship the dollar.
The younger generation is going to the dogs.	

ANSWERS TO SECTION B

1. All six items should be checked.
2. Yes Yes Yes
3. No No No
4. MODEL I agree that the statement may apply to some of these people, but not to all.
5. *but not all* (in each item)
6. MODELS A. Some referees have been known to show favoritism. B. Some politicians are conscientious, hard working, and capable. C. Some long-lasting marriages are happy.
7. MODEL It must be possible to prove that there are no exceptions at all.

8. Any answer you provided will fulfill the requirement.
9. MODEL It is impossible to generalize truthfully that all members of a group are lazy, happy-go-lucky, or good to their pets.

Unit 5—Avoiding the *either . . . or* Fallacy

A: COMMENTARY

Sometimes only two choices exist. For instance, either we'll go to the movie or we won't. But often there are more than two: We can go to this movie or to another movie or to a concert or to the library or to the basketball game or to bed.

A favorite tactic in discussion is to act as though only two possibilities exist when there really may be three or more. Someone says, "Either you're right and I'm wrong, or vice versa." Actually, perhaps each person is partly right. Or someone says, "If you don't feed the birds, they'll starve." Actually, the birds may go to a neighbor's feeder or find some seeds in a nearby weed patch.

In Section B we'll look at several statements of the *either . . . or* position, which is a fallacy we should try to avoid if our ideas are to gain and hold respect.

B: EXERCISES

1 **George is an atheist. He doesn't belong to any church.**
   A. Is it possible to believe in God without being a member of a church?

   _____

   B. Using your dictionary if necessary, tell what an agnostic is. _____

   _____

   C. Is it possible that George is an agnostic rather than an atheist? _____

2 The opening statement in exercise 1 implies that a person must be either a church member or an atheist. As we have seen, other possibilities exist. A false choice is often called an *either . . . or* fallacy.
   A student says to her roommate, "Either you admit that you're wrong or I'm going to pack up and leave."

   Suggest one or two other possibilities. _____

   _____

   _____

58

3 **It's how much you learn that matters, not the grades you get.**
This statement is less clear-cut than the first two, but it seems to imply that there is no relationship between grades and the amount of learning. Do you believe that, in general, grades show how much a person has

learned? _____ Explain your answer. _____

_____

_____

4 **Grades don't always reflect how much a person has learned in a course, but they usually do show whether the student has mastered what the teacher thinks is important.**

Is this statement fairly accurate, in your opinion? _____

Give an example to justify your answer. _____

_____

_____

5 **If we don't have a world government, there just won't be any world in 2000 A.D.**

Is this statement an example of the *either . . . or* fallacy? _____
Name one possible alternative to world government and no world at all.

_____

_____

6 **Either the world's population has to be held to about six billion or everybody will starve.**

Name a possible alternative to this *either . . . or* fallacy. _____

_____

_____

_____

7 **If we don't spend more on arms than our enemies do, we are doomed.**
Write two sentences, giving two possible alternatives to this fallacy.

_____

_____

_____

_____

_____

8 **If taxes don't come down, there'll be a revolution.**

Name an alternative. _____

_____

9 When in a discussion you hear someone say or imply that there are only two choices, you should ask yourself _____

_____

10 When in a discussion or in writing a paper you are tempted to say or to imply that there are only two choices, you should first ask yourself _____

_____

C: ASSIGNMENTS

• In conversations, news broadcasts, political speeches, or advertising, try to find one or more examples of the *either . . . or* fallacy. As a class, discuss the examples you have found. Or write a brief paper about one or more of them.

ANSWERS TO SECTION B

1. A. Yes   B. MODEL   One who does not know whether God exists.   C. Yes
2. MODEL   They may talk the matter out. The roommate may decide that she is wrong. The student may just go to a movie.
3. Yes or no (as you prefer)   MODEL   (for a *yes* answer)   Capable teachers give grades carefully, and usually do thus reveal fairly well each student's mastery of the material.
4. Yes or no (as you prefer) Give yourself credit if you provided an example.
5. Yes   MODEL   An international police force might be able to preserve peace.
6. MODEL   New sources of food or still greater agricultural yields may become possible.
7. MODEL   1. Better quality of armament, rather than the amount of money spent, must be the major criterion.   2. Moves toward peace may be more effective than accelerating the arms race would be.
8. MODEL   Taxes may stay about where they are—at a level where no revolution is seriously threatened.
9. MODEL   "What other possibilities exist?"
10. MODEL   "What other choices may there possibly be?"

Unit 6—Logical Relationships

A student wrote:

My goal is an auto mechanic.

A moment's thought would have told the student that a mechanic is not a goal. What the student meant was this:

My goal is to become an auto mechanic.

The original statement isn't "wrong" grammatically, and it can be understood. But it isn't logical. The beginning and the end of the sentence don't fit together neatly. The reader might suspect, rightly or wrongly, that the person who puts such a sentence together may not do a good job in putting an engine together.

In the exercises in Sections B and C, think about what the sentence says and what the writer probably means. Then rewrite to make the intended meaning clear.

B: EXERCISES

1 The outcome will end in disaster.

_____

2 His physical condition was in bad shape.

_____

3 Her only reason for going to college is a job.

_____

4 Babies often get what their tears are crying for.

_____

5 My widowed mother was very difficult to bring up five children.

_____

6 Alcoholic beverages are taught to be taken not even in moderate amounts.

_____

7 The bloody accident was perfectly terrible.

_____

8 Lightning does sometimes strike twice in the contrary of popular belief.

_____

9 We read articles out of three magazines.

_____

10 The fire was put out before the fire spread by use of a foam extinguisher.

_____

_____

C: ASSIGNMENTS

• Rewrite on a separate sheet of paper, or discuss in class.

1. Put the baby on the stove a bottle.
2. A school's athletic program ties together an opportunity for school spirit.
3. A woodpecker was pecking away at the hole which was his food.
4. He told his wife that they could have no vacation that year with a sad look on his face.
5. The musical accompaniment was the most beautiful that I almost ever heard.
6. The deaf mute tried to tell the guests about the fire signaling frantically.
7. She did not believe that the honor system should be reinstated for several reasons.
8. Marty's "home run" was really a foul ball because I saw it go to the left of the pole.
9. The waiter was serving customers wearing his hat.
10. A good example of his physique was fullback on the football team.

ANSWERS TO SECTION B

1. MODEL   The outcome will be disastrous.
2. MODEL   He was in poor physical condition.
3. MODEL   Her only reason for going to college is to get a job.
4. MODEL   Babies often get what they cry for.
5. MODEL   My widowed mother had great difficulties in bringing up five children.
6. MODEL   The school teaches that alcoholic beverages should not be taken even in moderate amounts.

7. MODEL   The bloody accident was terrible.
8. MODEL   Despite popular belief, lightning does sometimes strike twice in the same place.
9. MODEL   We read articles in three magazines.
10. MODEL   By use of a foam extinguisher the fire was put out before it spread.

Unit 7—Appropriateness of Language

A: COMMENTARY

Motto
I play it cool and dig all jive;
That's the reason I stay alive.
My motto, as I live and learn,
Is to dig and be dug, in return.[1]

In that short poem, Langston Hughes was using *jive* to mean "language." There are several kinds of language, although the lines between them are not always easy to draw.

We hear or read *formal* language in some lectures, most textbooks, reports to stockholders of corporations, and other relatively serious and impersonal kinds of communication. *Technical* writing is usually formal; it is customary in scientific reports and journals and, slightly popularized or simplified, in magazines like *Science* or *Scientific American. Literary* writing is often formal, but frequently is not; its language tends to be rather innovative or experimental and is often intended to make a reader react emotionally.

A few writers and speakers use *excessively formal* language. They "perform their ablutions" instead of taking a bath, or (writing for the sports page) they say that a shortstop "perpetrated a miscue" instead of "fumbled an easy roller."

We hear or read *semiformal* language in most college lectures, some textbooks (such as this one), and a high proportion of magazine and newspaper articles.

Informal language, also called *colloquial*, is what most of us use most of the time, especially in talking with our family and friends or in writing letters to persons we know well. Informal language often includes some *slang*, which according to *Webster's Third International Dictionary* is "composed typically of coinages or arbitrarily changed words, clipped or shortened forms, extravagant, forced, or facetious figures of speech, or verbal novelties usu. experiencing quick popularity and relatively rapid decline into disuse."

[1] Reprinted by permission of Alfred A. Knopf, Inc. from *The Panther and the Lash: Poems of Our Times,* by Langston Hughes. Copyright by Langston Hughes.

Language is used in ways called *standard* and *nonstandard*. Examples of standard language are *they were, it isn't, he and I did it*; nonstandard language might substitute *they was, it ain't, me an' him done it*. Formal and semiformal speech and writing almost always are expressed in standard language. Informal language more often uses nonstandard forms, although it is quite possible to be pleasantly informal and at the same time use only standard forms.

Now read "Motto" again. The speaker in Hughes's poem is saying that to "play it cool," to be successful, a person needs to understand and use more than one kind of language. To "dig and be dug," a person shouldn't be satisfied with knowing just the language with which he or she grew up. To "stay alive" a person needs to "dig all jive."

The point of view in this book is that it is indeed desirable to "dig" as much "jive" as one can master. One kind of language is not always better than another, but one kind is likely to be more appropriate than another in any given situation. Appropriate English is good English, and a person needs to be able to use more than one kind in order to select what is appropriate for each occasion.

B: EXERCISES

1 It is morning. You feel your shoulder being shaken. You say, "Ahh, whatza matter? Ofergoshsakelemmesleepenurfiminuteswilya?"
2 Half an hour later you stop at Joe's Diner for breakfast. You say, "Hi, Joe. Coupla fried eggs and black coffee, please."
3 Your first class of the day. You say, "Good morning, Professor Hamilton. I'm sorry that I was late this morning, but I overslept."
4 When Professor Hamilton picks up your term paper, he may read: "When one considers the environmental influences that helped to shape the personality of Edgar Allan Poe, one finds oneself more in sympathy with this misunderstood author than was his first biographer, Rufus W. Griswold."
5 You earn a little money by playing in a dance combo. One night you see on the dance floor an elderly man with a long, flowing beard. You say to the drummer in a quiet moment, "Hey Pete, dig that far-out dude!"
6 Sunday, at church, in communion of silence, you whisper, "Our Father who is merciful beyond human understanding, hear the prayer of your humble servant."

1 In the passage above, which two paragraphs make use of formal language?

_____ and _____

2 Which one is semiformal? _____

3 Of the other three paragraphs, which one includes an especially slangy quotation? _____

4 Would it be more appropriate or less appropriate to write the quotation in the first paragraph like this: "**I should definitely prefer to be allowed an additional five minutes of repose**"? _____ Why? _____

_____

_____

5 Comment on the appropriateness of this rewriting of the quotation in the fourth paragraph: "**Poe had a sort of weirdo childhood. If you know all the ins and outs of it, it makes you feel real sorry for the kid.**" _____

_____

_____

6 No doubt God "digs all jive" and is as likely to answer one style of prayer as another. However, do you consider this version of the sixth paragraph appropriate: "**Sure hope you're listenin', Pops**"? _____ Why or why not? _____

_____

7 Here are three versions of the same sentence:
   A. **It seems to me that after a country is torn up by war, the things that have to be rebuilt first are the bridges and roads and hospitals and so on.**
   B. **The first requisite in the rebirth of a ravished land must be the infrastructure: bridges, roads, waste disposal facilities, hospitals.**
   C. **OK, so there's this country that war has turned to practically nothin'. What's to be done? First you gotta start with roads and bridges to haul stuff in on, and you gotta rebuild the hospitals, and get rid of the stinkin' garbage.**

   Which sentence is the most formal? _____ Which the least? _____

8 In what circumstance might the language of sentence C be appropriate?

_____

9 Which of the three sentences might be most appropriate in a statement from a committee reporting to Congress? _____ Why? _____

_____

_____

65

10 If you were talking with a history instructor about the after-effects of war, which of the sentences might be appropriate for one of you to say? _____ Why? _____

_____

11 Many high school and college instructors used to insist on formal language in any papers written for their classes. Today most are likely to prefer a semiformal style, or even an informal style that follows standard usage.

Why, in your opinion, has this change taken place? _____

_____

_____

_____

12 Why, in your opinion, do most instructors still prefer standard usage instead of expressions like *you was* or *between you and I?* _____

_____

_____

_____

C: ASSIGNMENTS

• Copy one or two sentences illustrating each of the following kinds of language, and note where you found each. Be prepared to discuss in class (or in writing) the appropriateness of each to its context. Suggestions of possible sources follow:

1. Informal English (talk shows on radio or television, a conversation with a close friend or with children, a letter you have received from a relative)
2. Semiformal English (a lecture in class, class discussion, a news broadcast)
3. Formal English (a public lecture, a speech by the President, an article in a scholarly magazine, an editorial)
4. Technical English (specialized magazines such as *Sky and Telescope* and *Turkey World,* lectures in specialized subjects such as computer programming)
5. Literary English (a literature textbook, a best-selling novel)
6. Slang (very informal conversations with friends)
7. Nonstandard English (examples may be heard on the street and in other public places)

ANSWERS TO SECTION B

1. 4 6
2. 3
3. 5
4. Less appropriate MODEL In the circumstances this sentence would be unhumanly stiff.
5. MODEL For most school or college literature papers this version would be far too informal. It also is not very informative.
6. Probably no, but the question asks your opinion. MODEL (for a *no* answer) The sentence sounds irreverent.
7. B C
8. MODEL Sentence C might be appropriate in conversation with close friends.
9. B MODEL Most reports to Congress or any such body are expected to be in relatively formal language.
10. A MODEL The sentence is semiformal, natural, informative, not at all stiff.
11. MODEL The modern American life style is much more relaxed than it used to be, and writing style reflects that general informality. (*Give yourself credit for a different reason, too.*)
12. MODEL The schools reflect the educated community, including the business community, which in general prefers standard usage. (*Give yourself credit for a different reason, too.*)

Unit 8—Editing and Proofreading

A: COMMENTARY

Anything written or printed for others to see is more attractive if it is checked for accuracy. Many students create a bad impression of themselves and their writing because their editing and proofreading are careless, indifferent, even sloppy. Perhaps without even being aware of the reason, many an instructor, wavering between one grade and another, may decide on the lower because of a student's careless error or two, or choose the higher because a paper is carefully edited and proofread.

Many workers in business and industry, too, are hurt by carelessness in written work even when that work is not extensive. It is doubtful that the boss looked, with favor on the cereal company employee who in January stamped 30FEB as the expiration date on fifty thousand boxes of cereal. And this sign in the Weir-Cook Airport in Indianapolis didn't stay up long: FLY BIG TO

CALIFORNIA 3 TIMES DAILY ON THE TWA 1011. Nor did this sign put up by the Minnesota Highway Department: NO DUMPING ALOUD.

Editing, as used here, refers to the stage in writing before the final draft. It consists especially of doing these things:

1. checking for accuracy anything questionable, such as factual information and quotations
2. making sure that paragraphs or other sections are in the best possible order and are bound together with suitable transitions
3. checking sentences to see that they really say what the writer intends and that they cannot easily be misinterpreted
4. checking spelling, punctuation, and similar mechanical matters

Proofreading refers to the careful scrutiny that should be given the final copy of every paper, since even good writers and typists may be guilty of mis-copying, omission or repetition of words, transposition of letters or words, or slip-ups in punctuation.

Editing requires constant thinking, constant questioning. Proofreading requires constant alertness for details. Both processes may be helped if a slow reading aloud can be made part of the procedure.

Some of the sentences in Sections B and C are from student compositions, others from newspapers or other printed sources. Some are reminiscent of fillers in the *New Yorker*, whose editors delight in calling amusing blunders to the attention of their readers.

B: EXERCISES

1 **Advertisers should not include any false misinformation.**

In editing a manuscript, one must watch for slips in thinking. The person who wrote the sentence above probably started to write *false information* but then substituted *misinformation* without getting rid of *false*. The sentence should read:

_____

2 **This program is absolutely essential. What's more, it is necessary.**

Careful editing of the sentence above would probably result in the deletion of _____.

3 **Mr. Gordon has been in charge of press arrangements for almost every major news event in the history of the United States.**

Since the United States recently celebrated its bicentennial, Mr. Gordon must be (how old?) _____.

4 Milwaukee is the golden egg that the rest of the state wants to milk.

Does milk come from eggs? _____

5 Waterbased paint spots can be removed by running under water.

What ridiculous picture does the sentence above bring to your mind?

---

6 Yugoslavian Airlines are about to start trans-Atlantic jet flights, at first to Australia.

On what continent is Yugoslavia? _____ To fly from Yugoslavia to Australia, is a plane likely to cross the Atlantic? _____

7 Occasionally a careful editor will note that the wrong word has been used.

In the following sentence the wrong word is _____.

We found it necessary to have the apartment completely overdone because of the leaks from the plumbing upstairs.

8 This court ruling is enough to make your head stand on end.

In the sentence above the wrong word is _____.

9   **WIPE WITH DUMP CLOTH**
                     DO NOT EMERGE IN WATER
                     MADE IN JAPAN

Since the cutting board to which the label above was attached was made in a foreign country, the errors in printing are understandable and readily forgivable. In an English-speaking country the words _____ and _____ should be _____ and _____.

10 Exercises 10–13 contain miscellaneous errors that a good proofreader should be able to spot easily. The number of mistakes is indicated in parentheses. To make a correction in a word, neatly cross out the wrong word and write the proper form above. Correct punctuation within the line.
   Hear in the Untied States we have fredom of the press.   (3)

11 **Miss. Hart told police she was kidnaped by by two men at Gunpoint between Decatur and Springfield.   (3)**

12 **"This is whear most politicans make there biggest misteak, the speaker said   (6)**

13 Laywers poured over the the documents with grate care.   (4)

14 Edit and proofread:

You are invited to attend our Nineth Annual Science Fair and inspecked the many and numerous displays construcked by the adult science students in our shcool. Much planing and countless hours of work has been put in to this project—golden hours that would have been waisted in other worthless projects.

C: ASSIGNMENTS

• The sentences below need editing and proofreading. They may be faulty for any of a number of reasons, such as fuzzy thinking, incorrect use of words, unnecessary repetition, misspelling, or careless copying. What changes should be made in each?

1. Unemployment in California dropped slightly last month and the number of people out of work correspondingly increased.
2. The stage setting is unusually attractive, with credit going to Melvin Mann for the construction of Linda Miles for the design.
3. We had lead the horse into the barn.
4. When the bout ended, the crowd of seventy-five hundred gave both fighters a boxing.
5. The police chief reminded the dog owners that all dogs must be kept on leash retroactive to the first of the month.
6. The extensive accumulation of information on the responsibility of the employer to the employee suggests the need for some emphasis and information on the responsibility of the employer to the employee.
7. Watkins hit a sinking line drive to center field and Pirtle caught the ball off his shoetops as he slid along on his knees.
8. That was a low blow between the belt.
9. The bankers' pockets are bulging with the sweat of the honest workingmen.
10. Thoes people are absolutely right to a certain extent.
11. I am in favor of letting the status quo stay as it is.
12. Both of these pictures by Tintoretto were painted before his death.
13. Among the others, were a retried Army kernel who earlier had been a military policemen, a jail matren, and another women.
14. HELP WANTED Spanish and English speaking person for grocery store work must be conscious and willing to work
15. Houck said that peope not knowledgeable about buffalo had been critical of their commercial laughter "because it appears to be cutting down on they're numbers. That is untrue Houck said.
16. Area low enforcement officers said that CB radios sometimes interfears with their work

ANSWERS TO SECTION B

1. Advertisers should not include any misinformation. (*or* . . . false information)
2. the second sentence
3. over two hundred years old
4. No
5. MODEL   I see a paint-spotted man running through a shower.
6. Europe   No
7. overdone
8. head
9. dump, emerge   damp, immerse
10. Here, United, freedom
11. Miss, by (delete), gunpoint
12. where, politicians, their, mistake," said.
13. Lawyers, pored, the (delete), great
14. Ninth, inspect, and numerous (delete), constructed, school, planning, have, into, (change *would* to *might*), wasted, other (delete)

PART TWO

THE SENTENCE

The sentence is in some ways less complicated than most people think.

In this section we will first explore the two statements—the two kinds of basic sentences—that all of us utter almost every time we speak or write. Then we will move on to see different ways of combining those statements so that we can say exactly what we mean, say it clearly, and say it effectively.

Unit 9—The Basic Sentences of English

A: COMMENTARY

Each day users of the English language speak and write literally billions of different sentences. Yet at the base of nearly all those sentences are two statements that we make over and over. Almost everything that we ever say is only a variation of one of the two statements. Here is one of the statements:

Somebody or something does something.

This statement may take shapes like these:

Dogs bark.
Monkeys climb trees.
People make monkeys of themselves.
People give elephants peanuts.

Here is the other statement:

Somebody or something is or seems to be something.

This statement may take shapes like these:

Dogs are animals.
Collies are large.
Collies look gentle.

Remember that these are *basic* sentences. That means that we may make additions to them. It is the additions that make our sentences seem so different from one another. Here are two of the sample sentences above, with additions:

Some *dogs bark* so much at night that they keep the neighbors awake.
Because of their soft fur, smiling faces, and swishing tails, *collies look* very *gentle* despite their obvious strength.

Now let's look at the separate parts of our basic sentences.

Subject	*Verb*
Somebody or something	does something.
Dogs	bark.

Notice that the person or thing that *does something* is the subject of the sentence. And the word that tells what is done is the verb.

In a sentence like *Monkeys climb trees* or *Elephants eat peanuts* the last part tells, for instance, what is climbed or what is eaten. This part completes the *does something* in some sentences and so may be called a completer or a complement—which means the same thing. The more common name, however, is direct object.

Subject	*Verb*	*Direct Object*
Elephants	eat	peanuts.

75

The second basic sentence type is different in two ways from the first.

Subject	Verb	Complement
Somebody or something	is or seems to be	something.
Dogs	are	animals.
Collies	are	large.
Collies	look	gentle.

Note that again we start with a subject that indicates somebody or something. This time the verb doesn't mean *does something* but means *is or seems to be*. And the completer can be a word like *animals*—a noun or a pronoun—that names somebody or something, or it can be a descriptive word—an adjective— like *large* or *gentle*. (Once in a while it may also be an adverb, as in *The collies are downstairs*.)

In Section B we'll look at some more examples of basic sentences.

B: EXERCISES

1 **Benito Pablo Juárez spoke.**

In the sentence above, which words name somebody or something? _____

_____ Which word tells what that somebody

or something did? _____

2 In a basic sentence of the sort we are examining, the beginning part names somebody or something and is called the subject. The other part tells what the subject does and is called the verb. In the example in exercise 1 the

subject is _____ and the verb is _____.

3 *Subject   Verb   Direct Object*
  Juárez   led   the Mexicans.

Very often the second section of a basic sentence has not only a verb but also one or more words that tell who or what was led, eaten, damaged, or whatever the verb says. That part is called the direct object, as the example above shows.

In the sentence *Juárez opposed the wealthy* the direct object is _____

_____.

4 *Subject   Verb   Complement*
  Juárez   was   intelligent.
  He   seemed popular.
  He   is   the Mexican national hero.

The sentences above are of the second basic type. Do the subjects again mean *somebody or something?* _____ Does the verb again mean *does something?* _____

5 In sentences of the second type the verb shows no action. It means *is or seems to be* (or, in a different number and tense, *are, was, were, seemed,* and so on). In the sentence *Juárez was president* the verb is _____.

6 The complement in sentences of the second type may be an adjective that describes the subject. In exercise 4 the complements of this sort are _____ _____ and _____. It may also be a noun (or the equivalent of a noun) that classifies the subject or calls it by some other name. In exercise 4 the complement of this sort is _____ _____ _____ _____. (Here the last word is really the complement, but the other words go with it to provide more details.)

7 In exercises 7–11 you will be completing some basic sentences by putting in missing basic parts. You may use any words that make sense.
    Here, write in the missing subjects.

  A. _____ froze her hands.

  B. _____ swim.

  C. _____ chose the vegetables.

8 In these basic sentences of the first type, supply suitable verbs.

  A. The boys _____.

  B. The girls _____ the boat.

  C. Squirrels _____ the farmer's corn.

9 Supply suitable direct objects in these sentences of the first basic type.

  A. Drinking drivers kill _____.

  B. The voters elected _____.

  C. Richard and I built _____.

10 The following incomplete sentences are of the second basic type. Complete them by writing in some verbs with the meaning of *is or seems to be.* (Use plural forms and past tenses if necessary.)

  A. Many rivers _____ muddy.

  B. Amelia Earhart _____ a famous flyer.

  C. These oranges _____ unusually sweet.

11 Supply adjectives or nouns to complete these sentences of the second basic type.

A. **Lemons taste** _____.

B. **Lemons are** _____.

C. **John Quincy Adams was** _____.

12 In some of the examples above we have added words like *the, these, many, her, unusually.* Such additions may be made without any changes in the basic pattern. Write in some such additions that make sense in the following paragraph:

_____ robins were building _____ nest. _____ male

and _____ female both carried grass, twigs, and mud. They

_____ put _____ materials _____. _____

nest _____ took shape.

C: ASSIGNMENTS

• Complete these sentences of the first basic type. Add whatever other words are necessary (like *a, the, some, quickly*).

1. Chemists _____. 2. _____ hurry. 3. _____ buy _____.
4. _____ shoved _____. 5. _____ defeated _____.
6. _____ fly. 7. _____ fly _____. 8. The trumpeter
_____ _____. 9. Camels _____ _____. 10. _____
_____.

• Complete these sentences of the second basic type. Add whatever words are necessary.

1. _____ is a flower. 2. _____ are flowers. 3. John Glenn was _____.
4. Susan is _____. 5. Susan seemed _____. 6. A carp _____ a fish.
7. Carp _____ always hungry. 8. Carp always _____ hungry. 9. This
milk _____ sour. 10. _____ _____ a heroine.

ANSWERS TO SECTION B

1. Benito Pablo Juárez   spoke
2. Benito Pablo Juárez   spoke
3. the wealthy

4. Yes   No
5. was
6. intelligent, popular   the Mexican national hero
7. MODELS   A. Bonita   B. Fish   C. The cook
8. MODELS   A. fished   B. rocked   C. ate
9. MODELS   A. pedestrians   B. a governor   C. a garage
10. MODELS   A. are   B. was   C. taste
11. MODELS   A. sour   B. yellow   C. a President
12. MODELS   Two, their, The, the, carefully, the, together, The, finally

Unit 10—The Sentence Fragment with an Incomplete Verb

A: COMMENTARY

Many students mistake sentence fragments for complete sentences. The purpose of this unit is to make clear one of the important differences.

Almost every complete sentence must have a subject and a complete verb. Usually the verb causes the trouble. Although a verb is often only one word, such as *is*, *ran*, or *explained*, more than a single word is sometimes needed.

Specifically, if the main verb ends in the suffix *-ing*, for instance *carrying* or *speaking*, a helping word, technically called an auxiliary verb, is required. One part of the auxiliary must be a form of *be* (*am, is, are, was, were, be, been*). So we may say, for instance, *am carrying, was speaking, may be carrying, must have been speaking.*

Similarly an auxiliary verb is needed with a past participle, which is sometimes called an *-en* verb because it has that ending in a few verbs such as *spoken* and *eaten*. The same auxiliaries are used as with *-ing* forms, and *have, has,* and *had* also occur frequently. For example: She *had spoken* her lines. The eggs *were eaten.* The house *has been sold.* The petition *was denied.*

Sentence fragments are not always undesirable. In fact, professional writers use them fairly often, especially in writing dialog, since most of us speak occasional fragments in conversation. Professionals may also use fragments for other purposes, such as transitions: *Now for the victim's side of the case* or *On the contrary.* Most teachers, though, prefer that students avoid using fragments (except maybe in dialog) until they have demonstrated mastery of the complete sentence.

B: EXERCISES

1 A. **Men brought beer.**
  B. **The men brought some beer to the hilltop.**

C. **Several men wearing blue jeans and odd-looking hats were with some difficulty carrying cases of beer to the top of the hill.**

The subject and whatever words belong with it are called the *complete subject,* which is the first part of a sentence that is in the normal order. The verb and the direct object or other complement, as well as any other words belonging with the verb, are called the *complete predicate,* which is the second part of a sentence in normal order. In sentences A, B, and C above draw a line between the complete subject and the complete predicate. (These three sentences are examples of the first basic type, as described in Unit 9.)

2 A. **Karl Marx was a radical.**
   B. **A German, Karl Marx, was the theorist of the radicals.**
   C. **A German, Karl Marx, who wrote** Das Kapital, **had written the** Communist Manifesto **much earlier.**

Again, draw a line between the complete subject and the complete predicate.

3

        Complete Predicate
        Verb
Men   carried cases of beer.

Most often the verb part of a complete predicate is a single word. In the example above, the verb is _____.

4

          Complete Predicate
     Verb   *Direct Object*
  A. **Men were carrying**   cases of beer.
  B. **Men had been carrying**   cases of beer.
  C. **Men may have been carrying** cases of beer.

Sometimes the verb part of a complete predicate has to be two, three, or four words. In sentence A above, the verb is _____ _____, in B it is _____ _____ _____, and in C it is _____ _____ _____ _____.

5 Look again at sentences A, B, and C in exercise 4. Note that the verb *carrying* has a helper or helpers (called auxiliary verbs) in each sentence. In A the auxiliary verb is _____; in B the auxiliaries are _____ and _____; in C they are _____, _____, and _____.

6 A verb form ending in *-ing* cannot serve alone as the main verb of a sentence. It must have as an auxiliary a form of the verb *be* (*am, is, are, was,*

or *were*) or a phrase containing a form of *be* (*may be, will be, were being, had been,* and so on). In sentence A of exercise 4 the form of *be* is _____, and in B and C the form of *be* is _____.

7 **Men carrying cases of beer.**

The group of words above is not a complete sentence. It is only a sentence fragment. To make it complete we would have to add (what kind of verb or phrase?) _____ before *carrying.*

8 **Several men, in blue jeans and odd-looking hats, with some difficulty carrying cases of beer to the top of the hill.**

The fact that a group of words is long does not make it a complete sentence. The group above is only a sentence fragment because _____

_____.

9 A. **A woman was entering the library.**
   B. **A gray-haired woman with an armload of books entering the library from the Fifth Avenue side.**

Which of the groups of words above is a complete sentence? _____

10 **A woman _____ entering the library.**

Besides *was*, which of the following auxiliaries could be used to make a complete sentence of the words above? _____
A. is   B. were   C. will be   D. has been   E. have   F. may have   G. may have been

11 **Trees broken by the ice.**

In addition to the *-ing* form of a verb (technically called a present participle), there is another form that needs a helper. This is sometimes called an *-en* form because it ends in *-en* in such verbs as *break* (*broken*), *speak* (*spoken*), *freeze* (*frozen*), *drive* (*driven*). It is more generally called a *past participle*. Most often it ends in *-ed*, just as the past tense does.

The same auxiliaries that help out the *-ing* form may also help the *-en* form, and so may *have, has,* and *had.* In the sentence at the beginning of this exercise we could use as auxiliaries the following: _____
A. is   B. were   C. will be   D. have been   E. are   F. has been   G. may have been

12 **The house painted white.**

Even though the verb in the group of words above does not end in *-en*, it is here a past participle and needs an auxiliary to be complete. (Obviously *The house painted white* does not mean much. It does not make a complete statement.)

Using the same list of auxiliaries as in exercise 11, tell which ones may

go before *painted* in the sentence above. _____

13 Some of the following examples are complete sentences, but others may have no verb at all or else only an incomplete verb. Place an X before each complete sentence.

_____ A. **The boys played.**

_____ B. **The happy children.**

_____ C. **The playing children.**

_____ D. **The children were playing.**

_____ E. **The children playing hopscotch on the sidewalk in the hot sun.**

_____ F. **The soldiers given passes.**

_____ G. **The soldiers having been given passes for the weekend.**

_____ H. **The soldiers were given passes for the weekend.**

14 Write sentences as follows:
A. Say that you are in the process of finishing your assignment. Use the

word *finishing* with an auxiliary. Underline the auxiliary. _____

_____

B. Say that Tom sings while you are trying to study. Use the *-ing* form of

sing with an auxiliary. Underline the auxiliary. _____

_____

15 Now write these sentences:
A. Say that Dr. Reynolds advised the students, but use *the students* as the

subject of the sentence. Underline the auxiliary you use. _____

_____

B. Say that lightning has struck the house, but use *house* as the subject.

Underline the two words you use as the auxiliary. _____

_____

C: ASSIGNMENTS

• Some of the following statements are complete sentences; others are not because their verbs are not whole. Determine which statements are complete sentences. If a statement is a complete sentence, underline the main verb twice and add a period. If a statement is not a complete sentence, find the partial verb and make it whole by doing one of two things:

A. Add to it an auxiliary word or phrase such as *is, are, was, were, will be, may have been, could be,* or *might be.* For example:

were
Birds ∧ singing in their cages

was
The run ∧ scored by the catcher

B. Use a caret (∧) and write your corrections above the line. Cross out any words you replace.

sang
Birds ∧ ~~singing~~ in their cages

1. The roads being icy and slippery

2. Melba was studying her part in the play

3. The package containing no directions whatsoever for assembling the sprayer

4. The toddling child was stopped at the brink of the cliff

5. The man hit by the stray bullet

6. After the show we strolled down toward Fisherman's Wharf

7. The men hunting for a good place to have dinner

8. The speaker adjusting the microphone

9. The Gettysburg Address delivered by Lincoln on the occasion of the dedication of the battleground

10. Ned loading the boat, checking his equipment, and shoving off without his oars

11. The burning brush near the road threatened to stop traffic

12. The newspaper printed by the journalism students

13. I was astonished by your remark

14. Having a flat tire on the freeway proved to be inconvenient and dangerous

15. Having a flat tire on the freeway proving to be inconvenient and dangerous

ANSWERS TO SECTION B

1. A. Men/brought   B. men/brought   C. hats/were
2. A. Marx/was   B. Marx,/was   C. *Kapital*,/had
3. carried
4. were carrying, had been carrying, may have been carrying
5. were, had been, may have been
6. were, been
7. an auxiliary (*or* a helper)
8. MODEL   it does not have a complete verb
9. A
10. A. is   C. will be   D. has been   G. may have been
11. B. were   C. will be   D. have been   E. are   G. may have been
12. A. is   C. will be   F. has been   G. may have been
13. X's before A, D, H
14. MODELS   A. I am finishing my assignment.   B. Tom is singing while I am trying to study.
15. MODELS   A. The students were advised by Dr. Reynolds.   B. The house has been struck by lightning.

Unit 11—Appropriate Sentence Length

A: COMMENTARY

A good sentence may be one word long. For instance, *Hurry!* (which has the understood subject *you*) may be the very best sentence for its purpose.

Or a good sentence may be fifty or one hundred or even more words in length. Novelist William Faulkner sometimes wrote sentences that stretched all the way from here to there—sometimes over a page.

On the average, today's sentences of professional writers come out about twenty words each, although the range in any single piece of writing may be considerable. The sentences of writers of a hundred or two hundred years ago were considerably longer. Modern writers are convinced that very lengthy sentences are difficult to understand. They also believe that many consecutive short sentences are choppy.

The exercises in Section B deal with ways of adding useful information to short sentences and with ways of combining series of very short sentences. Units 12 to 14 provide additional suggestions for combining.

B: EXERCISES

1 **We will come home next Tuesday.**

In general does the sentence above seem satisfactory? _____

2 In most circumstances the sentence in exercise 1 would be quite satisfactory. But suppose that you are the mother or father of the writers and have no idea of their travel plans, where to meet them, and so on. What are two

or three questions you might like to have answered? _____

_____

_____

3 **We will come home next Tuesday on TWA flight 227, arriving at 3:05 P.M.**

Note how much more information has been crammed into about ten additional words. This information, of course, was added not to make the

sentence longer but rather for the purpose of _____

_____.

4 **My last examination was difficult.**
  We won last night.
  A friend was hurt.

Choose one of the sentences above and rewrite it, adding some details that

a friend or relative of yours might like to know. _____

_____

_____

5 Choose another of the sentences in exercise 4 and expand it.

_____

_____

6 Read these two selections, both of which contain only short sentences.

   A. The sound of footsteps came closer. Terrified, I sat up in bed. My ears seemed to bend toward the sound. My heartbeat was loud in the room. Out on the sidewalk the feet scraped concrete as they moved. Then, fully awake, I saw what time it was. Five o'clock! I heard the clang of metal against metal. Of course, the garbage collector! I fell asleep laughing.

   B. In the early days a journey up the Mississippi was difficult. It was not by steam. It took three or four months. That was to get from New Orleans to St. Louis. By 1836 things had changed. The change was for

the better. One could then make the trip in six days. Steam had provided a great new source of power.

In which paragraph can we defend the short sentences on the ground that the paragraph deals with disconnected, fragmentary, abrupt thoughts?

_____

7 In exercise 6 what makes the short sentences in B seem inappropriate?

_____

8 Using paragraph B in exercise 6 as our example, let's consider some of the ways that short sentences can be combined.

One of these ways is to change one of the sentences into a phrase starting with a preposition. (*To, in, on, near, for, of, before, after,* and *with* are examples of words often used as prepositions.) If we were to change the second sentence into the prepositional phrase *before steam,* how could this phrase be used in the first sentence? Rewrite the first sentence to include the new phrase. _____

_____

9 Another way to combine sentences is to change one of them into a verbal phrase. Such a phrase usually starts with an *-ing* form of a verb (for example, *staying here all day*). It may also start with an infinitive, which is generally signaled by *to* (for example, *to finish very early*). Or it may start with an *-en* verb form, called a past participle (for example, *broken in the mail*).

Change the third sentence of paragraph B in exercise 6 into the verbal phrase *taking three or four months.* Attach that phrase to your revision of the first two sentences. Write the new sentence. _____

_____

_____

10 What could be done with the next sentence (starting with *That was*)?

_____

_____

_____

11 The next sentence is *By 1836 things had changed.* The sentence after that one could be reduced to a phrase and attached to it. Write the phrase.

_____

12 Sometimes two sentences can be combined in this way: Decide which seems

to be the less important of the two. Then decide whether *because, when, where, if, so that, after, before, while,* or some other such word can be put in front of the less important sentence so that it will make sense when joined with the other. For example, in our paragraph change the last sentence into the clause *because steam had provided a great new source of power.* Combine it with the preceding sentence. Write your answer.

_____

_____

13 In this exercise we have looked at four ways to combine short sentences. In exercise 8 we saw that sometimes a whole sentence may be changed to a

_____. In exercise 9 we saw that a sentence

may be changed to a _____. In exercises 10 and 11 we

noted that sometimes several words may simply be _____
And in exercise 12 we saw that sometimes a word like *because,* (name four

other suitable words) _____, _____, _____,

or _____ may be used to link sentences logically.

14 Revise each example as indicated in parentheses.

A. **We played eighteen holes of golf. We played in the morning.**

(Delete some words.) _____

_____

B. **I veered sharply to the right. I was trying to avoid a head-on collision with the oncoming car.** (Make the second sentence a verbal phrase of

the first. Start with *Trying.*) _____

_____

C. **The wind died away. The hurricane had finally moved northward.**

(Put a suitable one of these words before the second sentence as you

write the combination: *if, while, because, after, although, until.*) _____

_____

D. **The freezing rain made the narrow road treacherous. It was an icy ribbon.** (Combine the sentences by use of a prepositional phrase. Perhaps

the combination will end like this: *a treacherous* _____ of

_____ .)

_____

_____

C: ASSIGNMENTS

• Add to these short sentences in order to provide information of the sort that an interested reader might like to have.

1. Several trees were damaged.
2. I went to a concert.
3. The park is beautiful.
4. Snow is predicted.
5. She won an award.

• Revise the following paragraphs.

1. O. E. Rölvaag came to America. There was no work in New York. He was poor. He soon decided to leave New York. He went to Minnesota.
2. Cheese is made from cows' milk. Also the milk of goats, sheep, horses, buffalo, llamas, and yaks is used. Cheese-making is an ancient art. It dates back to biblical times. Today's commercial cheeses are more uniform in quality and taste. They usually taste like plastic.
3. Nearly all animals are competitive. Observation establishes this. Perhaps it is in the nature of man to be competitive too. Perhaps we should not try to eliminate competition from our lives. Perhaps we should simply provide substitutes for destructive competition. War is destructive competition. Most games make good substitutes for war. Perhaps we could find other nondestructive substitutes for war. We might eliminate war in this way.

ANSWERS TO SECTION B

1. Yes
2. MODEL   How are you coming? When will you arrive? Shall we meet you, and if so, where?
3. MODEL   providing details that someone might need to know
4–5. MODELS   My last examination, in mathematics, was rather difficult for me because I had not had time to review. We won the basketball game last night, 74–69, but the outcome was in doubt until the last minute. My friend Jack was hurt, although not seriously, when he stepped on a rusty nail.
6. A
7. MODEL   The passage seems jerky and disconnected.
8. Before steam, a journey up the Mississippi was difficult.
9. Before steam, a journey up the Mississippi was difficult, taking three or four months.
10. MODEL   *That was* could be deleted, and the rest could be attached to the sentence in exercise 9.
11. for the better

12. One could then make the trip in six days because steam had provided a great new source of power.

13. prepositional phrase   verbal phrase   deleted (*or* left out)   when, where, if, so that, after, before, while (four of these)

14. A. We played eighteen holes of golf in the morning.
    B. Trying to avoid a head-on collision with the oncoming car, I veered sharply to the right.
    C. Because (*or* After) the hurricane had finally moved northward, the wind died away.
    D. The freezing rain made the narrow road a treacherous ribbon of ice.

Unit 12—Compounding in Sentences

A: COMMENTARY

In Unit 10 we looked at the basic sentences that we use over and over, and in Unit 11 we saw some of the ways by which very short sentences may be combined. In this unit we'll examine the kind of combination known as compounding or coordination.

These words refer to joining parts of equal importance. In speaking and writing we do this constantly, referring to *ham and eggs, snow and sleet, Dick and Jane, come hell or high water,* or *red, white, and blue.*

Often we combine two nouns or noun equivalents as compound subjects or compound objects. Instead of saying *Jack went up the hill and Jill went up the hill,* we economize by compounding: *Jack and Jill went up the hill.* Instead of saying *I brought some salt and I brought some pepper,* we again save some time by saying *I brought some salt and pepper.* We may also have compound adjectives, more often called coordinate adjectives: Instead of saying *The stripes are yellow and the stripes are green,* we say *The stripes are yellow and green.*

We also combine whole sentences that are on the same topic and that seem to be of about equal importance. We may take some sentences like these:

> **I brought some salt and pepper.**
> **Juanita furnished the bacon and eggs.**

and combine them as a compound sentence by adding a comma and an appropriate connecting word:

> **I brought some salt and pepper, but Juanita furnished the bacon and eggs.**

Compounding results in saving words and time, in getting rid of unnecessary repetition, and in eliminating choppy, short sentences. Writers, however, must be sure that the parts they compound really do belong together. They must make sure also that they do not compound so much that they come out with monotonous *and . . . and* sentences.

B: EXERCISES

1 **My father likes spaghetti. My mother likes spaghetti.**

According to the sentence above, do my father and mother both like the

same kind of food? _____

2 To avoid repeating *likes spaghetti* in exercise 1, we can compound the two subjects and come out with a single sentence:

_____ _____ _____ _____ **like spaghetti.**

3 **My uncle prefers ravioli. He also prefers lasagna.**

Do the words *my uncle* and *he* refer to the same person? _____

4 We can compound the two direct objects in the sentences in exercise 3 and come out with this sentence:

My uncle prefers _____ _____ _____.

5 **Spring grass is light green. It is also very soft.**

Here we can compound the adjectives, with this sentence as the result:

Spring grass is _____ _____ _____ _____ _____.

6 Often we put two or more basic sentences together without making any large changes. For instance, consider these two sentences:

The bomb shattered windows for blocks.
It apparently killed no one.

To be compounded, basic sentences need to be closely related. Does that

seem to be true of our examples? _____

7 In compounding, we usually need to think about which one of the following connectives will make best sense as a link: *and, but, for, or, nor, yet,* or

so. To connect the basic sentences in exercise 6, the most logical connective is _____.

8 We generally put a comma before the connective in a compound sentence. Write the sentence that we get by compounding our two basic sentences (exercise 6).

_____, but

_____.

9 **The population of the United States in 1880 was fifty million. In the next sixty years it more than doubled.**

Sometimes in writing a compound sentence we decide that no connective is needed. In that case we simply punctuate with a semicolon (;). If we compound in that way the examples at the top of this frame, we come out with: _____; _____

_____.

10 **This morning's round-table discussion was on office regulations. I think these discussions should be held in the late afternoon.**

The first sentence above concerns the topic of a discussion. The second is about desirable times for similar discussions. These topics (are/are not) _____ closely related. They (should/should not) _____ be combined as a compound sentence.

11 The clauses of a compound sentence should be of about equal importance. Is there such a relationship between the clauses of the following sentence?

_____ If not, which clause is more important, the first or the second?

_____

Moby Dick **is the story of a man's battle with a white whale, and the story takes place mainly in the South Seas.**

Is the above sentence a good compound sentence? _____

12 Though the clauses in the above sentence are closely related, they are not of equal importance. The second clause might be treated as just a modifier of the first. Complete this revision of the sentence:

Moby Dick, **which takes place mainly in the South Seas, is**

_____.

13 Sometimes there is a relationship between the clauses of a compound sentence that is wrongly left unexpressed, as in this example:

The drive between Barstow and Kingman is a difficult one, and we make the trip at night.

In this sentence there is apparently a relationship between the fact that the trip is made at night and the idea that the drive is difficult, but the relationship is not expressed.
Here is a revision of the sentence:

The drive from Barstow to Kingman is a difficult one, and we make the trip at night to escape the heat.

In the revision the addition of the phrase _____
makes clear the relationship between the clauses.

14 Is the revised example in exercise 13 a good compound sentence? _____

15 As we saw in exercise 7, it is important to use the most logical connective between the clauses of a compound sentence. Here is one in which a better word than *and* may be found:

I wanted to hand in my paper late, and the instructor said that he had no provision for late papers.

Remember that the available connectives are *and, but, for, or, nor, yet,* and *so.* Instead of *and,* we should use _____ in the sentence above.

16 Some people, especially in speaking, have a tendency to string independent clauses together with a series of *and*'s and *so*'s as connectives, as in this example:

We packed our picnic lunch, and we all piled into the car, but Bob had forgotten about gas, and none of us had any money, so we got out again, and Hilda said we could walk to the park, so we did.

Are all of the following three points reasons for avoiding sentences such as the example above? _____

A. **Such sentences are monotonous and stylistically uninteresting.**
B. **They give no clue to the relative importance of each part.**
C. **They are usually a mark of immature expression.**

17 Revise the example in exercise 16 according to the following pattern. Keep the clauses in their original order. It will be necessary to omit some connectives.

After we _____, we all piled into the

car. However, because _____ gas, and none of

us _____, _____ got out again. Then, at Hilda's sug-

gestion, we _____.

C: ASSIGNMENTS

• Combine the following sentences by the use of compound subjects, compound objects, or coordinate adjectives.

1. Judy likes to play basketball. Zelda likes to play basketball.
2. Dad paid the electric bill. He paid the telephone bill. He paid the rent.
3. This mower is well built. It is unusually sturdy.
4. Cabbage plants are relatively tough. They are fairly frost resistant. *state of bring*
5. Bryan is a star athlete on the track team. He also excels on the basketball court.
6. Swimming is one of my favorite sports. Gymnastics is another of my favorite sports.

• Here are several pairs or groups of sentences. Decide whether the sentences in each pair or group can sensibly be compounded, and if so, write the result.

1. We should get a new car. New cars are very expensive.
2. Teacups are sometimes made of porcelain. Our stove has a porcelain top.
3. One meaning of *ramp* is "a sloping way or path." Another is "a wild onion."
4. The safety catch on a rifle keeps it from being fired accidentally. Safety precautions are very important.
5. Shagbark hickories are easy to recognize. They are tall trees with unusually rough bark.
6. The clock continues to run. There is less than five minutes left.
7. The leaves of tobacco next go to the stemmery. The stems and other unusable parts are discarded there.
8. We may be able to win the game now. We may have to settle for a tie.
9. There must have been a strip mine here. The ground over several acres is deeply furrowed.
10. LaGarde has four fouls. He will have to play very cautiously.

• Rewrite these *and . . . and* sentences.

1. There are two kinds of wild turkeys, and one of them is a native of Mexico and Central America, and the other is from the eastern part of the United States, and this is the larger of the two.
2. Texas has long stretches of sandy beaches, and these are on its Gulf Coast, and they are popular for swimming, and they also provide access to much good deep-sea fishing.
3. I pulled a muscle in my thigh and so I was not able to move very well and I limped along with the ball for a while and then I was tackled again and this time I hurt the other leg.

ANSWERS TO SECTION B

1. Yes
2. My father and mother
3. Yes
4. ravioli and lasagna
5. light green and very soft
6. Yes
7. but (*or* yet)
8. The bomb shattered windows for blocks, but it apparently killed no one.
9. The population of the United States in 1880 was fifty million; in the next sixty years it more than doubled.
10. are not   should not
11. No   First   No
12. the story of a man's battle with a white whale
13. to escape the heat
14. Yes
15. but (*or* yet)
16. Yes
17. (had) packed our picnic lunch   Bob had forgotten   had any money   we walked to the park

Unit 13—Subordinating Less Important Ideas

A: COMMENTARY

This unit reinforces a point that you have already studied in earlier units: When two sentences of unequal importance are combined, the one with the less important idea should normally be placed in a subordinate construction. Sometimes, of course, the ideas are of about equal importance and may be compounded, or sometimes it is impossible to tell which is more important.

The dance ended. Jay and Kathy went home.

In the sentences above, from the standpoint of Jay and Kathy, the more important idea is that Jay and Kathy went home. When we combine the sentences, then, we should subordinate the first one, perhaps like this:

After the dance ended, Jay and Kathy went home.

We have used the word *after*, which is here called a subordinating conjunction. *After the dance ended* is a subordinate clause (also called a dependent clause). The main part of the sentence, *Jay and Kathy went home*, may be called a main clause or a dependent clause.

Some other subordinating conjunctions are *before, while, whenever, since, because, although, if, even if, even though,* and *so that.*

Section B elaborates on this explanation, and also pays some attention to occasional misuse of the subordinating conjunctions *because, while, since,* and *where.* It also recommends against long chains of subordinate clauses.

B: EXERCISES

1 **A tidal wave unexpectedly hit the coast, and a thousand people were drowned.**

From the human standpoint, which of the clauses in the above sentence would seem to be more important, the one before the comma or the one after? _____

2 Does the form of the sentence in exercise 1 indicate that one clause is more important than another? _____

3 The more important idea in a sentence should normally be placed in a (main/subordinate) _____ clause.

4 The less important idea should be placed in a _____*clause*_____ clause.

5 Here are the two clauses of the original example:
_____WHen_____ a tidal wave unexpectedly hit the coast
a thousand people were drowned

Would the word *when* in the blank above express the logical relationship between the two clauses? _yes_

6 **When a tidal wave unexpectedly hit the coast, a thousand people were drowned.**

Note the punctuation in our revised sentence. It shows that after a subordinate clause like that in the example, the normal punctuation mark is a _____,_____ .

7 Which of the following clauses relates the more important happening? _____A_____

A. **our team won the tournament**
B. **we did not expect to win a single game**

8 Put together the two clauses in exercise 7. Start your sentence with *Although*. *We didn't expect to win a turkey* *we did*

9 It is important to use the subordinating conjunction that makes your meaning most clear. For instance, consider the italicized subordinating conjunction in this sentence:

The astronauts landed safely *because* I saw the news on television this evening.

Did the astronauts land safely because someone watched television? *yes?*

10 There are many ways to correct a sentence like the one in exercise 9. Here is one way. Complete the revision.

I saw on television that *the astros landed safely*.

11 **Hank makes thirty dollars while Henry makes only twenty at the same job.**

In the above sentence could *while* mean either "in the same time that" or "although"? _____

12 _____ would be a better conjunction than *while* if the meaning is simply that Hank makes more money than Henry.

13 **Since you left town, your brother is very happy.**

Like *while, since* may sometimes be ambiguous. In the sentence above, *since* may mean either "because" or "during the time after." The reader has no way of deciding which meaning is intended. One meaning may be made clear in *Since the time you left town, your brother has been very happy.* The following sentence, using the word *because*, shows the other meaning:
because you left town your bro is very happy.

14 **Did you see in the paper where Sue and Bill got elected?**

In the above sentence *where* seems to refer to a place where the election occurred. Is this probably what the speaker meant? _____

15 Rewrite the example from exercise 14, substituting *that* for *where*.

_____

16 Write four sentences using each of the following words in turn as a subordinating conjunction: *because, while, since, where.* Be sure that in your sentences each conjunction can have only one meaning.

A. _____

_____

B. _____

_____

C. _____

_____

D. _____

_____

17 The wind changed direction when the eye of the storm passed because the storm was rotating in a circle that was counterclockwise since the storm was in the Northern Hemisphere, though it would have rotated clockwise in the Southern Hemisphere.

The above example contains a long chain of subordinate clauses. Such a sentence is (effective/ineffective) _____.

18 The example in exercise 17 is ineffective for which three of the following reasons? __B__ __C__ __A__

A. There are too many loosely related ideas.
B. So many subordinate clauses make effective emphasis impossible.
C. Such a sentence is unpleasant to read.
D. In general, long sentences are undesirable.

19 There is no actual ambiguity in the example in exercise 17, but chains of subordinate clauses do sometimes obscure the meaning, as in this example:

The child had a tantrum because his mother left the house because she wanted to shop for groceries.

The above sentence has two possible meanings:

A. The child had a tantrum because the mother left the house.
B. The child had a tantrum because the mother left the house to shop for groceries (but might not have objected to her leaving the house for another reason).

Is it possible to tell which meaning is intended? _No___

20 Does the following revision of the sentence clear up the ambiguity? _Yes__

The child had a tantrum when the mother left the house to go grocery shopping.

97

C: ASSIGNMENTS

• Most of the following sentences are faulty in some way. Copy the fifteen numbers, leaving space enough for a revised sentence. Indicate which of the following statements best describes the sentence by writing A, B, C, or D alongside the corresponding number. Then rewrite each faulty sentence, correcting the fault.

> A. **Neither clause is subordinated although one clause is less important that the other.**
> B. **The wrong clause is subordinated.**
> C. **The subordinating conjunction is misused.**
> D. The sentence is correct.

1. Harvey didn't pass the test because his wife said so. C
2. The railroad signal lights were working, and the truck ran into the speeding train.
3. Did you see in the paper where the new freeway has been approved? C
4. The police officer tore the wire from the timing mechanism although the bomb went off. B
5. After the sun set, the comet's brilliance increased.
6. The police officer gave me a ticket, and I had considered him my friend. A
7. The fire trucks arrived immediately although seven people died in the fire.
8. When the helicopter troops arrived, the guerrillas fled.
9. Mary favors the new bond proposal while Jack is bitterly against it.
10. The professor gave a pop quiz on the difficult chapter, and most of the students failed.
11. The Giants lost in the last inning because my brother saw the game.
12. I am sure that the pianist hit a couple of wrong notes, although she played brilliantly and received a standing ovation at the end.
13. The speaker frankly revealed the unpleasant truth, and the audience applauded.
14. The show "Stars over Hollywood" received fairly good ratings, and it was canceled by the network.
15. Since you scolded him, the dog has been sulking in his house.

• Rewrite the sentences that have long, ineffective, or possibly ambiguous strings of subordinate clauses.

1. We left after the touchdown that won the game for us after the opposing team failed to make its point after its last touchdown.
2. Because the library was closed, I studied in my room because it was cold in the study hall.
3. Jim failed the test because he cheated and was caught because he hadn't studied.
4. Your fear that you will study so late that you will oversleep the examination that is scheduled for 8:15 A.M. is well justified.

5. The professor closed the windows because the students were having a pep rally in the street because the big game was the next day.
6. Williamson will vote for anyone who opposes the incumbent mayor, who openly supported Senator James, who favors state lotteries.
7. I like the proposed new calendar because it would put every holiday on the same day of the week because the number of working days in the year would be divisible by seven because that is the number of days in the week.
8. Although I am very much in favor of your proposal, I cannot support it at this time.
9. Any parking lot that has so many exclusions that patrons are afraid that they will be arrested for parking in it is poorly conceived.
10. The editor asked that I interview the man that led the demonstration that caused so much trouble.

ANSWERS TO SECTION B

1. the one after
2. No
3. main
4. subordinate (*or* dependent)
5. Yes
6. comma
7. A
8. Although we did not expect to win a single game, our team won the tournament.
9. No
10. the astronauts landed safely
11. Yes
12. Although
13. Because you left town, your brother is very happy.
14. No
15. Did you see in the paper that Sue and Bill got elected?
16. A. Give yourself credit if the subordinate clause actually expresses a causal relationship.
    B. Give yourself credit if you can substitute for *while* one but not both of these meanings: "during the time that," "although."
    C. Give yourself credit if you can substitute for *since* one but not both of these meanings: "during the time that elapsed after," "because."
    D. Give yourself credit if your *where* means "in the place that."
17. ineffective
18. A B C
19. No
20. Yes

Unit 14—Other Ways to Combine Sentences

A: COMMENTARY

Here are two ordinary basic sentences:

Uncle Bob is a native of Colorado.
He has lived in that state most of his life.

One way to combine such sentences is to change one of them into a clause using *who* or *which*:

Uncle Bob, who is a native of Colorado, has lived in that state most of his life.

That sentence can be trimmed a bit further:

Uncle Bob, a native of Colorado, has lived in that state most of his life.

The words *a native of Colorado* are called an appositive. An *appositive* is a second identification of someone or something and comes right after the first identification. It is like a *who is* or *which is* clause except that those words are missing.
Now note these two sentences:

Uncle Bob is a rancher.
He is wealthy.

Such sentences can be combined by moving the adjective from one sentence into the other:

Uncle Bob is a wealthy rancher.

Finally, we'll take another look at a kind of combination already noticed in Unit 13.

The fire trucks arrived.
The small blaze was soon extinguished.

If we examine these sentences, we see that there is a time relationship. First the fire trucks arrived, and then the blaze was put out. We can combine the sentences in this way:

After the fire trucks arrived, the small blaze was soon extinguished.

Besides *after*, some of the other words that can be used in such combinations are *when, while, since, because, although, if*, and *so that*.
One caution: Do not confuse a clause like *After the fire trucks arrived* with a complete sentence. It is only a fragment and needs to be attached to a sentence to be complete.

B: EXERCISES

1 **Celtuce is a cross between celery and lettuce.**
It produces huge amounts of succulent green leaves.

One way to combine the two sentences above is to change the predicate of the first sentence to a *which*-clause. The sentence that results is this:

Celtuce, which is _cross between celery & lettuce_ ,
produces huge amounts of succulent green leaves

2 **One of my favorite television programs is *The Ralstons*.**
It is aired every Tuesday night.

Combine the sentences above, putting a *which*-clause at the end.

The Ralstons, which is aired e T
N is one g my favorite programs.

3 **Billy March plays the leading part in the show.**
He is my favorite actor.

It is possible to change either one of these sentences into a *who*-clause. Write the combination twice (once for each possibility).

Billy March, my favorite plays the
leading part in the show,

4 Look back at the sentence you wrote for exercise 1. Change the *which*-clause to an appositive by deleting the *which is*.

5 Rewrite one of your sentences for exercise 3, using an appositive.

6 **Terry gave the child a basketball.**
It was red and blue.

Combine the sentences above by moving the two adjectives from the second sentence to the first.

7 In exercises 7-9 use the clues provided for a combination of the two sentences.

The library is closed on Thursdays.
I cannot check my references today.

Because _____

_____.

8 The fruit trees were not damaged.
The temperature fell to 31°F.

_____ although

_____.

9 The museum is open tomorrow.
The children would like to go there.

If _____, _____

_____.

10 In exercises 10 and 11 add a sentence to each of the fragments.

A. While the highways were still crowded, _____

_____.

B. _____

because my parents wanted me to have a good education.

11 A. _____

when the funeral services were over.

B. _____

although the players were getting more proficient.

12 For review, write combinations of these pairs of sentences.

A. Ray Bradbury read a great deal as a boy. He says that the author of *Tarzan* was then his favorite author.

_____

_____

B. Later Bradbury became a writer of science fiction. He is famous.

_____

_____

C. He wrote hundreds of short stories, articles, and books. He never created a character as world-renowned as Tarzan.

C: ASSIGNMENTS

• Combine the following pairs or groups of sentences. If more than one sort of combination is possible, explain any differences in meaning or emphasis.

1. Madrid is the capital of Spain. It has a population of over three million.
2. Philip II was a king of Spain four centuries ago. He chose Madrid as the location for his court.
3. At that time Madrid was only a town. It was small. It was relatively isolated.
4. Today Madrid is a manufacturing center. It is commercially important. It makes automobile engines, electronic equipment, and plastics.
5. Natives of Madrid call themselves *gatos*. The word means "cats." Like cats, they walk around late at night.
6. Their dinner hour is 10 P.M. This seems late to most Americans.
7. Curtain time in the theaters is usually 11 P.M. Playgoers usually don't get to bed until 2 or 3 A.M.
8. The traditional siesta makes up for the small amount of sleep at night. A siesta is an early afternoon nap. Many offices and stores close at siesta time.

ANSWERS TO SECTION B

1. a cross between celery and lettuce, produces huge amounts of succulent green leaves
2. One of my favorite television programs is *The Ralstons*, which is aired every Tuesday night.
3. Billy March, who plays the leading part in the show, is my favorite actor. Billy March, who is my favorite actor, plays the leading part in the show.
4. Celtuce, a cross between celery and lettuce, produces huge amounts of succulent green leaves.
5. Billy March, my favorite actor, plays the leading part in the show.
6. Terry gave the child a red and blue basketball.
7. Because the library is closed on Thursdays, I cannot check my references today.
8. The fruit trees were not damaged although the temperature fell to 31°F.
9. If the museum is open tomorrow, the children would like to go there.
10. MODELS A. we delayed our departure for an hour or so
   B. I early learned to value schooling

11. MODELS A. All of us went to Rhoda's house
            B. We still kept losing games
12. MODELS A. Ray Bradbury, who read a great deal as a boy, says that the author of *Tarzan* was then his favorite author.
            B. Later Bradbury became a famous writer of science fiction.
            C. Although he wrote hundreds of short stories, articles, and books, he never created a character as world-renowned as Tarzan.

Unit 15—Arranging Items in a Logical Order

A: COMMENTARY

Items in a sentence should be arranged according to some principle.

1. *Arrangement by chronology.* Ordinarily it is a good idea to list events in the order in which they occurred.

> POOR: Two shots rang out, and the gangster fell dead after he had unexpectedly reached for his gun.

> BETTER: The gangster unexpectedly reached for his gun, two shots rang out, and the gangster fell dead.

2. *Arrangement according to importance.* The most important item may be given first, then the next most important, and so on.

> POOR: Harold had the second-best paper, Karen the best, and Fred the third-best.

> BETTER: Karen had the best paper, Harold the second-best, and Fred the third-best.

3. *Arrangement by climax.* This arrangement turns Number 2 upside down. It builds up to the most important.

> ANTICLIMACTIC: The impact of the new tax will be felt in state, nation, and city.

> CLIMACTIC: The impact of the new tax will be felt in city, state, and nation.

4. *Arrangement by alphabetical order.* If a list of persons' names (or sometimes names of cities, states, or other places) is to be given in a sentence, and if there is no reason for some other arrangement, it is often best to list them in alphabetical order. Many people are sensitive about listings of names and dislike having their own near the bottom unless placed there by the impartial alphabet.

There are other ways of arranging the items in a sentence. The important thing to remember is that whenever you write a list, some kind of order is better than no kind of order.

B: EXERCISES

1 Failure to arrange items in a list in some logical order can result in awkwardness or confusion. For instance, consider this sentence:

In the lobby a person yelled "Fire!" but before that a bystander asked for water after someone had fainted, and the huge theater crowd stampeded.

Though the meaning of this sentence can be figured out, it loses all its force because the events are out of their proper order. Complete the revision of the sentence by filling in the blanks:

In the lobby, someone _____, a bystander asked for _____,

a person _____ _____, and the huge theater crowd

_____.

2 The order in the revised sentence is (alphabetical/chronological)

_____.

3 Here is a list of the causes of an automobile accident:
   A. **the coming off of the left front wheel**
   B. **a driver who had a severe cold and was less alert than normal**
   C. **streets that were glazed with ice**
   Which of the factors is so important that it probably would have caused

   the accident without the other factors? _____

4 What is probably the second most important cause of the accident? _____

5 The least important cause, then, was probably B. Complete this sentence, using in the order of their importance the three causes listed in exercise 3.

   The main cause of the accident was, of course, the _____

   _____, but _____

   _____ and _____

   _____ probably were contributing causes.

6 Other arrangements are possible for a sentence such as the above, but any arrangement will depend on the writer's first putting the items in the series into some logical order.

Would the following version of the sentence be acceptable? _yes_____

Though the driver's severe cold and the icy streets were undoubtedly contributing causes of the accident, the main cause, of course, was the coming off of the left front wheel.

The series in the above sentence is arranged in the order of climax.

7 As exercise 6 shows, sometimes the order of climax may be very effective. If you were walking through a swampy region, which of these dangers would you consider most threatening: the clinging mud, water moccasins, or

mosquitoes? _____

8. A. **When I was trudging through the swamp, the black mud sucked at my shoes and coated my legs, I had to slap constantly at bloodthirsty mosquitoes, and deadly water moccasins twice stuck up their heads no more than five feet away.**
   B. **When I was trudging through the swamp, I had to slap constantly at bloodthirsty mosquitoes, deadly water moccasins twice stuck up their heads no more than five feet away, and the black mud sucked at my shoes and coated my legs.**

Which sentence is more effective, A or B? __A___ Why? _Order_____

9 State in a sentence that the following persons aided in the Salvation Army drive for funds. Do not give anyone special recognition. Mr. Horace Young,

Miss Susan Bley, Mrs. Kate Meadows, Mr. Ted Blount. _____

10 Here are activities often involved in the beginning of a college lecture:

A. **The lecture begins.**
B. **The class bell rings.**
C. **The professor clears his throat.**
D. **The professor goes to the lectern.**

Although sometimes the order may vary, what do you consider the probable

chronological order? _B___ _D___ _C___ _A___

11 Using the items listed in exercise 10, write a sentence about the beginning of a college lecture.

_____

_____

_____

12 In a sentence, list three or four important things you have accomplished in the past year, naming the most important first.

_____

_____

_____

13 Rewrite your sentence for exercise 12, this time building up to the most important item.

_____

_____

_____

C: ASSIGNMENTS

• Analyze a sample of the writing in an article or two in a recent issue of a good-quality magazine. Find and copy five sentences in which there is a list of some kind. Try to decide what principle the writer has used in arranging each list.

• Write sentences according to the following patterns:

1. List your favorite spectator sports as indicated in the following patterns:

I like to watch many sports, but __bAse__, __foot__, and especially __BksEt__ are my favorites.

I like to watch many sports, with _____ being my favorite and _____ and _____ not far behind.

2. List the causes of highway deaths, as indicated by the following patterns:
Many factors contribute to deaths on the highways, the most important of which are _____, _____, and _____. Of the causes of deaths on the highways, _____, _____, and, in my opinion the most important of all, _____, are avoidable.

3. List in three phrases or clauses within a sentence the reasons why you are now a student. Use whatever order you think most effective.

4. Write a sentence in which you list in chronological order the three or four things you did after awakening this morning.

ANSWERS TO SECTION B

1. (had) fainted, water, yelled "Fire!" stampeded
2. chronological
3. A
4. C (although it might conceivably be B)
5. coming off of the left front wheel, streets that were glazed with ice, a driver who had a severe cold and was less alert than normal
6. Yes
7. water moccasins
8. A   MODEL   It builds up to the greatest danger.
9. Miss Susan Bley, Mr. Ted Blount, Mrs. Kate Meadows, and Mr. Horace Young aided in the Salvation Army drive for funds.
10. B, D, C, A
11. MODEL   The class bell rings, the professor goes to the lectern and clears his throat, and the lecture begins.
12–13. Give yourself credit if you followed the instructions.

Unit 16—Emphasis

A: COMMENTARY

Underlining (which corresponds to printed italics) and using exclamation marks are the most obvious ways to attain emphasis. Since both may easily be overdone, however, those methods are not stressed in this unit.

One good way to emphasize is to vary the normal word order by moving the part to be emphasized away from its normal position in the sentence.

NORMAL ORDER:	The *beaten and bleeding* old man limped along the road.
EMPHATIC:	The old man, *beaten and bleeding*, limped along the road.

Another method of gaining emphasis is by completing the essential grammatical structure or idea at the very end of the sentence.

NORMAL ORDER:	The sentry allowed the farmer and the child to pass. He stopped the old beggar.
EMPHATIC:	The sentry allowed the farmer and the child to pass. The old beggar he stopped.

A sentence in which the essential grammatical structure or the essential meaning is not completed until the end is called *periodic*.

One other means of attaining emphasis consists of building to a climax in a series or a whole sentence. Unit 15 illustrates this method.

Not all sentences can or should be emphatic. A college freshman was once addicted to trying for emphasis by underlining significant words. Although this habit is generally frowned upon, a person can be forgiven for underlining an *occasional* word. The problem with this student was that the habit grew; the time came when he was underlining about half of his words. Remember, too, that even the more respectable means of gaining emphasis can be overdone.

B: EXERCISES

1 **The crippled transport circled *over the field*.**

   What group of words stands out in the above sentence? _____

   _____

2 The most obvious way of emphasizing part of a sentence is to italicize it or underline it. In fact, the method is so obvious that most professional writers usually avoid it.

   What group of words is emphasized in the following sentences?

   Adverb **Over the field the crippled transport circled.**

   _____

3 The normal word order in a sentence is subject first and then predicate. Does the sentence in exercise 2 follow this order? ~~Yes~~ No

4 **I like Ned and Henry. Warren I dislike.**

   Which word stands out in the second sentence? _____

5 Rephrase the second sentence of the example in exercise 4 to put the words in their normal order.

   _____ I dislike _____

6 Did *Warren* stand out in the original version of the sentence because it was out of its normal position? Yes

7 Does putting an element out of its normal order in a sentence tend to make the displaced element stand out? Yes

8 A *periodic sentence* is one in which the essential grammatical parts or the essential meaning is not complete until the end. The essential grammatical parts are the basic parts that we have discussed in earlier units: subject,

verb, and complement (when needed). In which sentence below do the subject and verb come last? ___B___

A. **The cry of the owl echoed through the empty spaces of the abandoned haymow.**
B. **Through the empty spaces of the abandoned haymow the cry of the owl echoed.**

9 It is also sometimes possible to change a sentence so that the verb comes before the subject. This, too, adds emphasis.

Through the empty spaces of the abandoned haymow echoed the cry of the owl.

In this example, the verb _____ comes before the subject _____.

10 Are the examples in exercises 8B and 9 both periodic? ___yes___

11 Does saving the main thought until the end of the sentence tend to throw increased emphasis upon that thought? ___yes___

12 Which sentence below is periodic? ___A___

A. **In my opinion, all drunk drivers should be imprisoned.**
B. **All drunk drivers should be imprisoned, in my opinion.**

13 For which one of the following reasons does placement of the phrase *in my opinion* tend to weaken the emphasis in 12B? ___yes___
A. Placing *in my opinion* at the end of the sentence indicates that the writer has no confidence in his or her own opinion.
B. The important part of the statement is *all drunk drivers should be imprisoned*. Placing *in my opinion* last makes that little phrase seem especially important and weakens the whole sentence.

14 Rewrite each of the following examples to emphasize the italicized part.
A. He could see water in every direction. **He could not see *land*.**
(Rewrite the second sentence.)

_____

B. **The thief crept down the stairs *like a cat*.**

_____

C. **I did not need *advice*.**

_____

15 The following sentences have normal word order. Rewrite each one as a periodic sentence.

A. **Stop teasing the dog unless you want to get bitten.**

_____

B. **Death came after the days of creeping flood, after the nights of bitter cold, after the days and nights of wretched sickness.**

(Make _death_, the subject, the very last word.)

_____

_____

_____

C. **Listen to me if you want freedom, if you want security, if you want dignity.**

_____

_____

16 Write emphatic sentences as follows:
A. State that your opinion is that your community should have no curfew. Use the phrase _in my opinion_.

_____

B. State that everyone who wants good schools should vote for you.

_____

C: ASSIGNMENTS

• Using methods of emphasis discussed in Section B (exclusive of underlining), rewrite each of these sentences to make it more emphatic.

1. The soldiers trudged through rain, mud, and filth.
2. I like chocolate and cherry ice cream. I cannot stand strawberry.
3. An obviously bruised and battered child crouched in one corner of the room.
4. Words of wisdom come from the mouths of babes, according to an old saying.
5. Crowds greeted Maximilian as if he had just returned from the tomb.
6. The snow fell softly but relentlessly all through the night and all through the next day and through another night.
7. The incumbent is favored in the Illinois primary, although her opponent is given a chance at what would be a major upset if it were to occur.

ANSWERS TO SECTION B

1. over the field
2. Over the field
3. No (Part of the predicate is at the beginning.)
4. Warren
5. I dislike Warren.
6. Yes
7. Yes
8. B
9. echoed, cry   (*Not* owl—the owl didn't echo.)
10. Yes
11. Yes
12. A
13. B
14. A. Land he could not see.
    B. Like a cat the thief crept down the stairs.
    C. Advice I did not need.
15. A. Unless you want to get bitten, stop teasing the dog.
    B. After the days of creeping flood, after the nights of bitter cold, after the days and nights of wretched sickness, came death.
    C. If you want freedom, if you want security, if you want dignity, listen to me.
16. A. Give yourself credit for any answer that puts *in my opinion* fairly early in the sentence.
    B. Give yourself credit if the last words of your sentence are *vote for me* or some variation of that clause.

Unit 17—The Passive Transformation

A: COMMENTARY

In Unit 9 we saw that one of the basic types of sentences is one that says *Somebody or something does something*. In that unit one of the sentences that we looked at was this:

Subject	*Verb*	*Direct Object*
Juárez	led	the Mexicans.

Grammarians say that that sentence is in the active voice. They note that the subject (*Juárez*) is performing some kind of action (*led*) that affects somebody or something else (*Mexicans*).

Sometimes, however, we are less interested in who performs an action than we are in the person or thing affected. In our example, we may be more

interested in the Mexican people than in their leader. The language permits us
to turn our basic sentence upside down:

$$\begin{array}{ccc} \textit{Subject} & \textit{Verb} & \textit{Obj Prep} \end{array}$$
The Mexicans were led by Juárez.

Notice that the word that was the direct object has become the subject. The
verb *led* has been replaced by *were led*, which uses a form of *be* and a past
participle. Such a verb is said to be in the passive voice. And the word that
was the subject has become the object of the preposition *by*.

Grammarians say that the new sentence, like its verb, is in the passive
voice. That means that the subject of the sentence is the passive receiver of
the action, not the one who acts.

Section B explores some of the uses of the passive voice, but suggests that
in most sentences the active voice is stronger.

B: EXERCISES

1 **Mr. Scott designed the complex traffic interchange badly.**

In the example above, did the subject act? That is, did Mr. Scott do
something? _____

2 In exercise 1 what one word tells what the subject did? _____

3 When a verb shows that the subject is active—that is, doing something—the
verb is understandably said to be (active/passive) _____.

4 If the writer wanted to emphasize not *Mr. Scott* (the one who acts) but
interchange (the thing acted upon), the sentence could be turned upside
down, with *interchange* as the new subject. The sentence would then be:

The complex traffic interchange was badly designed by Mr. Scott.

To a person who used the interchange every day the significant fact might
be that it was badly designed. For such a person might the last three words
of the sentence be omitted? _____

5 In the new sentence (exercise 4) the subject is *interchange*. Does the subject do anything? In other words, does the subject act? _____ Is the verb
the same as the active verb in the original sentence? _____

6 When a verb shows that the subject is passive—that is, the subject does not
act—the verb is understandably said to be (active/passive) _____.

7 Sentences in either the active or the passive voice may be "right." It is a matter of emphasis. When we want to emphasize that the subject is performing some action, it is best to use the (active/passive) _____ voice. But when we want to emphasize the person or thing that is acted upon, it is preferable to use the (active/passive) _____ voice.

8 Although the active voice and the passive voice are equally respectable, the fact is that inexperienced writers tend to use the passive voice too often.

Which of the following sentences seems stronger? _____

A. **All the old favorites were played by the band, a nostalgic speech was made by the president of the alumni association, and a good time was had by all.**

B. **The band played all the old favorites, the president of the alumni association made a nostalgic speech, and everyone had a good time.**

9 In which sentence (exercise 8) are the verbs in the passive voice? _____

10 Which sentence below is stronger? _____ Which is in the active voice? _____

A. **The difficult fugue was played by Harry in his most brilliant style, and after the number was finished, he was applauded by the audience, as well as by the orchestra.**

B. **Harry played the difficult fugue in his most brilliant style, and at the end both the audience and the orchestra applauded.**

11 The active voice is not *always* more effective than the passive. In the following sentences is it probably more appropriate to emphasize the concert or the authorities? _____

A. **The concert was held in the auditorium.**
B. **Authorities held the concert in the auditorium.**

C: ASSIGNMENTS

• Many weak passive constructions reduce the effectiveness of the following passage. Revise it, changing most of the passives to actives.

His first real speech was to be made by him before an audience. The text of the speech had been laid on the table, and the speech itself was now being rehearsed with only occasional glances at the text. His whole life could be affected by the success or failure of this speech. It had been written weeks ago, but now it seemed inadequate. It was now being tried by him with little reference to the text in the hope that delivered without being read it would sound better. He was told by the clock on the wall that time was running out. A chance would have to be taken. It was too late for the speech to be revised.

• Write five effective active-voice sentences, such as *Juárez led the Mexicans.* You may want to use these words as your subjects, although you may choose others: *Henry Aaron, a pair of cardinals, Gloria Steinem, the author, our cat.*

Now rewrite each of your five sentences in the passive voice, and decide which version seems stronger and in general more effective.

• Write three passive voice sentences in which the performer of the action need not be named at all. Examples: *Daniel Walker was elected. A suspect has been arrested.*

ANSWERS TO SECTION B

1. Yes
2. designed
3. active
4. Yes
5. No   No (It now has an auxiliary, *was.*)
6. passive
7. active   passive
8. B
9. A
10. B   B
11. The concert

Unit 18—Eliminating Ambiguity: Adjective Clauses

A: COMMENTARY

There is often a special danger of ambiguity in a sentence that follows this pattern:

Noun + phrase modifier + clause modifier + verb

EXAMPLE: The clown   with the illuminated nose   that is amusing the children   is a student.

The danger is that often the clause modifier may seem to modify either the noun or the phrase modifier. In the example we can't be sure whether it is the clown or only his nose that amuses the children. The ambiguous clause is *that is amusing the children.*

Ambiguity does not always result from following the pattern, but when it does, it can usually be cleared up in more than one way. In the example, a simple substitution of *who* for *that* will do the trick, since *who* and *whom* refer only to persons, not to noses. Alternatively, we can change the order of parts and write *The clown that is amusing the children with his illuminated nose is a student.*

B: EXERCISES

1 A sentence is ambiguous if it has more than one possible meaning.

   Is the following sentence ambiguous? _____

   The woman with the football player, who was carrying an embroidered handbag, waved to us.

2 Note that in the above sentence the subject, *woman,* has two modifiers following it. One is a prepositional phrase (*with the football player*). The

   other is a dependent clause beginning with the pronoun _____.
   Two modifiers like these (a phrase and a clause) following a noun often create ambiguity.

3 Our example in exercise 1 seems to say either that the woman was carrying the embroidered handbag or that the football player was doing so. Let's assume that the football player wouldn't carry a handbag, embroidered or otherwise. We'll revise the sentence to show clearly that the woman was carrying it:

   The woman with the embroidered handbag, who was standing by the football player, waved to us.

   Notice that we have made some changes in the modifiers but kept the probable original meaning of the sentence. Is the revised sentence ambiguous? _____

4 *Who* and *whom* refer to (persons/things) _____.

   In the revised sentence can *who* refer to *handbag?* _____

5 Here is another ambiguous sentence:

   The man with the scar that I called your attention to is here.

   Can the word *that* refer to both persons and things? _____

6 In exercise 5 can *that* refer to either *man* or *scar*? _____

If we substitute *which* for *that*, could *which* also refer to either the man or

the scar? _____

Is the following sentence clear? _____

The man with the scar which I called your attention to is here.

7 Is this revision also clear, but with a different meaning? _____

The man with the scar, whom I called your attention to, is here.

8 **The house beside the road where two men were robbed burned down last night.**

In this ambiguous sentence the word *where* could refer to either *house* or

_____.

If *where* were changed to *in which*, the resulting clause (*in which two*

men were robbed) would have to refer to (house/road) _____.

If *where* were changed to *on which*, the resulting clause would have to

refer to (house/road) _____.

9 The following sentence is ambiguous. Revise it in such a way that the word *who* can refer only to *man.*

The man with the woman who is wearing the green beret is a reporter for the local paper.

_____

_____

10 Revise this sentence in the simplest way, making it clear that the monkey, not the old man, was chattering and turning somersaults.

The monkey with the old man that was chattering and turning somersaults was entertaining to the children.

_____

_____

_____

C: ASSIGNMENTS

• Compose sentences that begin in the ways indicated below. After you have written each, examine it to see whether anyone could possibly misunderstand it. If so, revise to eliminate the ambiguity.

1. The man on the roof that
2. The woman with the artist who
3. A car belonging to a driver that
4. A person with a doctor who
5. A meeting in a park where

ANSWERS TO SECTION B

1. Yes
2. who
3. No
4. persons   No
5. Yes
6. Yes   No   Yes
7. Yes
8. road   house   road
9. MODEL   The man who is talking with the woman and wearing the green beret is a reporter for the local paper. (*Or*   The man wearing the green beret who is standing with the woman is . . .)
10. The monkey with the old man, which was chattering and turning somersaults, was entertaining to the children.

Unit 19—Eliminating Ambiguity: Adverbial Modifiers

A: COMMENTARY

Some errors in expression are more amusing than confusing. For instance:

Flying low over Berkeley, the football stadium came into view.

No one would seriously interpret this sentence to mean that the football stadium was aloft, but everyone is amused by such inadvertencies of careless writers.

Some sentences, such as the one above, can be corrected by naming in the modifier the person or thing acting:

While I was flying low over Berkeley, the football stadium came into view.

Ambiguous or ridiculous sentences having elliptical clauses (clauses with words left out) can be improved by completing the clause:

FAULTY: **While deciding what to do with the ticking package, an alarm went off inside it.**

BETTER: **While we were deciding what to do with the ticking package, an alarm went off inside it.**

Other faulty sentences can be improved by moving the modifier to another position in the sentence.

FAULTY: **Singing and playing in the yard, I quietly watched the children.**

BETTER: **I quietly watched the children singing and playing in the yard.**

The first rule for avoiding such ambiguous or ridiculous sentences is to be alert—if you recognize them, you can easily correct them.

B: EXERCISES

1 **Skating gracefully across the ice, a large moose appeared on the right bank of the lake.**

This sentence seems to say that the _____ was skating gracefully across the ice.

2 The error in exercise 1 is that no one is named who could skate or see the

_____.

3 **Skating gracefully across the ice, Sonia saw a large moose on the right bank of the lake.**

The revision above names _____ as the person who skated and saw the moose.

4 **While putting the mail into the mailbox, our dog bit the postman.**

In this sentence the dog seems to be putting the _____ into the

mailbox, but of course the writer means that the _____ was doing it.

5 The example in exercise 4 contains what is called an *elliptical* or *incomplete subordinate clause* (*while putting the mail into the mailbox*). The clause is elliptical because it lacks a subject and part of the verb. Elliptical clauses are perfectly acceptable except when they give rise to ambiguity. When one causes ambiguity, it should be expanded. Consider this revision:

While the postman was putting the mail into the mailbox, our dog bit him.

In this sentence the original elliptical clause has been expanded by the addition of the words _____ _____ _____.

Is the ridiculous situation of the original sentence corrected in this one?

_____

6 **In scoring the winning touchdown last Saturday, three school records were broken by Sam.**

In the absurd sentence above, _____ seem to have scored the winning touchdown. Actually, of course, _____ scored it.

7 In the example in exercise 6 the verb is in the passive voice. That is, the subject (*records*) is acted upon, and the person doing the acting (*Sam*) is named as the object of the preposition *by*. When a verb is in the active voice, the subject acts.

Rewrite the example in exercise 6 in the active voice, with *Sam* as the subject. _____

_____

8 Is the meaning of your revised sentence clear? _____

9 **Blowing lazily in the wind, we watched the tall sycamores.**

Is this an ambiguous sentence? _____

10 Sometimes such a sentence can be made clear by changing the position of the adverbial modifier, placing it last in the sentence instead of first.

We watched the tall sycamores blowing lazily in the wind.

Is the revised sentence clear? _____

11 **The man who takes his evening walk along this street frequently stops to talk with other passersby.**

Is it possible to tell here whether *frequently* refers to the walking or to the talking? _____

12 Adverbial modifiers such as *frequently* have a surprising ability to move about in a sentence. Here is the same sentence repeated in short form several times:

A. **Frequently the man . . .**
B. **The man who frequently . . .**
C. **. . . takes his evening walk along this street frequently stops to talk . . .**

D. . . . stops to talk frequently . . .

E. . . . stops to talk with other passersby frequently.

With so many possibilities, it should be easy to avoid this kind of ambiguity.

The only ambiguous sentence in the group above is sentence _____.

13 Which three of these sentences are ambiguous or ridiculous because of some kind of faulty relationship between a modifier and the word modified? _____ _____ _____

A. Honking madly, Kemp heard the car careening down the street.
B. Talking rapidly to divert the attention of the intruder, I edged toward the door.
C. The two boys who play in the vacant lot nearly every morning wake up the whole neighborhood.
D. While running for mayor, many signs for the candidates were put up all over town.

14 Now complete each of these sentences in any way that makes sense.

A. Having lent all my money to my brother, _____

_____ .

B. In carelessly closing the car door, _____

_____ .

C. After completing my assignment, _____

_____ .

15 Complete these sentences in any way that makes sense. If it is necessary to move the italicized word to another place in the sentence, do so.

A. The policeman who stops motorists along this road *frequently*_____

_____ .

B. The professor who takes the roll at the beginning of the class *normally*

_____ .

C: ASSIGNMENTS

• Revise the ambiguous or ridiculous sentences in any way that makes good sense. Two sentences are all right as they are.

1. Having finished our lunch, Bert took me back to work.
2. When only two years old, my father bought me a bicycle.
3. While attending a movie, our house burned down.

4. Since the board members were all present at nine o'clock the meeting began.
5. Happily pulling taffy in the kitchen, the kitten silently watched the children.
6. Having repaired the tire, I hastily put away the tools.
7. The director said on the stage everyone must be alert.
8. After counseling the students to use their own judgment in the selection of their president, they all cheered.
9. Before completing the building of the dam, the engineers were confronted with a major flood.
10. Unable to write after breaking her arm, secretarial assistance was necessary for Ms. Johnson.

ANSWERS TO SECTION B

1. moose
2. moose
3. Sonia
4. mail, postman
5. the postman was   Yes
6. records   Sam
7. In scoring the winning touchdown last Saturday, Sam broke three school records.
8. Yes
9. Yes
10. Yes
11. No
12. C
13. A, C, D
14. MODELS   A. I could not buy even a sandwich.
             B. Nadine almost caught the bottom of her long skirt.
             C. I relaxed for an hour. (Give yourself credit if the respective sentences make clear who did the lending, who closed the car door, and who completed the assignment.)
15. MODELS   A. The policeman who frequently stops motorists along this road may have saved the lives of several children.
             B. The professor who normally takes the roll at the beginning of the class was the lecturer today.

Unit 20—Parallelism

A: COMMENTARY

Parallelism is also called parallel structure. It is attained when a word, phrase, or clause is accompanied by one or more similar words, phrases, or clauses. For example, in describing a person we may say that he or she is *short* and *fat* (two adjectives). If we say, though, that he or she is *short* and *carrying excessive poundage*, we violate the principles of parallelism and write a sentence that is both more wordy and somewhat harder to understand.

Four instances in which parallelism is needed are these:

1. in a series (two or more items)

    EXAMPLE: **She is tall and slender. He is short, fat, and bald.**

2. with correlatives (connectives used in pairs, generally *either . . . or, neither . . . nor, both . . . and; not only . . . but also*)

    EXAMPLE: **Either they will fire the manager or they will renew his contract for just one year. (*Not parallel:* They will either fire the manager or they will renew his contract for just one year.)**

3. after linking verbs (usually *is, are, was, were, been*)

    EXAMPLE: **Seeing is believing. To see is to believe. (*Not parallel:* Seeing is to believe.)**

4. in comparisons

    EXAMPLE: **I like swimming better than diving. (*Not parallel:* I like swimming better than to dive.)**

Occasionally writers use parallel structure when they should not. This error is a variation of faulty parallelism:

   FAULTY: **After a snack after the dance we went home. (The two *after*-phrases result in hard reading.)**
   BETTER: **After the dance we had a snack and went home.**
   FAULTY: **The comedy was lively, well acted, and entertained the audience.**
   BETTER: **The comedy was lively and well acted; it entertained the audience.**

A special caution is needed concerning the use of *and which, but which, and who,* and *but who.* An *and which* or *but which* clause may follow only an earlier *which* clause; an *and who* or *but who* requires an earlier *who.*

   NOT PARALLEL: **We were tossed by gigantic waves and which threatened to swamp our little boat.**

PARALLEL: We were tossed by waves which were gigantic and
which threatened. . . .

ALSO CORRECT

AND LESS WORDY: We were tossed by gigantic waves which threatened. . . .

Professional writers and speakers, striving for special effects, often make
conscious use of elaborately parallel structure. Examples could be cited from
such modern writers as Winston Churchill, Thomas Wolfe, Alan Paton, and
William Faulkner. Here is an older example, from the great orator Daniel
Webster, set typographically to make clear the several instances of parallelism
in a single sentence:

When my eyes shall be turned to behold for the last time the sun in
heaven, may I not see him shining
    on the broken and dishonored fragments of a once glorious Union;

on States   dissevered,
               discordant,
               belligerent;
on a land   rent   with civil feuds
               or drenched, it may be,   in fraternal blood.

This example shows that complete parallelism is not invariably needed—that
an artist varies structure to avoid monotony but still keeps the framework of
parallelism. Note that the three phrases starting with *on* vary in length and in
the details of structure and that *it may be* modifies the rhythm and provides a
momentary pause before the climactic *in fraternal blood*.

B: EXERCISES

1 You probably never would be tempted to write a sentence like the following:

Sarah is courageous, industrious, truthful, and honor.

Write the word that does not make good sense in that sentence.

_____ It should be changed to what word? _____

2 In exercise 1 you realized almost automatically that the last word in the
example should be like the other three describing Sarah. We can say that
Sarah is courageous, that she is industrious, and that she is truthful, but, as

you saw at once, we cannot say that she is _____. We need a
word that is parallel (similar in use) to *courageous, industrious,* and *truthful.* Those words are adjectives, but *honor* is usually a noun. To attain

parallelism you decided to change the noun *honor* to the adjective _____.

3 Often faulty parallelism is less obvious than it is in exercise 1.

I wish that I knew more about pinochle and how to play bridge better than I do.

In this example, *more about pinochle* and *how to play bridge better than I do* are different kinds of phrases. One way to make them parallel is to write: **I wish that I knew more about playing pinochle and** (What word?)

_____ .

4 Another but more wordy way to achieve parallelism in the example in exercise 3 is to write: **I wish that I knew how to play** (What seven words?)

_____ .

5 **He dresses well, tall, and truly distinguished in appearance.**

In this example, *dresses* is a verb, and *tall* and *distinguished* are used as adjectives. Once more we have at least two ways to attain parallelism:

A. **He dresses well, is** (What seven words?) _____

_____ .

B. **He is** (What eight words?) _____

_____ .

6 **Without a college background one cannot enter a profession such as a doctor, lawyer, or teacher.**

This example shows a different kind of faulty parallelism. Is a doctor a

profession? _____ Is a lawyer a profession? _____ Is a teacher a pro-

fession? _____

7 To correct the example in exercise 6 we must make parallel the words represented by *profession* and by *doctor, lawyer, teacher*. Two ways of doing this are:

A. **Without a college background one cannot enter a profession such as**

medicine, _____ .

B. **Without a college background one cannot become a** _____

_____ **such as** _____ .

8 Let's try to summarize what we have found out about parallelism. In a sentence, if two or more parts function in the same way, they should be

stated in (the same grammatical form/different grammatical forms) _____
_____.

For example, if a series starts with an adjective, the other parts of the series

should be _____. If two phrases or clauses have the same

function, they should be (the same kind/different kinds) _____
of phrases or clauses.

9 In each group below underline the item that is not parallel to the others.

A	B	C
for God	having drive	thievery
for country	possessing talent	beggars
and family	plenty of money	cutthroats
	lacking interest	ruffians

10 Which sentence in each pair has parallel structure? _____ _____

A. Joe promised his parents to write often and that he would study hard.
B. Joe promised his parents that he would write often and that he would study hard.

A. Any student normally intelligent and who works hard can pass this course.
B. Any student who is normally intelligent and who works hard can pass this course.

11 Again, which sentence in each pair has parallel structure? _____ _____

A. While I watched, the children played in the sand, waded in the pool, and frolicked in the grass.
B. I watched the children playing in the sand, wading in the pool, and as they frolicked in the grass.

A. To take care of tomorrow's adult students, we need to employ more teachers, more textbooks, and many more classrooms.
B. To take care of tomorrow's adult students, we need to employ more teachers, buy more textbooks, and secure the use of many more class-rooms.

12 **Maggie is either really near exhaustion or she is a superb actress.**
After correlatives (connectives that work in pairs, such as *either . . . or,
neither . . . nor, both . . . and,* and *not only . . . but also*) the sentence
elements should be parallel in structure. After *either* in the example above,

the words are _____; after *or* the words are

_____. These elements (are/are not) _____
parallel.

13 Rewrite the example in exercise 12 to give it parallel structure.

_____

_____

14 Write a sentence using a series that illustrates parallel structure. Your series should name three things that you like to do at the beach. _____

_____

15 Write a sentence using *not only* . . . *but also*. Be sure that it illustrates parallel structure.

_____

_____

C: ASSIGNMENTS

• Correct the lack of parallelism or the faulty parallelism in each of these sentences:

1. Irene sings admirably, plays the piano expertly, and graceful on the dance floor.
2. The money bought three loaves of bread, three pounds of hamburger, and fed the parking meter.
3. During the earthquake the church collapsed, the school burned to the ground, and I am terrified to think what may have happened to the dam.
4. As the ship neared the pier, the band struck up a tune, the crowd began to sing, and some people even dancing.
5. I believe in justice for all, universal freedom, and honorable officials.
6. I being almost faint from hunger, the road stretching interminably ahead, and the engine was overheated, I feared that I could not possibly reach São Paulo by nightfall.
7. To spend ten weeks in this hellhole was asking too much of any person.
8. Marvin enjoys playing basketball better than to play water polo.
9. For him for his personal use from his sister from Indiana came a brown leather suitcase.
10. We could now see the ship limping along the edge of the world, and which our binoculars revealed was smoking at the stern.

• Construct three sentences in which you use parallel structure in a series.

• Construct a sentence with *either* . . . *or,* one with *both* . . . *and,* and one with *not only* . . . *but also*. Be sure that the elements after these correlatives are parallel.

• Construct two sentences illustrating parallel structure after linking verbs.

• Write two comparisons that illustrate parallel structure.

ANSWERS TO SECTION B

1. honor   honorable
2. honor   honorable
3. bridge
4. MODEL   pinochle and bridge better than I do
5. A. tall, and is truly distinguished in appearance
   B. well dressed, tall, and truly distinguished in appearance
6. No   No   No
7. A. law, or education (*or* teaching)
   B. professional person   a doctor, lawyer, or teacher
8. the same grammatical form   adjectives   the same kind
9. A. and family   B. plenty of money   C. thievery
10. B   B
11. A   B
12. really near exhaustion   she is a superb actress   are not
13. Either Maggie is really near exhaustion or she is a superb actress.
14. MODEL   At the beach I like to swim, to sunbathe, and to look for shells.
15. MODEL   Not only has your senator supported labor constantly, but also she has introduced two strongly pro-labor bills.

Unit 21—Complete Comparisons

A: COMMENTARY

This unit deals with the slight or not-so-slight ambiguity that sometimes results when a comparison is not finished. Here are some examples:

> AMBIGUOUS: **Gerald likes Ross better than Bill.**
> BETTER: **Gerald likes Ross better than *he does* Bill.**
> *or*
> **Gerald likes Ross better than Bill *does*.**
> AMBIGUOUS: **Alaska is larger than any state in the Union. (Alaskans would be outraged to be excluded from the states.)**

BETTER:	Alaska is larger than any *other* state in the Union.
ALSO CORRECT:	Quebec is larger than any state in the Union.
AMBIGUOUS:	Franklin D. Roosevelt was President longer than any-body. (Was Roosevelt a nobody?)
BETTER:	Franklin D. Roosevelt was President longer than any-body *else*.
MISLEADING:	Baird's paint lasts longer. (Longer than what?)
PERHAPS MORE ACCURATE:	The new Baird's paint lasts longer than any that Baird has ever made before.
AMBIGUOUS:	Sally's eyes are bluer than Harriet. (Is Harriet blue?)
BETTER:	Sally's eyes are bluer than Harriet's.

Although not ambiguous, another construction is often considered objectionable:

POOR:	This year's class is as big, if not bigger, than last year's. (As big *than?*)
BETTER BUT A BIT AWKWARD:	This year's class is as big as, if not bigger than, last year's.
STILL BETTER:	This year's class is as big as last year's, if not bigger.

B: EXERCISES

1 Glenn and his father often had nasty little quarrels, sometimes caused by misunderstanding each other. For instance, Tuesday night Glenn's father refused to give Pomeroy (their dog) any of his meat, and Glenn, who had shared his own meat with the dog, said, "I like Pomeroy more than you." The father burst out angrily, "I know you do! In fact, I think you don't like me at all!"

This quarrel might not have started if Glenn had used a comparison correctly. Which two of the following three meanings could Glenn's sentence have? _____ _____

A. I like Pomeroy more than I like you.
B. I like Pomeroy more than you do.
C. I like neither Pomeroy nor you.

Assuming that Glenn wanted a peaceful evening, which should he have said, A, B, or C? _____

2 In comparisons there are often unstated words or phrases that almost everyone will understand. For example, what is the unstated verb at the end of the following sentence? _____

She plays golf better than Hal.

When there is no possibility of ambiguity, such a sentence is perfectly correct despite its unstated word.

3 But when the *better than, more frequently than* type of sentence names two persons after the main verb and there is no verb at the end of the sentence, ambiguity can result.

In the following sentence how many persons are named after the verb? _____

S   V
Sam tutors Frank more frequently than Harry.

Is there a verb at the end of the sentence? _____ Can the sentence mean than Sam tutors Frank more frequently than he tutors Harry? _____ Can it also mean that he tutors Frank more frequently than Harry does?

_____

4 **Sam tutors Frank more frequently than ₁ Harry ₂.**

Where in the above sentence (at ₁ or ₂) would you put the words *he does* to make the sentence mean that Sam tutors both Frank and Harry but Frank more frequently? _____

Where would you put the word *does* to make the sentence mean that both Sam and Harry tutor Frank but that Sam does it more frequently?

_____

5 When a *better than* sentence names only one person after the main verb, no ambiguity is likely. Here are two sentences:

A. **Jim plays badminton better than Jack.**
B. **Jim imitates Hank better than Jack.**

In which sentence are two persons named after the main verb? _____

Which sentence is ambiguous? _____

6 Sentence B in exercise 5 could be understood in either of two ways. Revise the sentence to show that both Jim and Jack imitate Hank. _____

_____

7 **I think that Janice sings the song better than anybody.**

Does this sentence seem to say that Janice is a nobody? _____

Can the sentence be corrected by adding *else* at the end? _____

8 **Whales are larger than any mammals.**

It happens that the whale is a mammal. It obviously cannot be larger than itself. The addition of the word _____ before *mammals* will make a correct statement.

9 **This team is as good if not better than last year's.**

Here is a different kind of problem in comparison. Admittedly the sentence above is not ambiguous. Admittedly this kind of construction is heard frequently in informal conversation. In formal writing and speaking, however, because it sounds as if someone is saying *This team is as good than last year's,* we need to use *as.* One possible revision is this:

This team is as good _____ or even better than last year's.

10 The sentence we have just written is, unfortunately, a little awkward. Better would be this revision:

This team is as good as last year's or even _____.

11 **Marjorie's car is more streamlined than Bill.**

In the above sentence Marjorie's car seems to be compared with (Bill's car/Bill himself) _____.
Always be sure to compare things of the same class. Bill usually cannot be compared with a car.

The correction is simple. Can the sentence be made logical by changing *Bill* to *Bill's?* _____

12 **White-O Shoe Polish is whiter.**

In the sentence above, White-O Shoe Polish appears to be compared with something. But is it? _____ If White-O is whiter, it must be whiter than something. But here we are not told *than what.* Often advertisers use this kind of construction deliberately in order to give the impression of quality or excellence without actually claiming anything specific. This is an ignoble use of language, to be avoided by persons who want to be clear, not deliberately confusing.

13 Which of the following sentences are correct? _____

A. **Sally entertained Helen better than Orinda.**
B. **The Amazon is larger than any river.**
C. **Marie did better on the test than anyone else in the class.**
D. **This photograph is as good as that one, or even better.**

E. **My model airplane went higher than Pete.**
F. **Lite-Up Cigarette Lighters are better.**

14 Write a sentence of your own in which you compare the population of New York City and other American cities. Use the words *larger, any,* and *other* in your comparison. Be sure that *American* is in your sentence.

_____

_____

15 Complete this sentence: **I like Hemingway better** _____

_____.

16 Write a sentence containing the phrase *as well as or even better than.*

_____

_____

17 Revise your sentence to make it less awkward.

_____

_____

18 Use one word to complete this sentence: **Delbert's short novel proved to be better than** (the short story of what other person?) _____.

C: ASSIGNMENTS

• Find the errors in the comparisons below and rewrite each sentence correctly. (If a sentence can be interpreted in more than one way, select one plausible interpretation.) Then write another sentence for each, using the same kind of comparison as that in the corrected version.

1. Creighton knows our company's finances better than anyone.
2. Helen likes opera better than Mark.
3. In my opinion, Gray Company outboard motors are as good if not better than any.
4. The audience liked this concert more.
5. The population of Denver is larger than Salt Lake City.
6. Your suggestion is better than Elbert.
7. Strongwear tires are safer.
8. The lakes of the West are deeper than the East.
9. Larry thinks his arms are stronger than Mike.
10. This type of book binding is distinctly inferior to that book.

ANSWERS TO SECTION B

1. A, B   B
2. does
3. two   No   Yes   Yes
4. 1   2
5. B   B
6. Jim imitates Hank better than Jack does.
7. Yes   Yes
8. other
9. as
10. better
11. Bill himself   Yes
12. No
13. C, D
14. MODEL   New York City's population is larger than that of any other American city.
15. MODEL   I like Hemingway better than I like any other author.
16. MODEL   Connors played as well as or even better than Fuqua.
17. MODEL   Connors played as well as Fuqua, or even better.
18. MODEL   Roberta's (Give yourself credit if you used the *possessive* form of any suitable noun or pronoun.)

PART THREE

DICTION

Professional writers devote much time to finding the words that say most accurately and vividly whatever they want to express. Polish-English novelist Joseph Conrad, for instance, would sometimes search an hour or more for the word that would precisely fit the meaning and mood he wanted to convey. English poet Elizabeth Barrett Browning used to build little pyramids of words in the margin and would come back later to pick the most appropriate word from the pyramid. And American humorist Mark Twain made possibly the most famous of all comments about words when he said that the difference between the right word and the almost right word is as great as the difference between the lightning and the lightning bug.

Even for the nonprofessional, choice of words is important for effective communication. In this section we will discuss concrete and abstract words, denotations and connotations, and figures of speech, and then devote considerable attention to common words that are often confused with one another.

Unit 22—Concrete and Abstract Nouns

A: COMMENTARY

The basic difference between a concrete and an abstract noun is easy to understand: A noun is concrete if it names something that you can see, touch, taste, smell, or hear. It is abstract if it names anything else. Note how much easier it is to perceive with the imagination the words in the left-hand column than those in the right-hand column:

Concrete Nouns	Abstract Nouns
skyscraper	truth
zebra	democracy
milk	envy
firecracker	surprise
honeysuckle	friendship

At times, however, the same noun may be more abstract than at other times. Consider, for instance, the word *home* in the following sentences:

They built their *home* **in a forest.**
Tom has no *home.*
Home **is where the heart is.**

In the first sentence, *home* refers to a physical structure that can be seen, touched, lived in. It is quite real, quite concrete. In the second sentence, *home* means a kind of dwelling, but not a particular structure that can be seen. It could be an apartment, a cabin, or a mansion. It is less concrete than the first *home*, but less abstract than that in the third sentence, where *home* represents a state of mind rather than any structure at all.

Both concrete and abstract words have their uses. In general, concrete words are easier to understand, because they represent things that most readers can picture in their minds. *Before you leave the house, turn off the lights* is easier to understand than *Before making your departure from the premises, effect the termination of the illumination. House* and *lights* are concrete, but *departure, premises, termination,* and *illumination* are abstract.

An abstract word, for instance *premises,* is useful because sometimes we do not need to name a particular kind of land or building or perhaps cannot even do so. The law, for example, makes much use of words like *premises* so that every possible kind of locale will not need to be mentioned over and over. And all of us use, again and again, abstract words like *love, friendship,* and *government,* with reasonable assurance that our readers or audience will know at least approximately what we are talking about. The use of a single abstract word can sometimes save a paragraph of examples or explanation.

Inexperienced writers, however, tend to use too few concrete words, too many abstractions. The best advice is this: Use abstract nouns when you must, but if you find your pages crawling with *-ation* and *-ness* and their kin, see whether you can't transform some of the fuzziness into shapes, some of the invisibility into visibility, some of the vegetation into azalea blossoms.

B: EXERCISES

1 Which of the following nouns are mainly concrete and which abstract? Encircle the concrete nouns. Underline the abstract nouns.

horse	idea	notebook	airplane	republic
honor	dust	respect	apathy	highway
lumberjack	tendency	truthfulness	emotion	graph

2 Which of these sentences is easier to understand? _____

A. His intransigence led to an altercation and subsequent incarceration of both participants.
B. Jack's bullheadedness led to a fistfight and finally to the jailing of both Jack and the drunk he was fighting.

3 In sentence B above, the words *bullheadedness, fistfight, jailing,* and *drunk* call up rather vivid sense impressions. They represent concrete things or events that you can perceive in your imagination. Nouns that call up such images are called (concrete/abstract) _____ nouns.

4 A noun that does not call up vivid sense impressions but that names abstract qualities, conditions, or actions is called (a concrete/an abstract) _____ noun.

5 Abstract nouns have an important place in the language. Our communication would be severely limited without such terms as *democracy, affection, conviction, anger, capitalism, communism, prerequisite, electives, sonata,* and *athletics,* but because abstract nouns generally do not call up the sense impressions, it is well to avoid them when concrete nouns are appropriate.

Which word(s) in parentheses would be better in the following sentences?

A. Here is a (hyacinth/decoration) _____ for your hair.
B. (Mammalian life/Squirrels, raccoons, and foxes) _____

_____abound(s) in these woods.

6 We entered the edifice and prepared to engage in those rites characteristic of our religious persuasion.

Rewrite the above sentence using concrete nouns instead of abstract.

---

7 Sometimes abstract words hide fuzzy thinking. Some people may say, "We believe in freedom of religion," but then object when some religious group not their own propose to build a church across the street. These people honestly think that they favor religious freedom, but when the

abstraction is translated into concrete terms, (finish the sentence) _____

---

8 Arguments between "capital" and "labor" occur often in the United States. But when negotiators (who are real, concrete people) sit down at the bargaining table (which is a real, concrete table), they necessarily talk in terms of such things as (name two or three concrete things that they may discuss)

C: ASSIGNMENTS

• Listed below are a number of abstract words or phrases. You are to change each of them into a more concrete expression or sentence. For example, one change that can be made in *loyalty of an animal* is this: *My dog, Plato, was the only living creature that greeted me warmly when I got out of jail.*

1. loyalty of an animal
2. a nervous condition
3. drunkenness
4. stubbornness
5. an accident in traffic
6. carelessness
7. waste of scarce material
8. show of affection
9. narrow escape from defeat
10. a generous act

ANSWERS TO SECTION B

1. Concrete: horse, notebook, airplane, dust, highway, lumberjack, graph.
   Abstract: idea, republic, honor, respect, apathy, tendency, truthfulness, emotion.
2. B

3. concrete
4. an abstract
5. A. hyacinth   B. Squirrels, raccoons, and foxes
6. MODEL   We entered the church and prepared to worship.
7. MODEL   their conviction shrivels; often, it seems, "good" things are good for other people, not for themselves.
8. MODEL   dollars and cents, safer machine tools, or even cleaner restrooms

Unit 23—Connotations of Words

A: COMMENTARY

If you look up the word *father* in your dictionary, you will find some such definition as "a male parent." A dictionary definition gives the *denotation* of a word: an objective, unemotional, detached explanation of meaning. The denotation "a male parent" is not likely to make anyone regard a father either favorably or unfavorably.

A *connotation*, in contrast, represents what a word suggests to an individual or a group. *Father*, for instance, to most persons probably has connotations of kindness, helpfulness, and firmness; it may call up memories of a friendly dining table, trips to the zoo, and the giving of advice and encouragement. To others, because their experiences have been different, it may have quite different connotations such as laziness, indifference, incompetence, intoxication. To still others, the connotation of *father* may be highly religious. It is doubtful that any two persons have exactly the same connotations for *father* or for any other word that they know well.

Despite such differences, the connotations of words chosen by writers and speakers affect the way that *most* readers or listeners react to a statement. In simple terms, the connotations of a given word may be

1. *relatively neutral*—not causing much emotional reaction
2. *relatively favorable*—causing a favorable reaction
3. *relatively unfavorable*—causing an unfavorable reaction.

For example, *child* and *children* are relatively neutral, even though some persons may react favorably or adversely to them. Words like *little darling, angel,* and *cherub* (unless used with obvious irony) are mainly favorable. *Little ruffian* and *brat* tend to cause an unfavorable reaction.

Most of the writing in school or college is intended only to report or explain, not to sway readers emotionally. For that reason, a student should ordinarily try to use relatively neutral words. But sometimes a paper or a speech is designed to persuade an audience, to make people favor or oppose something. The author is then likely to choose the words that will help him or her to influence the audience emotionally.

Almost all advertising uses nouns, adjectives, adverbs, and verbs intended to make the reader think highly of the product. Most political speeches contain highly connotative words that are intended to show what a fine person the candidate is and how incompetent or even deceitful the opponent is.

B: EXERCISES

1 The denotation of a word is the direct or explicit meaning. A denotation of the word *home* is (dwelling place/haven of rest) _____.

2 Connotations, on the other hand, are associations that cluster around the word. Put a check mark beside each of the following items that is for you a connotation of *home:*

_____ place of rest

_____ That's where the old folks stay.

_____ place of refuge

_____ place of love and warmth

_____ where the heart is

_____ destination

_____ an ugly, cheerless place

3 According to a dictionary, the denotation or basic meaning of *automobile* is "a self-propelled vehicle; especially, a four-wheeled passenger vehicle that carries its own source of power and travels on roads or streets." Some connotations might be: status symbol, symbol of wealth, instrument of death, an important item in the country's economy, a waster of natural resources. Would a desk dictionary be big enough to give *all* the connotations of even the one word *automobile?* _____

4 Would the connotations of *automobile* be the same for an eighteen-year-old and for a wealthy person of sixty-eight? _____

5 It is not true that a rose by any other name would smell as sweet, for our reactions to the rose have been conditioned by all the connotations that have clustered around the name *rose* for hundreds of years.

Our reactions to things are to some extent conditioned by our reactions to the words that stand for the _____.

6 As speakers and writers we must be aware of connotations. If we write, for instance, that certain politicians are *notorious* for their support of social legislation, we are using a definition of *notorious* ("well known") that we can find in some dictionaries. However, we have spoken so much of notorious *outlaws* and notorious *criminals* that, if we were to use the term in connection with politicians, we might unintentionally give the wrong impression of their activities. Usage has given the word *notorious* an unfavorable

_____.

7 We cannot and should not try to avoid connotations entirely. There are legitimate occasions for playing on the emotions. The mention of a hitching post may evoke a pleasant memory for an old-timer from a country town. The mention of a hearse may arouse in some people associations with funerals, funeral flowers, their own grief when a dear one died. Imaginative

writing of all kinds depends heavily on the _____ of words for its effect.

8 Mrs. Alfred, a bank teller, was confronted one day by a man dressed in a tee shirt and Levis who passed a note across the counter, along with a paper bag. On the note was scrawled, "Fill this bag with twenty-dollar bills."

It was plain that the man was unarmed. A gun in a pocket would have created a bulge.

Nevertheless, the teller gave him all her twenty-dollar bills, later explaining that, although the man appeared unarmed, he might have had an accomplice, and there were several customers in the bank who might have been injured if the teller had refused to turn over the money.

If you were favorably impressed by Mrs. Alfred's actions, you might say

that she was (cautious/timid/cowardly) _____. If you were

mildly unfavorable, you might say she was _____. If you were

very unfavorably impressed, you might call her _____.

9 The three adjectives refer to the same event, but they give a very different evaluation of Mrs. Alfred. Is Mrs. Alfred herself changed by one or the

other of the adjectives? _____

10 Is it possible for Mrs. Alfred's reputation to be affected by the adjective

used to describe her? _____

11 The fact that Mrs. Alfred's reputation could be affected by words used to

describe her means (Which of the following?) _____

A. **that unfavorable words should never be used.**

B. that no judgment of an act should ever be attempted.

C. that one should be sure of one's ground before using an unfavorable word.

12 We should always remember that the words we use to refer to people or things influence _____ toward these people or things.

13 The following description of a coat for little girls is in a mail order catalog. Make two lists based on it: one of at least four neutral words or phrases giving factual information, and another of at least four words or phrases intended to sway the customer emotionally.

Great-looking nylon coat, economically priced. Sleeve length easily adjusted as she grows. Always a proper fit! Lining is warm acetate taffeta quilted to polyester interlining. Trim of acrylic on polyester backing. Attractive double-breasted styling. Two neat front patch pockets. Self-fabric belt with a buckle she'll love. Machine washable at cold temperature.

Neutral: _____ _____

_____ _____

_____ _____

Emotional: _____ _____

_____ _____

_____ _____

14 The following excerpt from a political speech contains several expressions favorable to the speaker and several others unfavorable to the opponent. List some of each.

My opponent would irresponsibly trade off the solid accomplishments of my administration for pie in the sky. I have adhered to the time-honored American principles of the worth and dignity of the individual. My program is affirmative; his is negative. He looks upon the people—upon *you*, my fellow-citizens—as weaklings, incapable of making your own personal decisions.

Favorable to the speaker: _____

_____ _____

_____ _____

Unfavorable to the opponent: _____

_____ _____

_____ _____

15 In exercises 15, 16, and 17 are three statements that are slanted in one way or another. Try to rewrite each in relatively neutral terms.

(From a student newspaper) **Student malcontents disrupted the Student Senate session Thursday night with carping criticism of the hardworking officers who managed the fund-raising drive.**

_____

_____

_____

_____

16 **Unruly children at the theater kept savagely hissing the villain and unrestrainedly cheering the hero during last night's showing of "The Face on the Bar Room Floor."**

_____

_____

_____

_____

17 **When attacked by a drunk, Ted Nackard wisely elected to defend himself, expertly hitting the sot over the head with a beer bottle just hard enough to floor him. Taking no chances, he hit the inebriated man in the face after the drunk had fallen. Having disciplined the wino but not wanting to bother the police, he then left the scene.**

_____

_____

_____

_____

_____

C: ASSIGNMENTS

• Is each of the following statements (listed in pairs) favorable or unfavorable toward the subject? Try to rephrase each in relatively neutral terms.

1. Then the little brat kicked me. Then the frightened and confused little tot pushed at me with her foot.
2. Goon squad hits factory. Heroes of the picket line strike factory.
3. Jack was the life of the party last night. Jack was an obnoxious exhibitionist last night.

4. Professor Blakely is a reserved individual. Professor Blakely is a snob.
5. This visionary scheme is socialistic. This inspired plan is a forward-looking piece of social legislation.

• Examine several advertisements and a political column or editorial. Make a list of words that are important for their connotations. Explain how the connotations affect the impact or the argument.

ANSWERS TO SECTION B

1. dwelling place
2. Give yourself credit regardless of which items you checked.
3. Probably not
4. No
5. things
6. connotation
7. connotations
8. cautious   timid   cowardly
9. No
10. Yes
11. C
12. attitudes (*or* feelings)
13. Neutral: nylon, Sleeve length . . . adjusted, acetate taffeta quilted to polyester interlining, acrylic on polyester backing, double-breasted, Two . . . front patch pockets, Self-fabric belt with a buckle, Machine washable at cold temperature.   Emotional: Great-looking, economically priced, easily, Always a proper fit, warm, Attractive, neat, she'll love.
14. Favorable to the speaker: solid accomplishments of my administration, time-honored American principles of the worth and dignity of the individual, affirmative. Unfavorable to the opponent: irresponsibly trade off, pie in the sky, negative (plus the whole last sentence).
15. MODEL   Some students interrupted the Student Senate session Thursday night with criticism of the officers who managed the fund-raising drive.
16. MODEL   Children at the theater kept hissing the villain and cheering the hero during last night's showing of "The Face on the Bar Room Floor."
17. MODEL   When struck by a man who staggered and showed other signs of intoxication, Ted Nackard hit back with a beer bottle, knocking the unidentified man to the floor. Then Mr. Nackard struck the man in the face and walked away without notifying the police.

Unit 24—Good and Bad
Figures of Speech

A: COMMENTARY

Whoever first said "as slow as molasses in January" was a genius of sorts. Sorghum molasses, always thick, becomes almost impossible to pour when it is cold. Anything or anyone that moves as slowly as molasses in January must be very slow indeed.

But not everything that is slow should be described with that phrase. For one reason, *as slow as molasses in January* has been said so often that it is trite —almost worn out. For another, some kinds of slowness are not enough like the slowness of molasses to make the comparison appropriate. One train, for instance, may be much slower than another, but no train in working order is very slow. At any rate the "movement" of a train is not similar enough to the movement of syrup for the analogy to be very accurate.

So a figure of speech can be trite or inappropriate. And if it happens to be connected to a second, unrelated figure, it becomes a mixed figure, which is often at least slightly ridiculous. Perhaps the most infamous example is "That snake in the grass is barking up the wrong tree"; most students know that snakes don't bark. Here are two other mixtures:

> **Although he was down for the count of nine, he refused to be checkmated.**
> **Keep your shoulder to the wheel and don't give up the ship.**

A good figure of speech, however, helps a reader to understand, perhaps even more quickly than a literal explanation would. For instance, Loren Eiseley, referring to problems that will arise if man tries to travel to distant parts of the universe, expressed one of them this way: "[A person's] life span is that of a mayfly in terms of the distances he seeks to penetrate." We know that the mayfly lives only a day. Eiseley uses that fact to show us, with just a phrase, that it would take hundreds or thousands of human lifetimes, even at the speed of light, to reach some of the more distant solar systems.

Satisfactory figures of speech come much more easily to some of us than to others. Poets seem best at finding them, but some scientists, like Eiseley, share the poet's gift of noting how two apparently unlike things are really alike.

B: EXERCISES

1 Some figures of speech are so useful that they have become part of our everyday language and we no longer even think of them as figurative. So we say:

the arms of a chair   the hands of a clock
to get in touch with   to turn over a new leaf
a warm invitation   a stream of letters
a crying need   a stubborn ailment

The fragments below may remind you of some other expressions of this sort:

the four _____ of a table   with the playfulness of a _____

Just before the mountains are the _____. the _____ tones of her voice (suggest a temperature)

2 Other figures (often comparisons using *as*) are tired, having been so long overworked. Perhaps all of us use some of them, especially in conversation when we have little time to think of a fresh comparison. So we may tritely describe a person as:

proud as a peacock   big as a house
hungry as a bear   mad as a hornet
strong as an ox   cool as a cucumber

Such overworked, tired phrases no longer have the desired effect and should be avoided in writing.

A good rule to follow is this: If a companion is quite familiar to you,

(use it/do not use it) _____.

3 Sometimes a comparison is not very appropriate. Sometimes, in fact, it may be so outlandish that it hinders communication. For instance:

Mr. Danziger looked like a Brinks armored truck as he stood up to present the award to the mayor—there were flashing lights and square corners all over him.

Is this description of Mr. Danziger vivid? _____

4 In exercise 3 assume that the basic purpose is simply to inform the reader that Mr. Danziger, an impressive-looking man, gave the mayor an award.

A. Is the vivid description of the man appropriate? _____
B. Does it actually detract from the intended meaning of the sentence? _____
C. Is the description honest? That is, does it show that Mr. Danziger is impressive in appearance? _____

5 What two familiar sayings (both of them figurative) are mixed in the following sentence?

Don't cross your bridges until they're hatched.

A. _____

B. _____

6 Which two of the following figures of speech are mixed? _____ _____

   A. Hitch your wagon to a star and keep your nose to the grindstone, and you will swiftly climb the ladder of success.

   B. I had trouble keeping my head above water; I was so desperate that I would grasp at a straw.

   C. She had two strikes against her when she sat down to take the examination, but most of her answers hit the nail on the head.

7 Rewrite the two mixed sentences in exercise 6. In each, keep one of the figurative expressions and expand it instead of using the part that mixes it up.

_____

_____

_____

_____

8 Now try something more difficult. The beginnings of several unfinished comparisons are given below and in exercise 9. Try to complete one or more in each frame, saying something that seems appropriate and that you have not read or heard before. (There are no "correct" answers for these items.)

   A. the old door, creaking like _____

   B. the canary, pert as _____

   C. a _____ oak

9 A. My friend smokes incessantly, like _____.

   B. The sky was as blue as _____.

   C. the _____ little stream

C: ASSIGNMENTS

• Here is a list of inadequate figures of speech. Try to suggest either a better figure of speech or an effective but nonfigurative way to express each idea.

   1. He was as mad as a hornet.
   2. They climbed the ladder of success, avoiding all pitfalls.
   3. She's happy as a lark.

4. It was a close shave, but he won by the skin of his teeth.
5. Jan tried to zero in on the promotion but didn't get to first base.
6. That's as scarce as hens' teeth.
7. She was white as a sheet.
8. He was as good as gold.
9. He bit off more than he could chew.
10. She is brown as a berry.
11. The sky was black as coal.
12. He was red as a beet.
13. She is wise as an owl.
14. It's all Greek to me.
15. He was walking on air.

• Here are a few more incomplete figures for you to try to complete originally and appropriately.

1. a craggy face like _____

2. as steady and dependable as _____

3. a temper like _____

4. a _____ temper

5. lined up in rows like _____

6. as pretty as _____

7. as lonely as _____

8. a solitary peak, standing like _____

9. the _____ of the waves

10. the _____ tractor, _____ as a _____

ANSWERS TO SECTION B

1. legs   kitten   foothills   warm (*or* icy)
2. do not use it
3. Yes
4. A. No   B. Yes   C. No
5. A. Don't cross a bridge until you come to it.
   B. Don't count your chickens until they're hatched.
6. A, C
7. MODELS Hitch your wagon to a star and the wagon may become a chariot streaking across the sky.   She had two strikes against her when she sat down to take the examination, but her perfect score shows that she hit a home run.
8–9. Give yourself credit for any of your answers that you feel are appropriate. The following have been suggested by students:

8A. the old door, creaking like an ungreased axle as the wind blew it back
and forth
B. the canary, pert as the kitten that was stalking it
C. a lordly oak
9A. My friend smokes incessantly, like a small munitions plant in wartime.
B. The sky was as blue as a baby's eyes.
C. the rustling little stream flowing over a taffeta bed

Unit 25—Some Nonstandard Expressions

A: COMMENTARY

This unit concerns a few expressions that are generally regarded as nonstandard
and therefore not suitable for most written or formal spoken English.

being as, being that Nonstandard: "*Being as* (or *that*) my father is almost
eighty, he doesn't work in the mine any more." Use *since* or *because* instead.

busted Nonstandard for *broke* or *broken.*

complected Standard English uses *dark-complexioned, light-complexioned,
sallow-complexioned* (or possibly just *dark, light,* or *sallow*) instead of the
regional *sallow-complected,* and so on.

considerable *Considerable* is an adjective: a *considerable* sum of money. It is
nonstandard as a noun or an adverb. For "bought *considerable*" say "bought
a large amount." For "hurts *considerable*" say "hurts considerably" or "hurts
a great deal."

could of, must of, and so on Some people hear *could've, might've,* and the
like and think that *'ve* is spelled *of.* Standard: *could have, may have, must
have, should have, would have.*

disremember Say "*forget*" or "*do not remember.*"

good and Expressions like *good and ready* or *good and tired* are informal,
perhaps nonstandard. Omit *good and.*

hadn't ought Standard: *ought not* or *shouldn't.*

he don't, she don't, it don't When in doubt about whether to use *don't* or
doesn't, ask yourself whether it is standard to say *do not* or *does not* in the
sentence. Use *don't* only to mean "do not."

in regards to Omit the *s.*

irregardless Standard: *regardless.*

kind of, sort of Not *kind of pretty, sort of unpopular,* but *rather* (or *somewhat*) *pretty, rather* (or *somewhat*) *unpopular.*

learn Not to be confused with *teach.* Standard: *She taught me to tell the
truth. I learned to tell the truth.*

literature Informal for *circulars, advertising.*

mad Standard for *insane,* informal or nonstandard for *angry.*

somewheres, anywheres, everywheres, nowheres Omit the *s*.
take and In expressions like "He took and hit her," omit *took and*.
without Not a substitute for *unless*. Say "unless it rains," not "without it rains."

B: EXERCISES

In the exercises below, rewrite each sentence in full, omitting any nonstandard expressions.

1 In regards to her appearance, I'd say she was sallow-complected and may of had a busted nose. _____

_____

_____

2 Being as an engagement ring costs considerable, maybe she don't really need one. _____

_____

3 The company sent me some literature about Eternal Life batteries, but I can't find it anywheres. _____

_____

_____

4 The lawyer seemed sort of friendly at first, but he got kind of mad when I told him I didn't have any money. _____

_____

_____

5 Irregardless of what the doctor tells him, he don't watch his diet.

_____

_____

6 Without your father learns you the difference between right and wrong, you'll be in trouble. _____

_____

7 **I disremember whether he took and ran off that day or not.**

---

8 **You hadn't ought to see him again till you're good and ready.**

C: ASSIGNMENTS

• The following paragraph includes many of the nonstandard expressions treated in this unit. Rewrite it in standard informal (but not stiff) English, or be prepared to discuss in class the changes you would make.

    Grandpa Higgins was tall and skinny and sort of sallow-complected. He had busted his left leg when he was young—or maybe it was his right leg—I disremember which. Anyhow, he limped considerable, but irregardless of that, he was a great woodsman and learned me most of what I know in regards to the outdoors. He could of been a great teacher if he'd of had more education. He never got mad at me when I made a mistake. I remember that when I was just a little fellow he learned me to make a willow whistle. I was supposed to take and rap a smooth, green willow stick until the bark would slip off in one piece. Without you hammered it gently for a long time, it would bust. In a few minutes I got good and tired, and even though it was nowheres near ready, I tried to push the bark off. It busted. I thought Grandpa would get kind of mad, but he just said, "Being as that piece of willow didn't cooperate, let's go get another one."

ANSWERS TO SECTION B

Your answers may differ slightly from those that follow. Give yourself credit if you replaced the number of nonstandard expressions indicated below in parentheses.

1. (4) In regard to her appearance, I'd say she was sallow-complexioned and may have had a broken nose.
2. (3) Since an engagement ring costs a considerable amount, maybe she doesn't really need one.
3. (2) The company sent me some information about Eternal Life batteries, but I can't find it anywhere.
4. (3) The lawyer seemed friendly at first, but he got rather angry when I told him I didn't have any money.
5. (2) Regardless of what the doctor tells him, he doesn't watch his diet.
6. (2) Unless your father teaches you the difference between right and wrong, you'll be in trouble.
7. (2) I don't remember whether he ran off that day or not.
8. (2) You shouldn't see him again till you're really ready.

Unit 26—Malapropisms

A: COMMENTARY

In Richard Brinsley Sheridan's play *The Rivals* a character named Mrs. Malaprop has trouble saying what she means. She may call someone "the *pineapple* of politeness" rather than *pinnacle*, or say "Lead on, we'll *precede*" instead of *follow*. A person she admires may be "a *progeny* of learning" instead of *prodigy*. Most of us, however, don't have such obvious troubles with words.

Nevertheless, if we are not careful, sometimes we use words that don't quite fit. For instance, look up the italicized words in the following sentences to see how they are misused.

1. I enjoyed *The Sun Also Rises, A Farewell to Arms,* and *The Old Man and the Sea,* but the *latter* book was definitely the best.
2. Why are you two *continuously* insulting each other?
3. He told us an amusing *antidote.*
4. She suffers from a *congenial* ailment.
5. Frank Lambert, now *diseased,* was a bank president.
6. It is considered *immortal* to undress in public.

Sometimes it is difficult to tell from a dictionary definition whether or not a word will fit in a particular context. For instance, consider the word *assassinate.* In one dictionary one of the definitions is "to kill by sudden or secret, premeditated assault." However, we do not ordinarily refer to the killing of a mosquito as an assassination, even though the killing may be sudden and premeditated.

To discover how a word may be used correctly, watch for the word in print and listen for it in lectures or conversations, as well as check its meaning in a reputable dictionary.

B: EXERCISES

1 Mrs. Jakes is in the hospital. She has *very close* veins.

A malapropism is generally the misuse of one word for another that is intended. In the sentence above, the speaker undoubtedly meant *varicose* rather than *very close.*

Which of the following sentences contains a malapropism? _____

A. You go ahead; I'll *precede.*
B. The sergeant *preceded* his men down the mined road.

2 There are several slightly different kinds of malapropisms. One is the confu-

sion of words that are somewhat alike. For instance, consider this example:

This is private property. Trespassers will be *persecuted*.

To *persecute* is "to annoy or oppress unceasingly with ill-treatment."
On the other hand, *prosecute* means "to take legal action against." The

writer of the example above probably meant _____.

3 **I like reading nonfriction better than friction.**

Instead of *nonfriction* and *friction*, the writer certainly meant _____

_____ and _____.

4 **I am attending the University of Colorado now. I was formally a student
at Indiana University.**

In the sentence above, the words *formally* and *formerly* are confused.

The word _____ means "at an earlier time." The word

_____ means "in a formal manner." The word _____
would be correct in the example.

5 Another kind of malapropism involves use of the wrong form of a word, as
in this sentence:

I *suspicioned* that he was the guilty person.

In the sentence above *suspicioned* is a (noun/verb) _____.
Suspected is the form normally used as a verb and would be more appropriate in the example.

6 One kind of malapropism is observed only in writing since it involves
homonyms, words sounding alike but spelled differently.

The bride walked down the *isle*.

Possibly this bride was indeed on a hilly island, but most brides walk down

the _____.

7 **"There's a statute of George Washington in the park."**
"You don't mean *statute*. You mean *stature*."

Both speakers are wrong, of course. The monument that stands in a park

is a _____. A *statute* is a _____. *Stature* means

"_____."

8 Sally has a cute appendicitis.

What is the malapropism in this sentence? _____ What word is meant? _____

9 Use *later* correctly in one sentence, *latter* in another.

_____

_____

10 Using a dictionary if necessary, write sentences to show the differences between these words:

A. **contemptible/contemptuous**   B. **livid/vivid**   C. **loose/lose**

A. 1. _____
   2. _____
B. 1. _____
   2. _____
C. 1. _____
   2. _____

C: ASSIGNMENTS

• One word in each of the following sentences is italicized. Using the dictionary if necessary, decide whether the italicized word is used correctly in the sentence. If it is not used correctly, try to find a word that would be correct in the context.

1. Mack is a *progeny* of learning.
2. The speaker made an *allusion* to Wylie's book.
3. Dick was *enthusiastic* about the new school dance band.
4. The program will be *continuous* from 4 P.M.
5. I *suspicion* that we have missed the freeway.
6. Alice was obviously *contemptible* of Charles's behavior at the party.
7. It's no fun to play if you are going to *flaunt* all the rules.
8. Our new coworker was *formally* with General Electric.
9. Perhaps the most *famous* American criminal was Al Capone.
10. The gossip about Jim will ruin his *character*.
11. The priest was at the *alter*.
12. A ninety-degree *angel* is a right *angel*.
13. Several *calvarymen* rode up noisily.
14. Louise played a few *cords* on the piano.

15. Every day she writes a few lines in her *dairy*.
16. People who move into a country are *immigrants*.
17. The *lightening* was flashing.
18. He smoothes the plank with his *plane*.
19. He *waived* the little flag vigorously.
20. Is society becoming more *permissible?*

ANSWERS TO SECTION B

1. A
2. prosecuted
3. nonfiction, fiction
4. formerly   formally   formerly
5. verb
6. aisle
7. statue   law (*or* ordinance)   height
8. a cute   acute
9. MODELS.   Our arrival was later than we had expected.
         Either revision or repeal is a possibility but I prefer the latter.
10. MODELS   A. 1. That was a contemptible act. I despise it.
              2. Some people tend to be contemptuous of those poorer than themselves.
           B. 1. Her face reddened, livid with anger.
              2. The story is a vivid account of an African safari.
           C. 1. I have a loose tooth.
              2. Try not to lose your scarf, Elaine.

Unit 27—Words Often Confused (I)

A: COMMENTARY

Study the definitions, illustrations, and comments below, and refer to them as needed when you do Sections B and C. If necessary, see your dictionary for further explanations.

a, an   Use *a* before a consonant sound, *an* before a vowel sound: *a* car; *an* automobile.

accept, except   You *accept* a gift. All *except* John agreed.

adverse, averse   *Adverse* means "unfavorable"; *averse* means "unwilling": an *adverse* decision; *averse* to using profanity.

advice, advise   *Advice* is a noun, *advise* a verb: give *advice*; to *advise* your friends.

affect, effect   To *affect* is to influence. *Effect* is usually a noun: the *effect* of the judge's ruling. As a verb, *effect* means "to cause, to bring about": The counselor *effected* a reconciliation.

all ready, already   *All ready* means "completely ready"; *already* means "earlier, previously."

all together, altogether   *All together* means "as a group"; *altogether* means "entirely" or "in all."

allusion, illusion   You make an *allusion* when you refer indirectly; an *illusion* is something not really there: a ghost is an *illusion*.

amateur, beginner, novice   *Amateurs* take part in an activity because they enjoy it even though they may not be very proficient; a *beginner* or a *novice* has had little experience with the activity.

amount, number   An *amount* is measurable, and a *number* is countable: the *amount* of flour; the *number* of sacks of flour.

anxious, eager   You're *anxious* about something that worries you and *eager* for something that you strongly want.

avocation, vocation   An *avocation* is a hobby; a *vocation* is a way to make a living.

beside, besides   I'll sit *beside* you. *Besides*, I'll comfort you.

breath, breathe   *Breath* is a noun, *breathe* a verb: to take a deep *breath*; to *breathe* deeply.

can, may   Although informally *can* is often used for *may*, formally *can* refers to ability to do, and *may* refers to permission or possibility: Yes, Jimmy, you *may* have some cookies if you *can* reach them.

capital, capitol   *Capitol* refers only to the building: has an office in the *capitol*. For all other meanings of the word, use *capital*.

censor, censure   To *censor* is to examine and perhaps delete for moral or other reasons; to *censure* is to blame or condemn. Both words may also be nouns.

cite, site   To *cite* is to refer to and perhaps to quote; a *site* is a location.

climactic, climatic   *Climactic* means "pertaining to climax"; *climatic*, "pertaining to climate."

complement, compliment   A *complement* completes; a *compliment* is words of praise: the *complement* of an angle; to pay a *compliment*.

compose, comprise   To *compose* is to put together or constitute; *comprise* means "consist of": Fifty states *compose* the United States. The United States *comprises* fifty states.

B: EXERCISES

1 The speaker made (a/an) _____ (allusion/illusion) _____ to the (amount/number _____ of Canadians killed in the war. (Beside/Besides) _____ referring to all those deaths, he (cited/sited) _____ figures on the number of wounded.

2 "(Breath/Breathe) _____ deeply" was the coach's (advice/ advise) _____. "There will be no (adverse/averse) _____ (affects/effects) _____ unless you take too many short (breaths/ breathes) _____."

3 (Climactic/Climatic) _____ conditions are important in some people's choices of (a/an) _____ (avocation/vocation) _____. They may be (adverse/averse) _____ to working in very hot or very cold areas, but will gladly (accept/except) _____ jobs in temperate zones, where temperatures will not (affect/effect) _____ them (adversely/aversely) _____.

4 It was (all ready/already) _____ two o'clock, although Brunton suffered from the (allusion/illusion) _____ that very little time had passed. (All together/Altogether) _____ he had been in the pit for five hours, and he was (anxious/eager) _____ to rejoin the other engineers at the (cite/site) _____ of the proposed dam.

5 Brazil (composes/comprises) _____ not just the well-known tropical rain forests but also a huge (amount/number) _____ of fertile farm lands. It is a country of contrasts. (Beside/Besides) _____ the hovel stands the mansion. The (capital/capitol) _____ city, Brasília, is new and was especially built for governmental purposes. The (capital/capitol) _____ building, as we would call it, is the National Congress Building.

6 Almost everyone would rather hear a (complement/compliment) _____ rather than (censor/censure) _____ for what he or she does. I know that in my fifteen years of playing tennis as (a/an) _____ (amateur/novice) _____ I have welcomed every (breath/breathe) _____ of praise. And of course if I am glad to hear someone say that I am doing well in my (avocation/vocation) _____, I'm even gladder to hear that I am doing my regular job well.

7 The speaker said, "A (censor/censure) _____ is (composed/comprised) _____ of one part malice, one part fear, and two parts pettiness. The (climactic/climatic) _____ part of the day comes when he or she can reject something (all together/altogether) _____. The (amateur/novice) _____ censor is anxious to avoid being considered too lenient, and is (all ready/already) _____ to condemn half of what he or she sees."

8 The arithmetic teacher told her pupils, "You (can/may) _____ easily find the (complement/compliment) _____ of an angle. Are you (all ready/already) _____ to learn how? Fine. We'll do the first problem (all together/altogether) _____. Angle A is 27 degrees. To find the (complement/compliment) _____, just subtract 27 from 90, and the difference, 63 degrees, is your answer. When I give the signal, you (can/may) _____ start the next four problems."

C: ASSIGNMENTS

• Pick out all the pairs of words discussed on pages 156–57 that have confused you even slightly in the past. Make up two or more sentences illustrating the use of each word. The number of sentences you compose should be large enough to make you feel confident of your mastery.

ANSWERS TO SECTION B

1. an, allusion, number, Besides, cited
2. Breathe, advice, adverse, effects, breaths
3. Climatic, a, vocation, averse, accept, affect, adversely
4. already, illusion, Altogether, eager, site
5. comprises, amount, Beside, capital, capitol
6. compliment, censure, an, amateur, breath, avocation
7. censor, composed, climactic, altogether, novice, all ready
8. can, complement, all ready, all together, complement, may

Unit 28—Words Often Confused (II)

A: COMMENTARY

Study the definitions, illustrations, and comments below, and refer to them as needed when you do Sections B and C. If necessary, see your dictionary for further explanations.

conscience, conscious *Conscience* is a noun: My *conscience* hurts me. *Conscious* is an adjective: The driver of the wrecked car was still *conscious*.

council, counsel A *council* is a group of people who meet to consider, debate, or instruct. *Counsel* is advice. Also, a lawyer is a legal counsel, or adviser.

credible, creditable, credulous *Credible* means "believable." *Creditable* means "deserving credit." *Credulous* means "naive, gullible, believing whatever one is told."

detract, distract To *detract* (from) is to reduce, to take something away: The muddy field *detracted* from the usual crispness of the marching maneuvers. To *distract* is to draw attention away: The scent of a rabbit does not *distract* a well-trained bird dog.

device, devise *Device* is a noun: a mechanical *device*. *Devise* is a verb: to *devise* a plan.

disinterested, uninterested Informally these words are used interchangeably, but formal writers prefer to define *disinterested* as "impartial": Football officials should be *disinterested* but not *uninterested*.

dual, duel *Dual* means "double": a *dual* carburetor. A *duel* is a battle between two opponents.

elicit, illicit *Elicit* is a verb meaning "to draw forth": to *elicit* praise. *Illicit* is an adjective meaning "illegal": *illicit* drugs.

eminent, imminent An *eminent* person is famous. Something is *imminent* if it will happen soon.

equable, equitable *Equable* means "unchanging, uniform, even": an *equable* temperament. *Equitable* means "fair, impartial": Laws should be *equitable*.

exceptional, exceptionable Something *exceptional* is unusual. Something *exceptionable* is objectionable.

fewer, less Use *fewer* if you can count whatever you are talking about, *less* if you cannot: *fewer* comments; *less* discussion.

genius, talent Genius is generally regarded as a higher quality than talent. *Genius* implies especially deep, broad, and creative ability, but *talent* is only a specialized aptitude in a particular field.

hanged, hung In formal language, executed people are *hanged* rather than *hung*.

healthful, healthy Something good for you is described in formal language as *healthful*: Wheat germ is *healthful*. *Healthy* means "having health": a *healthy* body.

historic, historical Something is *historic* if it is famous and very important in history: a *historic* court decision. *Historical* means "pertaining to history": *historical* writings.

human, humane   *Human* means "pertaining to people." *Humane* means "kind, tender."

imply, infer   To *imply* is to suggest, hint at. To *infer* is to deduce, conclude.

incredible, incredulous   *Incredible* means "not believable": an *incredible* exaggeration. *Incredulous* means "not believing": an *incredulous* look.

ingenious, ingenuous   An *ingenious* idea or invention is clever. An *ingenuous* person may be either naive or very frank and candid.

B: EXERCISES

1 The (Council/Counsel) _____ of Church Women said that it was not (credible/creditable/credulous) _____ that their minister would (imply/infer) _____ that a deacon would engage in such an (elicit/illicit) _____ activity as moonshining.

2 I (imply/infer) _____ from your remarks that the man who was (hanged/hung) _____ was really a good man, (human/humane) _____ in his treatment of animals, and (exceptional/exceptionable) _____ in his kindness of heart.

3 Judges should be (disinterested/uninterested) _____ in every case brought before them. Their responsibility is to help attorneys (elicit/illicit) _____ the truth from every witness, and to make sure that every decision reached in the court is (equable/equitable) _____ and just. If they succeed, they can sleep every night with a clear (conscience/conscious) _____.

4 This (device/devise) _____, which was invented by an (eminent/imminent) _____ surgeon, will permit a heart patient to remain (conscience/conscious) _____ during an operation and yet be perfectly motionless so as not to (detract/distract) _____ the surgical team.

5 "My car has (dual/duel) _____ mufflers," he told her, but she was completely (disinterested/uninterested) _____. He had an

(incredible/incredulous) _____ (genius/talent) _____ for boring his friends.

6 "I would like to (council/counsel) _____ you about a development that is (eminent/imminent) _____," said the tax lawyer. "There will be (fewer/less) _____ opportunities to take depletion allowances if HR 1711 becomes law, and that bill will also (detract/distract) _____ from our chances to make certain other deductions. But I'll try to (device/devise) _____ a formula that will cost you as little as possible."

7 There was (fewer/less) _____ soybeans in the bin than before, and the little that was left was hardly fit for (human/humane) _____ consumption. I was (incredible/incredulous) _____. I couldn't believe that hundreds of bushels of this (healthful/healthy) _____ food had simply vanished.

8 "A brilliant, devilishly (ingenious/ingenuous) _____ plan, Count. It takes full advantage of what we know of the Duke's calm, (equable/equitable) _____ temperament, and the poor fool is just (credible/creditable/credulous) _____ enough and (ingenious/ingenuous) _____ enough to fall for your scheme. I find no flaws in it—it's completely (unexceptional/unexceptionable) _____ from my point of view. He will certainly feel that he must challenge me to a (dual/duel) _____."

9 In one of his (historic/historical) _____ novels Thomas Costain tells of the (historic/historical) _____ moment when a remarkable young Greek, unquestionably a man of (genius/talent) _____, offered a (creditable/credulous) _____ explanation of the circulation of the blood and the need that a (healthful/healthy) _____ body has for uninterrupted circulation.

C: ASSIGNMENTS

• Pick out all the pairs of words discussed on pages 160–61 that have confused you even slightly in the past. Make up two or more sentences illustrating the use of each word. The number of sentences you compose should be large enough to make you feel confident of your mastery.

ANSWERS TO SECTION B

1. Council, credible, imply, illicit
2. infer, hanged, humane, exceptional
3. disinterested, elicit, equitable, conscience
4. device, eminent, conscious, distract
5. dual, uninterested, incredible, talent
6. counsel, imminent, fewer, detract, devise
7. less, human, incredulous, healthful
8. ingenious, equable, credulous, ingenuous, unexceptionable, duel
9. historical, historic, genius, creditable, healthy

Unit 29—Words Often Confused (III)

A: COMMENTARY

Study the definitions, illustrations, and comments below, and refer to them as needed when you do Sections B and C. If necessary, see your dictionary for further explanations.

its, it's *Its* is possessive: The dog dropped *its* bone. *It's* means "it is" or (sometimes) "it has": *It's* here. *It's* been here for three weeks.

judicial, judicious *Judicial* refers to courts of law: *judicial* proceedings. *Judicious* means "wise, prudent, like a judge."

leave, let To *leave* is to go away, or to allow someone or something to stay: *Leave* it there. To *let* is to permit: Please *let* me go.

liable, likely Both *liable* and *likely* refer to probability, but we generally use *liable* when what we are predicting may be considered bad: We're *likely* to get a good rain. We're *liable* to get a blizzard.

luxuriant, luxurious *Luxuriant* generally refers to growing plants, and means that they are lush and thriving. *Luxurious* means "rich, comfortable."

majority, plurality Although sometimes used interchangeably, *majority* often means "more than half of the total number," and *plurality* refers to the margin by which one candidate defeats another.

moral, morale *Moral* refers to the goodness or badness of human actions: a highly *moral* person. *Morale* is the state of spirits of a person or a group: The *morale* of the troops was excellent.

noted, notorious A *noted* person is famous, and a *notorious* person is infamous because of his or her wicked deeds. A scientist may be *noted*, but a criminal is more likely to be *notorious*.

oral, verbal Often used interchangeably, but some sentences would be more clear if a distinction were kept. *Oral* means "spoken": The agreement was *oral*, never written down. *Verbal* means "in words, whether spoken or written": His abuse was *verbal*, not physical.

personal, personnel A *personal* letter. The *personnel* in a large office.

practicable, practical *Practicable* means "feasible, capable of being successfully": a *practicable* way to get rid of the rattlesnake. *Practical* has several meanings, including "not theoretical," "level-headed," "capable of being used."

principal, principle If you remember that a princi*ple* is a ru*le*, and that *principal* is the spelling for most other meanings of the word, you should have no trouble: a *principle* of chemistry; the *principal* of a school; *principal* and interest; the *principal* sponsor.

prophecy, prophesy *Prophecy* is a noun: to make a *prophecy*. *Prophesy* is a verb: to *prophesy* the end of the world.

respectably, respectfully, respectively They live *respectably* (in a respectable manner); he spoke *respectfully* (with respect); we'll hear from Debbie, Frank, and Judy *respectively* (in that order).

stationary, stationery *Stationary*, an adjective, means "not moving." *Stationery*, a noun, means "writing paper."

than, then Thunder noisier *than* before. *Then* the rain came.

their, there, they're *Their* shows possession: Birds left *their* nests. *There* usually shows place: She stood *there*. *They're* means "they are": *They're* coming!

to, too, two They wanted *to* see the *two* elephants, *too*.

vice, vise Vice is wickedness. A *vise* is a tool for holding.

whose, who's *Whose* is possessive: the woman *whose* husband was late. *Who's* means "who is": *Who's* that man in the corner?

wreath, wreathe *Wreath* is a noun: a Christmas *wreath*. To *wreathe* is to encircle: to *wreathe* the cake with colored sugar.

your, you're *Your* is possessive: This is *your* life. *You're* means "you are": *You're* late.

B: EXERCISES

1 (Its/It's) _____ (to/too/two) _____ o'clock in the morning, and today is (liable/likely) _____ to be a hard day for us. (Whose/Who's) _____ ready for bed?

2 In our courts, backlogs of (judicial/judicious) _____ cases are greater (than/then) _____ ever. As a result we have (noted/

notorious) _____ criminals running loose, and (vice/vise) _____ increases steadily.

3 The (principal/principle) _____ herself helped to hang the (wreaths/wreathes) _____ in our school windows. Then she stood (stationary/stationery) _____ and admired her work. It was all a little silly, but it did wonders for the (moral/morale) _____ of the pupils.

4 My mother could not (leave/let) _____ the shrubs escape her regular attention. They grew (luxuriantly/luxuriously) _____, and soon (their/there/they're) _____ branches reached above her head and began to (wreath/wreathe) _____ their way around the upper columns.

5 José Martínez was (noted/notorious) _____ for his honesty. He never signed contracts with his customers; all his agreements were only (oral/verbal) _____. Through (judicial/judicious) _____ investments he had become a wealthy man, but he was always regarded as a highly (moral/morale) _____ person. He had no known (vices/vises) _____. He lived simply and (respectably, respectfully, respectively) _____, never (luxuriantly/luxuriously) _____ _____. After his death all who had known him spoke (respectably/respectfully/respectively) _____ of him.

6 (Your/You're) _____ (personal/personnel) _____ life is none of my business. If (their/there/they're) _____ are things you want (to/too/two) _____ keep hidden, you'll find that I won't be (to/too/two) _____ curious. With me it is a (principal/principle) _____ of conduct to (leave/let) _____ each person to his or her own way of life.

7 (Your/You're) _____ not (liable, likely) _____ to hear any favorable (prophecies/prophesies) _____ about the future of these companies. With all (their/there/they're) _____ problems with (personal/personnel) _____, their/there/they're)

_____ not going to find it (practicable/practical) _____ to expand.

8 Authors are usually (oral/verbal) _____, not physical. To them the pen is indeed mightier (than/then) _____ the sword, and an ordinary sheet of (stationary/stationery) _____ can be a beautiful thing on (whose/who's) _____ surface they may be able to compose a message that will last for generations.

9 Although almost any politician will (prophecy/prophesy) _____ or at least hint the end of the world if he or she is not elected, many are (practicable/practical) _____ enough to provide themselves with another means of livelihood if they do not obtain at least a (plurality/majority) _____ of the votes, although a two-thirds (plurality/majority) _____ is what they really hope for. In summary, (than/then) _____, they pray for a plurality, hope for a majority, but plan to survive defeat.

10 Try the wrench, the pliers, the clamps, and the (vice/vise) _____ (respectably/respectfully/respectively) _____.

C: ASSIGNMENTS

• Pick out all the pairs of words discussed on pages 163–64 that have confused you even slightly in the past. Make up two or more sentences illustrating the use of each word. The number of sentences you compose should be large enough to make you feel confident of your mastery.

ANSWERS TO SECTION B

1. It's, two, liable, Who's
2. judicial, than, notorious, vice
3. principal, wreaths, stationary, morale
4. let, luxuriantly, their, wreathe
5. noted, oral, judicious, moral, vices, respectably, luxuriously, respectfully
6. Your, personal, there, to, too, principle, leave
7. You're, likely, prophecies, their, personnel, they're, practicable
8. verbal, than, stationery, whose
9. prophesy, practical, plurality, majority, then
10. vise, respectively

Unit 30—Double Subjects
and Double Negatives

A: COMMENTARY

This unit concerns two of the most common types of nonstandard expressions.

One, the double subject, ordinarily consists of a noun and an unnecessary pronoun: My *mother she* always wanted to stay home at vacation time. The correction is simply to delete the pronoun:

> My *mother* always wanted to stay home at vacation time.

The double negative as a nonstandard form is illustrated in these sentences:

> They did*n't* do *nothing.*
> They did*n't* say anything, *neither.*
> They did*n't* want *nothing, neither.* (a triple negative)

Several hundred years ago such sentences were standard English, but today the speaker of standard English dispenses with all but one of the negatives. Shakespeare's Hamlet, in a play written close to four centuries ago, said, "Be not too tame neither." Today Shakespeare might write "Be not too tame either" or, even more likely, "Do not be too tame either."

Two kinds of double negative are still generally approved, however. One is the *not un-* construction, as in *a not unfamiliar sight.* Such a sight would supposedly be a little less common than a familiar sight.

The other kind of approved double negative employs the second negative for emphasis, but should seldom be used:

> Our troops will *never* surrender, *not* even if the walls of the castle fall.

B: EXERCISES

> S
>
1 **Captain Bridges would not follow his scouts' advice.**

   A. Does the sentence above seem grammatically complete? _____

   B. What is the subject? _____

>   S   S
>
2 **Captain Bridges he would not follow his scouts' advice.**
   A. Does the sentence above mean exactly the same thing as the example in

      exercise 1? _____

B. What are the two subjects in the sentence above? _____

_____

C. Is the second subject necessary? _____
D. Is the example in exercise 1 or that in exercise 2 the better sentence?

_____

3 The children in the front row they started throwing paper cups.
The children in the front row started throwing paper cups.
A. Which has a double subject, the first or the second sentence above?

_____

B. Which is the better sentence? _____

4 I did not not vote in any election last year, either.
No one is likely (except through carelessness) to write the sentence above.

Instead of two negative words (*not not*), only _____ is required.

5 I did not vote in no election last year, either.
A. Again in the example above only one negative word is needed. But this

example, like the one in exercise 4, has two negatives. They are _____

and _____.

B. The example should be written like this: _____

_____

6 I did not vote in any election last year, neither.

A. Once more the example has two negatives. They are _____ and

_____.

B. The example should be written like this: _____

_____

7 I didn't vote in no election last year, neither.

A. The three negatives in this example are _____, _____, and _____.

B. The example should be written like this: _____

_____

8 We didn't hardly have time.

In the sentence above, *hardly* and _____ both have negative meanings.
The sentence could be rephrased with only one negative in either of these

ways: *We hardly had time* or *We did _____ _____ _____.*

9 **We didn't scarcely have time.**

Like *hardly, scarcely* has a negative meaning. This double negative could be avoided by writing _____ _____ _____ _____ or ____ ____

_____ _____ _____.

10 Which of the following words are negative in meaning?
any no some none nobody anybody   no one   someone either neither hardly
scarcely ever never nothing something somewhere nowhere

_____ _____ _____ _____ _____

_____ _____ _____ _____ _____

11 **What I just said is not inconsistent with my first statement.**
A. The example above contains two negatives, one of which is the word

_____ and the other the prefix _____. This kind of construction, sometimes called the *not un-* construction, is considered satisfactory.
B. If we substituted *consistent* for *not inconsistent*, the meaning would be

(exactly the same/a little stronger and more positive) _____

_____.

12 **I will never touch a drop of liquor, not as long as I live.**
In the example above, *not* is really unnecessary since the negative idea is

contained in the word _____. However, for emphasis some such double negatives do occur, although they are rare.

C: ASSIGNMENTS

• Some of the following sentences are written in standard form, but most have double subjects or unjustified double negatives. Decide whether each is standard or nonstandard, and make necessary changes in the nonstandard ones.

1. My Aunt Carmen she flies to Puerto Rico every year.
2. When Aunt Carmen was a girl, she lived in Puerto Rico.
3. The apples that are in the basement they've started to rot.
4. We did not see nobody at first.
5. It is not unusual to see a guard in every room.
6. You can't hardly get there from here.
7. We will not go into the swamp, not even if you say you'll court-martial us.
8. We didn't see none neither, not nowhere.
9. The four girls in the helicopter they said that they didn't see none either.
10. If no one brought no can opener, we're in trouble.
11. They weren't scarcely out of sight of the camp when they began smoking.

12. Nobody wants none.
13. My grandfather he never had no television to watch when he was a boy.
14. If anybody has any complaints, he or she should not hesitate to let us know.
15. Neither of the bids wasn't really very low, but we felt we could do better.

ANSWERS TO SECTION B

1. A. Yes   B. Captain Bridges
2. A. Yes   B. Captain Bridges he   C. No   D. exercise 1
3. A. First   B. Second
4. one
5. A. not, no   B. I did not vote in any election last year, either.
6. A. not, neither   B. I did not vote in any election last year, either.
7. A. n't, no, neither   B. I didn't vote in any election last year, either.
8. n't   not have time
9. We scarcely had time   We did not have time
10. no, none, nobody, no one, neither, hardly, scarcely, never, nothing, nowhere
11. A. not, in-   B. a little stronger and more positive
12. never

Unit 31—Conciseness

A: COMMENTARY

Wordiness is a very common, though unintentional, time-wasting device. Avoid the boredom that wordiness creates; use only words that are necessary to express your idea.

WORDY: **Bill drove his car to the game. Hal took his car to the game also, and Jack used his own car for his transportation.**
BETTER: **Bill, Hal, and Jack all drove their cars to the game.**

Some wordiness is less noticeable than the example above. It involves the use of only one or two extra words that repeat an idea unnecessarily. For example, many people talk about *commuting back and forth*. The idea of *back and forth* is contained in the word *commute* and therefore can be left out. Others talk about *mental telepathy; mental* is redundant. Or someone asks you to *refer back* to page 16; *refer* can do the job alone.

Section B will call your attention to a number of other redundancies or other types of wordiness.

B: EXERCISES

1 **In my opinion I think that there is no point in further reducing trans-Atlantic flying time.**

The sentence above can be improved by eliminating the three words _____

_____ _____ or the two words _____ _____.

2 Sometimes when we are careless we are guilty of redundancies. That is, we say the same thing twice, for no good reason. For instance, in the sentence **Occasionally it sometimes snows in Florida** the words that mean the same

thing are _____ and _____.

3 In the next few exercises we'll glance at a number of fairly common expressions that are redundant. You are to cross out whatever word or words are not needed. However, if you find a redundancy that you yourself are guilty of, it will help you if you will repeat the reduced sentence (preferably aloud) at least three times.

  A. **I didn't hear you the first time. Please repeat that again.**
  B. **In the modern world of today we can easily learn about foreign countries.**
  C. **You now have all the essential information that you need.**

4 A. **That's the honest truth.**
  B. **What we want are the true facts.**
  C. **Where is he at?**
  D. **Where did she go to?**

5 A. **She cannot hardly cook her own meals.**
  B. **The house is rectangular in shape.**
  C. **The total effect of all this may be harmful.**
  D. **A poor widow woman lived down the street.**

6 A. **Reduction of taxes would be the most ideal solution.**
  B. **My father he says that Clark will run for the Senate.**
  C. **Where did you meet up with Mr. Pike?**
  D. **Send for this free gift today.**

7 A. **The two engines are identically the same.**
  B. **I personally dislike him.**
  C. **Take the first, third, fifth, and etc.**
  D. **In size she is petite.**

8 Sometimes we are guilty of redundancies because we aren't fully aware of

the meanings of certain words. *Commute,* already mentioned, is one example. Here are two more:

A. The *consensus of opinion* is that the law is unenforceable.
B. He has *ambivalent feelings* toward his father.

In A the idea *of opinion* is contained in the word *consensus,* for *consensus* means "agreement in opinions." Can *of opinion* be crossed out without harming the sentence? _____ In B the word *ambivalent* means "feeling two ways." Would it be correct to say just *He is ambivalent toward his father?* _____

9 Sometimes we become wordy because we have certain set phrases that we use even when they don't mean anything. For instance:

Like, you know, we were going only like fifty miles an hour, you know.

Copy the six unneeded words in that sentence: _____ _____

_____ _____ _____ _____

10 **All other things being equal, I think we should have the picnic at MacArthur Park.**

What is the phrase that is almost meaningless in the sentence above?

_____

11 Occasionally conciseness can result from combining two or more sentences.

Bill defeated his opponent in a speech contest. Beth bested her opponent also, and Janet was also victorious.

We can save words in this way: Bill, Beth, and Janet (finish the sentence) _____.

C: ASSIGNMENTS

• Rewrite each of the following sentences, keeping the thought of the original but making each more concise.

1. We live in the suburbs and commute back and forth to work.
2. In my opinion I think that final examinations should be done away with and abolished.
3. In this modern world of today, many diseases that our grandparents contracted and became ill with, diseases that kept them from being well, we moderns now do not have to contend with, partly because of vaccines that keep us from contracting diseases, partly because of principles of sanitation

having to do with cleanliness, and partly because of more healthful foods that are better for us when we eat them than those our grandparents used to eat.

4. In height Jim was six feet tall; in weight he weighed exactly two hundred pounds.

5. There was a movement that gained momentum and became a trend toward elaborate resorts where people go to play in the snow. From Squaw Valley in the West, which is located on the West Coast, to Lake Placid in the East, which is located on the East Coast, these resorts drew increasing thousands of skiers who were interested either in strenuous participation or in just watching.

6. I feel in a tired condition because I have been engaged in playing baseball.

7. The newspaper editorial published in the newspaper discussed the field of federal public housing, paid for not by private enterprise but by the federal government.

8. He made up his mind and decided to reiterate and repeat again his declaration stating that he had had nothing to do with the bus strike.

9. The speaker who was talking to the members of the audience of people who had come to hear her told the people who were there assembled that they were living their lives in dangerous times that were full of perils.

10. The autobiography of Franklin's life that he wrote himself is fascinating reading.

ANSWERS TO SECTION B

1. In my opinion, I think
2. Occasionally, sometimes
3. A. again   B. In the modern world of   C. that you need
4. A. honest   B. true   C. at   D. to
5. A. not   B. in shape   C. of all this   D. woman
6. A. most   B. he   C. up with   D. free
7. A. identically (or -ly the same)   B. personally   C. and   D. In size
8. Yes   Yes
9. Like, you know, like, you know
10. All other things being equal
11. all defeated their opponents in a speech contest

Unit 32—The Exact Word and the Right Amount of Detail

A: COMMENTARY

"Hey, Mike, where's the gizmo?"

"Where's the what?"

"The thing you just push on to get the things in."

"What things, Pete?"

"These damn screws."

"Oh, you mean the ratchet screwdriver."

Maybe Pete's failure to ask right away for the tool he needed didn't cause any serious problems. But sometimes a listener gets at least mildly annoyed because he or she has no idea of what a speaker is talking about. In a written message—say an order for goods—lack of exactness and specificity may cause a delay, the shipment of the wrong items, or at best a long-distance phone call to eliminate the confusion.

Professional writers often comment on their search for the exact word—*le mot juste*, the French call it. Authors know that the emotional impact of a sentence, a paragraph, or a poem may depend on the felicity of their choice of words. The nonprofessional is usually less interested in emotional impact: clarity is probably the goal. But clarity also depends on finding the words that say what one means. In this unit we are especially concerned with clarity.

Section B emphasizes three points:

1. Specific words are generally more clear than general ones. (See also Units 1 and 2.)
2. It is possible, though, to bring in specific details that are not really relevant.
3. Long or obscure words, unless they are the ones that most precisely reveal the meaning, should be avoided.

B: EXERCISES

1 **I'll bring the stuff to the meeting.**

Depending on the circumstances, the sentence above may or may not be satisfactory. If the speaker is talking with a fellow-worker who knows what meeting is meant and what "stuff" will be needed, is there likely to be any problem in interpreting the message? _____

2 Look again at the example in exercise 1. Suppose this time that the speaker's fellow-worker has been away from the office for a week and has just returned. Is it quite possible that he will not understand "stuff" and "meeting"? _____

3 **I'll bring the material to the session today.**
I'll bring the March sales statistics to the marketing conference.

Which sentence, the first or the second, is more likely to be clear to the fellow-worker? _____

4 **The members of *a well-known organization* had *a hassle* about *the problem.***

Improve the sentence above by substituting specific words and details for the italicized generalities.

_____

_____

_____

5 **The speech was interesting.**

Interesting is a useful word, but often a substitute says more precisely what we mean. List five other, more specific words that can replace *interesting* in describing a speech. _____ _____ _____

_____ _____

6 **The football game was interesting.**

List five other, more specific words that can replace *interesting* in describing a football game. _____ _____ _____

_____ _____

7 **The sunset was beautiful.**

Think of a sunset that impressed you. Try to describe it more specifically.

_____

_____

8 On a few occasions, specificity is overdone, as in this example:

The baby survived its fall of two stories when it fell into a bed of white pansies, purple, pink, and crimson hollyhocks, and yellow asters.

Do the details about the flowers add anything desirable? _____

9 Rewrite the example in exercise 8, deleting the inconsequentials.

_____

_____

10 Precipitation, in all probability, will occur during the early postmeridian hours.

Big or obscure words are probably useful or they would not have been created. Some persons, though, use them even when talking or writing about common things for which common words are much more appropriate. In simple language, what is the meaning of the sentence at the beginning of this exercise? _____

11 An excessive number of culinary artists cause irreparable impairment of the qualitative excellence of the *potage*.

Hidden in the sentence above is a familiar proverb starting with "Too many." What is the proverb? _____

C: ASSIGNMENTS

• Explain what is inexact, unspecific, or overdone in the language of each of these sentences. Rewrite each.

1. That music is real cool.
2. Holding the fatal telegram in her closed fist, the distraught mother fell back on the brocaded couch with the decorative pillows she had won years ago at the county fair and which were now threadbare with age.
3. A vehicle went down the ice-coated hill.
4. (from a letter of reference) The quality of Holman's work is OK.
5. I have been cogitating on your interrogation and shall now endeavor to expatiate a response.
6. We saw some interesting things in Yellowstone Park.
7. Our rural area provides a domicile for an abundance of wild life.
8. In the big city he soon learned to enjoy the wild life.
9. A person saw the incident and mentioned it to the long arm of the law.
10. He is a pig.

ANSWERS TO SECTION B

1. **No**
2. **Yes**
3. **Second**
4. MODEL The members of the Rotary Club had a long discussion about whether to increase their financial support of the day-care center.
5. MODELS fascinating, heart-warming, informative, useful, mind-boggling
6. MODELS exciting, thrilling, close, hard-fought, heartbreaking

7. MODEL   The sunset mingled vivid reds with long horizontal streaks of yellow.
8. No
9. MODEL   The baby survived its fall of two stories when it tumbled into a flowerbed.
10. MODEL   Rain is likely in the early afternoon.
11. Too many cooks spoil the broth.

PUNCTUATION AND OTHER MECHANICS

The most important use of all punctuation is to help make meaning clear to a reader. Punctuation marks are actually only a shorthand code that a writer and a reader should both understand. For example, as you know, when we come to, the end of a written sentence, we do not write "This is the end of the sentence." Instead, we make a little dot and with that tiny dot tell the reader that he or she has finished one sentence and perhaps can expect another.

When both writer and reader realize that each punctuation mark carries a certain meaning, written communication is much easier than it would otherwise be. The writer inserts the signals, and the reader interprets them.

When we speak, our voice provides the signals. We pause, or our voice rises or falls in pitch. But when we write, no one can hear us. All that we can do is to use those written signals—punctuation and capitalization mostly—that writer and reader both recognize as the substitutes for spoken signals. The units in this section explain these signals as clearly and simply as possible.

PART FOUR

PUNCTUATION AND OTHER MECHANICS

Unit 33—The Uses of Terminal Punctuation

A: COMMENTARY

You no doubt learned in elementary school most of the principles covered in this unit. In brief, they are:

1. A period is used after a sentence that makes a statement, after an indirect question, and after a request even when worded as a question.
2. Periods are used after most abbreviations and initials. Exceptions include letters (usually capitals) representing organizations, radio and television stations, and the like. Abbreviations should not be used excessively (see Unit 75). A few persons, such as the late President Harry S Truman, use no periods after one or more initials, since the letter is part of the legal name and is not just an initial.
3. Ellipsis marks are three spaced periods used to represent an omission from a quotation. If words are omitted from the end of a sentence, the three ellipsis periods are joined by a fourth, marking the end of the sentence.
4. A question mark is used primarily to mark a direct question, which is a group of words intended to obtain an answer: *Did the doorbell ring?* In contrast, an indirect question is actually a statement: *I asked whether the doorbell rang.*
5. A much more rare use of the question mark is to indicate doubt or uncertainty: *Our town was founded in 1792(?) by two veterans of the Revolutionary War.* The use of the question mark to show humor or irony is generally regarded as being in bad taste.
6. An exclamation mark is used at the end of a sentence, phrase, or word showing strong feeling, particularly when it would be spoken in a tone of excitement, anger, or other powerful emotion. The exclamation is usually short. Although comic strip writers and advertisers sometimes use !! or !!!, ordinary mortals content themselves with a single mark. A good writer usually avoids large numbers of exclamatory sentences because the effect on readers is rather deafening and eventually they pay little attention to the shouts.

B: EXERCISES

1 **The demand for adult education is increasing steadily.**

The sentence above illustrates what is probably the first rule you learned for punctuation. The sentence is in the form of a (statement/question) _____. After a statement in sentence form, the mark of punctuation required is a _____.

2 **I asked whether more adults were going back to school.**

This example is not quite like that in exercise 1, but the punctuation is the same. Notice that a question is asked indirectly. As a direct question it might be worded *Are more adults going back to school?* In that case a question mark would be used at the end. But an indirect question is really a statement and has a _____ at the end.

3 **Will you please tell me more about the changes in adult education.**

The sentence above is worded as a question, but is actually a polite request or mild command. A request or mild command, as the example shows, is punctuated with a _____.

4 **Dr. Rogers and Mr. S. M. Blake, Jr., are two of the teachers of adults.**

The first, second, and fifth periods above show that we use periods after most _____. The third and fourth periods show that we use periods after _____.

5 **Miss Marlin on station WBBM was discussing adult education programs of the UN.**

The sentence above shows that the title *Miss,* unlike *Mr., Mrs.,* or *Ms.,* (is/is not) _____ an abbreviation. It also shows that some abbreviations are not customarily followed by periods. Such abbreviations tend to be those written in (What kind of?) _____ letters.

6 **"No sort of scientific teaching . . . will ever teach men to share property and privileges with equal consideration for all. Everyone will think his share too small. . . ."**

—Dostoevski

Sometimes in quoting we wish to leave out certain words not relevant to our purpose. Such an omission is called an ellipsis. In the place where the words were omitted we use an ellipsis mark. The example above shows that the ellipsis mark consists of (How many?) _____ spaced periods. If the last part of a sentence is omitted, the ellipsis mark is the same, but a fourth period is needed to indicate _____.

7 **How large is Grand Forks?**
She asked how large Grand Forks is.

The first sentence above reminds you that a (What kind of?) _____ question is punctuated with a question mark. The second sentence reminds you that an _____ question ends with a period.

8 **Did she ask, "How large is Grand Forks?"**

The sentence above contains one direct question inside another direct question. The example shows that in punctuating such a sentence, we use (How many?) _____ question mark(s).

9 ACCEPTABLE: **Shakespeare was born on April 23 (?), 1564.**
  POOR: **After Helen fell on the freshly oiled street, she really looked happy(?).**

In the acceptable sentence above, the question mark shows that the exact date of Shakespeare's birth (has/has not) _____ been determined. In the other sentence, the question mark is intended to reveal that the word *happy* has been used ironically, as a feeble joke. Capable writers (should/should not) _____ be able to reveal their humor without resorting to such a device.

10 **No! I won't have a skunk in this house! Not even a deodorized one!**

An exclamation is an utterance expressing strong feeling. It is usually short and is punctuated with an exclamation mark. The examples above show that it (always is/need not be) _____ a complete sentence. They also show that after each exclamation (one/more than one) _____ _____ exclamation mark should be used.

11 In exercises 11–13 place a period, a question mark, an exclamation mark, or no mark when no mark is needed, at each place designated by a number.

   I wonder what time it is $_{\overline{1}}$
   At which gate will the 9:30 A $_{\overline{2}}$ **M** $_{\overline{3}}$ **flight arrive** $_{\overline{4}}$
   Will you please help me with my luggage $_{\overline{5}}$

12 **Miss** $_{\overline{1}}$ **Reynolds is working for a B** $_{\overline{2}}$ **A** $_{\overline{3}}$ **in history, isn't she** $_{\overline{4}}$
   What $_{\overline{5}}$ **In history** $_{\overline{6}}$ **I can't believe it** $_{\overline{7}}$
   Geoffrey Chaucer (1340 $_{\overline{8}}$ **–1400).**

13 **The F** $_{\overline{1}}$ **F** $_{\overline{2}}$ **A** $_{\overline{3}}$ **is active in our county** $_{\overline{4}}$
   Did you ask $_{\overline{5}}$ **, "When did France sign the treaty** $_{\overline{6}}$ **"** $_{\overline{7}}$
   Dr $_{\overline{8}}$ **Ladd has just returned from Washington, D** $_{\overline{9}}$ **C** $_{\overline{10}}$ $_{\overline{11}}$

14 **"Nothing is so galling to a people, not broken in from the birth, as a paternal or, in other words, a meddling government, a government which tells them what to read and say and eat and drink and wear."**
                                                                    —Macaulay

Copy the quotation above, omitting *not broken in from the birth* and *or, in other words, a meddling* and the last sixteen words. Use ellipses properly to show the omissions.

C: ASSIGNMENTS

• Supply the missing periods, question marks, and exclamation marks. If sometimes either one of two marks appears justifiable, be ready to defend your choice.

Dr Karch, like many doctors, did not write at all legibly Hasn't your own observation been that doctors write wretchedly But the members of the Professionals Club did not require good penmanship as a prerequisite for joining, and the doctors' credentials were impeccable "Let's get him before the Excelsior Club does" exclaimed Ralph Marshall, the chairman of the membership committee

So Ralph was authorized to invite the young doctor to join He sent the usual formal invitation Earlier the club members had reasoned, "Won't a formal written invitation be more impressive than a mere telephone call"

Ralph waited a week for the reply, which, like a sort of R S V P , he had requested At last An answer from Dr Karch Ralph tore the envelope open Except for the printed matter on the top of the small sheet of paper, he couldn't read a word of it

What could he do He didn't know whether or not the doctor was accepting And it would be too embarrassing to call up and ask

Then he had a brilliant idea Druggists needed to be able to decipher doctors' hieroglyphics, didn't they Else how could they fill prescriptions He decided to take the doctor's note to the corner drugstore, where he would simply say, "Will you read this for me, please" The pharmacist was busy when Ralph handed it to him, though, and took it into the back room before Ralph could utter a word

In a few minutes the pharmacist came out, carrying a small bottle of pink liquid He handed it to Ralph and said, "That will be six dollars, Mr Marshall"

ANSWERS TO SECTION B

1. statement   period
2. period
3. period
4. abbreviations   initials
5. is not   capital
6. three   the end of the sentence

7. direct   indirect
8. one
9. has not   should
10. need not be   one
11. 1. is.   2–3. A.M.   4. arrive?   5. luggage.
12. 1. No mark   2–3. B.A.   4. she?   5. What! (*or?*)   6. history! (*or?*)   7. it! (*or.*)   8. 1340 (or ?)
13. 1–3. No marks   4. county.   5. No mark   6. treaty?"   7. No mark   8. Dr. 9–10. D.C.   11. No mark
14. "Nothing is so galling to a people . . . as a paternal . . . government. . . ."

Unit 34—Commas to Prevent Momentary Misreading

A: COMMENTARY

All the examples in this unit illustrate one basic principle: The comma, judiciously placed, can often help the reader to interpret without unnecessary delay or rereading.

The comma is ordinarily a signal for a brief pause at a place where most speakers would hesitate. It represents a shorter pause than a semicolon or a period. We can't be absolutely safe if we use a comma where we would naturally pause slightly, but more often than not, following this practice will result in reasonably good punctuation.

Some teachers recommend that a comma always be placed after an opening phrase or adverbial clause, as in these sentences:

> **At the far right, you will see the color guard.**
> **After they turn the corner, the color guard will move ahead.**

The present tendency, however, is to use less punctuation than in past decades or centuries. Nevertheless, commas are advisable after opening phrases or clauses if there is any likelihood of misreading, as may be true in these examples:

> **After Easter lilies can be safely transplanted.**
> **When the kettle boiled over the burner was smelly white.**

In these sentences a comma after *Easter* and one after *over* would help the reader.

B: EXERCISES

1 **In the morning sun streamed in at the window.**

It is possible or probable that you had to read part of the sentence above more than once. Did you first believe that *morning sun* belonged together?

———

2 **In the morning, sun streamed in at the window.**

By use of a _____ we have made our example easier to read.

3 The first two exercises have illustrated the fact that the basic purpose of all

punctuation is to help the (writer/reader) _____.

4 We can eliminate momentary misreadings and thus help the reader if we insert a comma in each of the sentences below. Underline each word that should be followed by a comma. Read the sentence to yourself with the added punctuation to make sure that you have placed the comma intelligently.

  A. **Near the school buses always line up at four o'clock.**
  B. **When the dog attacked the snake crawled back into the bushes.**
  C. **In our school paper for examinations is furnished free of charge.**
  D. **Grandad reads his newspaper now and then he dozes in his old chair.**

5 **In Congress, as many people believe a speech that changes votes is rare.**

Some sentences are very difficult to understand without commas in the proper places. The example above may puzzle you for a little while. At last,

though, you discover that a comma after (What word?) _____ will make the sentence easy to understand.

6 **Whatever is is right.**

The sentence above (from Alexander Pope) can be clarified by placing a

comma after _____.

7 **that that is is that that is not is not is not that it it is**

The example above is a puzzle in punctuation. Have you seen it before?

_____ If your answer is "no," can you read the example with ease? _____

8 **That that is, is. That that is not, is not. Is not that it? It is.**

The rewritten puzzle shows that proper capitalization and punctuation

(finish the sentence) _____

———————————————————————————————————.

9 **Falling down the stairway the concrete floor knocked me unconscious.**

This exercise is intended as a caution. The sentence sounds as though the floor fell down the stairway. It is a bad sentence, and punctuation cannot make a bad sentence good. Such a sentence needs to be completely rewritten. If we insert a comma after *stairway*, will the example be a good sentence?

_____ Rewrite the sentence to make it clear.

_____

_____

C: ASSIGNMENTS

• Indicate where in each sentence a comma should be placed to prevent a possible misreading.

1. After Sue had gone there was a lull in the conversation.
2. After Sue had gone there was there a lull in the conversation?
3. The time has come for our legislators have dallied long enough.
4. After he had eaten Big Bear, the oldest warrior in the group, rose to speak.
5. As you remember the fringe on the surrey had come loose.
6. While I was sawing the logs seemed unusually knotty.
7. Ever since that night has lingered in my memory.
8. As the shiny new car approached Dad, staring unbelievingly, scrambled to his feet.
9. To compensate for this General Smith sent two more divisions to the front.
10. In retrospect Bob's actions seem strangest because we always had considered Bob level-headed.
11. The session over the class started to the exits.
12. To start with Judy seems the best prepared.
13. As you may have observed the decorations in front of our house are made of wood.
14. Once inside the visitor is sure the roof will fall on him.
15. After all the information was compiled in only two weeks.

ANSWERS TO SECTION B

1. (Most answer *Yes*, but *No* is possible.)
2. comma
3. reader
4. A. school,   B. attacked,   C. school,   D. now,
5. believe,
6. is
7. (Either *Yes* or *No*)   No (almost certainly)

8. MODEL   help to make sentences easier to read
9 No MODEL   When I fell down the stairway, the concrete floor knocked me unconscious.

Unit 35—Commas with Coordinate Elements

A: COMMENTARY

As used in grammar, *coordinate* means "of about equal importance and in similar grammatical form." Two or more parts of a sentence are often coordinate. Here are a few examples:

> He looked at the *straggly, unpruned* apple tree. (coordinate adjectives)
> She called *loudly*, almost *hysterically*. (coordinate adverbs)
> "I have nothing to offer but *blood, toil, tears*, and *sweat*."
>
> —Churchill (coordinate nouns)

> Churchill promised to fight *on the beaches, in the fields, in the streets, and in the hills.* (coordinate phrases)
> Please tell us *when we should come, what we should bring*, and *how we can find the place.* (coordinate dependent clauses)
> *Come early in the day*, and *bring clothes for hiking.* (coordinate main clauses, making a compound sentence)

In this unit we consider the punctuation of coordinate elements. The written language is based on speech, and to some extent the punctuation we use is too. Note that if you say aloud *a tall, slender building*, you pause slightly after *tall*. In writing, the comma represents the pause. *Tall* and *slender* are coordinate adjectives. In contrast, you do not pause so noticeably after *red* in *a red brick building.* No comma separates *red* and *brick*.

Series and compound sentences are made of coordinate elements. In speaking, you pause rather noticeably between these elements. For example, try saying *We climbed to the roof, jumped to the next roof, and hurried down the fire escape.* You paused distinctly after each *roof*. In contrast, if you say *We landed on the roof of a house*, you pause no more after *roof* than after other words.

Ordinarily most writers put commas between coordinate elements, although usage is not uniform. Almost any editor or teacher would insist on a comma in *a tall, slender building*, but a few would not. In many expressions, such as *a little white house*, the comma is now seldom used. In a series, the tendency to dispense with the comma before the *and* is increasing, as it also is before the conjunction in a compound sentence.

The comma before *and* in a series does have value in helping to differentiate a true series from a false one:

TRUE SERIES: **They spent a quiet, peaceful, and uneventful Fourth of July.**
FALSE SERIES: **They spent a quiet, safe and sane Fourth of July.** (*Safe* and *sane* go together as a team, as if they were really only one modifier.)

The comma in a compound sentence also sometimes prevents misreading:

The climb was slow but sure footing was always available. (A comma before *but* would prevent the temporary misreading *slow but sure.*)

In optional punctuation like that in a series or a compound sentence, follow your instructor's preference. He or she may recommend, for instance, that you use a comma between the parts of a compound sentence only when the clauses are long or when a comma will prevent a possible misreading.

B: EXERCISES

1 **a tall, slender building**
a red brick building

As you notice, a comma is likely to be used between words such as *tall* and *slender* but not between words such as *red* and *brick*. The reason is that *tall* and *slender* are coordinate adjectives modifying *building*. That is, they are the same kind of word (adjective) and are both used to modify *building*. One way to see that they are coordinate is to put *and* between them: *a tall and slender building*. That expression makes sense. Would it also make sense to say *a red and brick building*? _____

2 In *a red brick building*, *red* is an adjective: a building can be *red, redder, reddest* or *very red*. But *brick* is not an adjective: we don't say that a building or anything else is *bricker, brickest,* or *very brick*. *Brick* is actually a noun, then, even though it modifies the noun *building*. We place a comma between *tall* and *slender* because those words are coordinate, but we do not place a comma between *red* and *brick* because _____

3 **a small boy's grin**
a boyish carefree grin

Tell whether the first or the second example should be punctuated with a comma, and why. _____

4 **The Indian moved effortlessly silently.**
  The Indian moved very silently.

This time we are concerned with coordinate adverbs rather than adjectives, but the principle is the same. Tell whether the first or the second sentence should be punctuated with a comma, and why. _____

_____

_____

5 **The stripes in the flag of Hungary are red, white, and green.**

Coordinate elements often come in a series of three or more. The coordinate elements in this example are _____.

6 Look again at the example in exercise 5. Note that commas separate the items in the series. The comma before *and* may be considered optional, although many publishing houses and teachers prefer to use it, since in some sentences it prevents momentary misreading. Unless your own teacher tells you otherwise, however, you have two options: *red, white, and green* or

_____

7 **The kitten raced under the chair, onto the sofa, and halfway up the curtain.**
  Where Harris went, when he went, and why he went are all mysteries.

Coordinate elements need not be single words. Sometimes they are phrases, as in the first sentence above, or clauses, as in the second. According to these examples, are series of phrases and clauses punctuated in the same way as series of single words? _____

8 **Some hounds follow their prey chiefly by scent, but others rely mainly on sight.**

The sentence above is called compound. A compound sentence consists of two or more independent clauses, each of which could stand alone as a complete sentence. Since these clauses are of the same rank, they are also coordinate. When the connecting word *and, but, for, or, nor, yet,* or *so* joins the coordinate clauses, most editors and teachers recommend that a comma should be used. Copy the seven words that ordinarily should be preceded by a comma in a compound sentence. _____ _____ _____ _____

_____ _____ _____

9 In this exercise we have seen:
  A. that coordinate elements are two or more parts of a sentence that func-

tion (in the same way/in different ways) _____.

B. that coordinate elements may be single words, _____, dependent _____, or independent _____.

C. that it is customary to separate coordinate elements with _____.

D. that in a series or in a compound sentence the comma before *and* (or *but, for, or, nor, yet,* or *so*) is (optional/always insisted upon) _____ _____.

10 Select the four items that should be written with commas. Write the corresponding letters as your answers. ____ ____ ____ ____

A. strong silent soldier
B. large rose garden
C. sullen shame-faced smile
D. noisy clanging gates
E. noisy metal gates
F. gray filing cabinet
G. warm fragrant cookies
H. warmly affectionate glance

11 Write a sentence containing a series that names several of your friends. Punctuate correctly. _____

_____

12 Write a sentence containing a series of phrases such as *in the park*. Punctuate correctly. _____

_____

13 Write a sentence containing a series of dependent clauses such as *what she wanted*. Punctuate correctly. _____

_____

_____

14 Write a compound sentence about conflicting opinions that you and someone else have. Join the clauses with *but*. Punctuate correctly. _____

_____

_____

_____

C: ASSIGNMENTS

• Write five original expressions such as *a tall, slender building* that normally would be punctuated with a comma and five others such as *a red brick building* that would need no comma.

• Write two sentences containing a series of words, two with a series of phrases, and two with a series of dependent clauses.

• Write three compound sentences in which you use the connective *and, but, for, or, nor, yet,* or *so* to join the clauses. Write another compound sentence that consists of three or more independent clauses. If you have trouble thinking of content for some of your sentences, here are some random words as thought-starters: *aluminum, judgment, dashed, watery, cinnamon, playground, moved, morsel, punt, lover, lyric, bass, clarinet.*

ANSWERS TO SECTION B

1. No
2. MODEL   these words are not coordinate
3. MODEL   The second should have a comma because *boyish* and *carefree* are coordinate adjectives.
4. MODEL   The first should have a comma because *effortlessly* and *silently* are coordinate adverbs.
5. red, white, and green
6. red, white and green
7. Yes
8. *and, but, for, or, nor, yet, so*
9. A. in the same way   B. phrases, clauses, clauses   C. commas   D. optional
10. A, C, D, G
11. MODEL   Roy, Grace, and Maxine ate the asparagus.
12. MODEL   The children played in the house, on the lawn, and in the park.
13. MODEL   I do not know when she came, where she came from, or what she wanted.
14. MODEL   I have always favored the Equal Rights Amendment, but others consider it unnecessary.

Unit 36—Commas with Interpolated Elements

A: COMMENTARY

In writing, an interpolated element is a word or a group of words inserted within a basic sentence to provide a bit of extra information or clarification.

Although many textbooks supply separate rules for the various kinds of interpolations treated in this unit, it is simplest just to understand this basic principle that applies to all: Commas are used to set off parts of a sentence that are not essential to the central meaning. Two commas are needed if the element comes in the middle portion of the sentence, and one is needed if it comes at the beginning or end.

Section B explains what you may need to know about one kind of interpolation, the appositive. An appositive gives another name to someone or something:

Helen's mother, an ardent feminist, is running for Congress.

An ardent feminist is an appositive. (In Section B below, example A in exercise 1 and the sentence in exercise 9 contain appositives.) Usually an appositive is set off by commas, as the examples indicate. However, sometimes an appositive is necessary to identify a particular person or thing, and therefore is really part of the basic sentence. If, for instance, you have three cousins, you might write *my Cousin Bill* (or *my cousin Bill*, as some editors prefer) to show which one you mean, and would not use a comma to set off the appositive *Bill*. But if you have only one cousin and simply want to remind the reader of his name, you would correctly write *my cousin, Bill*. Similarly, since Nathaniel Hawthorne wrote several novels, you would correctly write: Hawthorne's novel *The Scarlet Letter* is. . . . Since Margaret Mitchell wrote only one novel, you would write: Margaret Mitchell's novel, *Gone with the Wind*, is. . . .

B: EXERCISES

1 What do these sentences have in common?

    A. **His first building, a small barn, turned out well.**
    B. **After that, Marge, we went to a diner.**
    C. **The pavilion, however, was closed for the winter.**
    D. **"Aren't you aware," he asked, "that only one decision is possible?"**

We first note a superficial resemblance. Each sentence contains two (What punctuation marks?) _____.

2 Read once more the examples in exercise 1. In each sentence is the part

between commas necessary for an understanding of the sentence? _____

3 Elements that are inserted within a sentence and that are not really essential to an understanding of the sentence (though they may add something to its meaning) are called *interpolated elements.* Copy the interpolated element from each example in exercise 1.

A. _____   C. _____

B. _____   D. _____

4 The examples in exercise 1 show that when an interpolated element is placed in the middle part of a sentence, it is normally punctuated with

(How many of what?) _____.

5 The interpolated elements in exercise 1 are of different kinds. That in A is an appositive; in B, a name of a person being addressed; in C, a transitional word; and in D, an interpolation in a speaker's words. Does the same principle of punctuation apply to all these kinds of interpolated elements?

_____

6 Still other kinds of interpolated elements exist, as in these examples:

QUALIFICATION OR EXPLANATION:	His retort, I believe, was unnecessarily sharp.
EMPHASIS:	The facts, I repeat, are undeniable.
CONTRAST:	The train, not the airplane, is what you should take on this trip.
PLACE NAMES:	In Fresno, California, she visited an old friend.
DATES:	On March 18, 1954, they were married.

Does the same principle of punctuation apply to these kinds of interpolated

elements? _____

7 They were married on March 18, 1954.
She stayed for a while in Fresno, California.
Marge, what do you think we did then?
On the other hand, consider this possibility.
No, I don't think so. (*Yes, no,* and mild exclamations like *well* are interpolated elements.)

In the sentences above, the interpolated elements come at the beginnings

or ends of sentences. When this happens, (How many?) _____ comma(s) is (are) required.

8 Summarize in your own words what this unit demonstrates about the punc-

tuation of interpolated elements. _____

_____

_____

_____

9 Exercises 9–14 require you to insert interpolated elements. Copy the whole sentence, including your interpolation, and punctuate correctly. The answers given at the end of the unit are model answers, not necessarily exactly like yours.

The first President (name) _____ opposed "foreign entanglements."

_____

_____

10 "My mother" (name of speaker) _____ said "is a blonde."

_____

11 He was born in Springfield (state) _____ on May 11 (year) _____.

_____

12 Tell me (name of person being addressed) _____ what you would do in my situation.

_____

_____

13 The future looked unpromising. (transition) _____ Craig still hoped that his luck would change.

_____

_____

14 Your petition (words of qualification, emphasis, or contrast) _____ is likely to be denied.

_____

_____

C: ASSIGNMENTS

• Exercises 1, 6, and 7 in Section B contain examples of about ten kinds of interpolated elements. Make up two sentences each to illustrate eight or more of the types. Compose some sentences that have the interpolation in the middle part and others that have it at the beginning or end.

• Where should a comma or commas be placed in each of these sentences?

1. Some mineral springs are near Boise Idaho.
2. That argument I insist is ridiculous.
3. "Are you insinuating" he asked "that I drink too much?"
4. Yes I believe so.
5. Yes Marie I believe so.
6. Yes I believe so Marie.
7. "Yes I believe so Marie" she said.
8. The sycamores moreover had been seriously damaged by anthracnose.
9. A rasp not a plane is the tool you need.
10. In August 1975 I first met Cleantha the best chess player in the state.
11. Your sister Cleantha is a much better chess player than your other sisters Henry.
12. Your sister Cleantha Henry is a much better chess player than your other sisters.
13. Your sister Cleantha is a much better chess player than your sisters Ruby and Annabel.
14. Your sister Cleantha is a much better chess player than your sisters Ruby and Annabel Henry.
15. Your sister the one named Cleantha was much better on August 24 1975 than any other player I saw in Grand Junction Colorado on that memorable day.

ANSWERS TO SECTION B

1. commas
2. No
3. A. a small barn   B. Marge   C. however   D. he asked
4. two commas
5. Yes
6. Yes
7. one
8. MODEL   At the beginning or end of a sentence an interpolated element is set off with one comma; in the middle it is set off with two.
9. The first President, George Washington, opposed "foreign entanglements."
10. MODEL   "My mother," Eileen said, "is a blonde."
11. MODEL   He was born in Springfield, Ohio, on May 11, 1954.
12. MODEL   Tell me, Leslie, what you would do in my situation.
13. MODEL   The future looked unpromising. However, Craig still hoped that his luck would change.
14. MODEL   Your petition, in my judgment, is likely to be denied.

Unit 37—Commas with Nonessential Phrases and Clauses

A: COMMENTARY

In many books essential phrases and clauses are called *restrictive*, because they tend to restrict or limit a meaning. Nonessential phrases and clauses are often called *nonrestrictive*. The terms *essential* and *nonessential*, however, are perhaps easier to understand.

Most of the phrases and clauses we'll look at in Section B are used as adjectives. That is, they tell something about a noun. For instance, in *Molly Mason, who operates a filling station, is a good friend of mine*, the clause *who operates a filling station* tells something about Molly Mason. In *The boy in the green sweater is Fred*, the phrase *in the green sweater* identifies the boy.

The point of this unit may be summarized in this way: Commas are used to set off phrases and clauses that are not essential to the meaning of a sentence. Commas are not used to set off phrases and clauses that are essential. In the preceding paragraph, *who operates a filling station* is not essential: the reader already knows that the sentence is about Molly Mason. But *in the green sweater* is essential—without it the reader or listener doesn't know what boy is meant.

If you are ever in doubt about whether a phrase such as *in the green sweater* or a clause such as *who operates the filling station* is essential or not, try reading the sentence without the phrase or clause. If the identification of the person or thing is still clear, the element is nonrestrictive (nonessential) and should be set off.

A second test is to note what your voice does when you say the sentence aloud. Note, for example, the difference in length of pause and in tone when you say these sentences aloud:

> **A boy in a green sweater entered the room.**
> **Fred Barclay, in a green sweater, entered the room.**

The kind of pause and intonation that you need in the second sentence indicates a nonessential element and therefore the need for a comma.

The punctuation of phrases or clauses used as adverbs causes little trouble. An adverbial clause at the beginning of a sentence is usually treated as nonessential and is set off with a comma: *While we were fighting,* Clayton Bray stepped between us. (The comma is sometimes omitted if there is no possibility of misreading.) Most often, an adverbial clause at the end of a sentence is not set off: Clayton Bray stepped between us *while we were fighting.* An adverbial phrase is now seldom set off unless a comma is needed to prevent misreading:

> **In the meantime Chris had gone to lunch.** (No commas are needed.)

From below, the leak was easily visible. (Comma prevents a momentary misreading. See also Unit 34.)

B: EXERCISES

1 **The girl on the left is a professional dancer.**

Suppose that the sentence above is part of a caption beneath a photograph of several girls. If the words *on the left* were omitted, would the reader know which girl is the dancer? _____

2 The punctuation (or lack of it) in the example in exercise 1 is correct. The example shows that we normally (set off/do not set off) _____ with commas a part of a sentence that is essential to its meaning.

3 **The girl who is shown on the left is a professional dancer.**

In exercise 1 we were concerned with the phrase *on the left*. This time we have inserted the clause *who is shown on the left*. Is this clause needed to show which girl is meant? _____ Is an essential clause set off with commas? _____

4 **Marlene May, in the culottes, is a professional dancer.**

In this sentence *Marlene May* provides a specific identification. The phrase *in the culottes* provides some additional information not essential to identifying her. A nonessential phrase is customarily (set off/not set off) _____ _____ by commas.

5 **Marlene May, who is wearing culottes, is a professional dancer.**

This time the nonessential element is the clause *who is wearing culottes*. Is a nonessential clause, according to the example, set off by commas? _____

6 An essential phrase or clause is one that in effect points to a person or thing in order to identify. It is ordinarily (set off/not set off) _____ by commas.

7 A nonessential phrase or clause, however, simply provides more information about someone or something already identified adequately. It is ordinarily (set off/not set off) _____ by commas.

8 **I visited the boy with the broken arm.**
I visited Tommy Meribella who had a broken arm.

Copy the sentence containing a nonessential element, and insert a comma in the appropriate place. _____

_____

9 Louise Lanier sitting on the floor began to laugh at the other girls.
The girl sitting on the floor began to laugh at the other girls.

Copy and punctuate correctly the sentence (or sentences) containing a nonessential element. _____

_____

_____

10 Lagging far behind Max and Judy got lost in the cave.
Max and Judy who were lagging far behind got lost in the cave.

Copy and punctuate correctly the sentence (or sentences) containing an element that needs to be set off. _____

_____

_____

_____

11 Counterpoint which is a melody added as an accompaniment to another melody was developed centuries ago.
The counterpoint that I like best is that of Pérotin.

Copy and punctuate correctly the sentence (or sentences) containing a nonessential element. _____

_____

_____

_____

12 Write a sentence in which *who comes late for dinner* is essential for identification. Punctuate correctly.

_____

_____

13 Write a sentence in which *who comes late for dinner* is a nonessential part. Punctuate correctly.

_____

_____

C: ASSIGNMENTS

• The following sentences are written without commas. Decide which ones contain nonessential phrases or clauses, and insert commas as needed.

1. The constellation Gemini a name that means "twins" was supposedly created by Zeus in honor of Castor and Pollux who were twin giants.
2. The Roman emperor whom most persons are likely to remember is Julius Caesar. Credit for this fame belongs at least in part to William Shakespeare who wrote a play about him. Caesar himself of course was renowned (or notorious) for centuries among schoolboys who had to translate his *Gallic Wars*.
3. Adult education about which we are hearing more each year is no new development. In 1826 for example a Connecticut man named Josiah Holbrook conceived a plan for a lyceum. This word which refers to the place where Aristotle taught a couple of millennia ago is sometimes confused with *chautauqua*. The chautauqua unlike the lyceum had a religious base. The original intent of the lyceum was to develop on an international scale an educational program that would have wide appeal to adults and to mature young people. Although lyceums did not flourish internationally they were so popular in the United States which in those years was highly interested in attaining that marvelous thing called *culture* that by 1834 almost three thousand lyceums were flourishing. Debates and lectures and essays usually homespun formed the major part of this early attempt at mass adult education. In a country that did not have radio or television or mass mobility the lyceum and later the chautauqua brought to the people information and ideas that otherwise might never have been theirs.

• With each phrase or clause below, make up two sentences, one in which the phrase or clause is essential and one in which it is nonessential.

1. on the beach
2. who was lying on the beach
3. staring at the ocean
4. whom we met at the door
5. which fell through the grating
6. who writes well
7. when the doorbell rang
8. where Mrs. Purcell found the mouse
9. clinging to the rafters
10. in a straitjacket

ANSWERS TO SECTION B

1. No
2. do not set off

3. Yes   No
4. set off
5. Yes
6. not set off
7. set off
8. I visited Tommy Meribella, who had a broken arm.
9. Louise Lanier, sitting on the floor, began to laugh at the other girls.
10. Lagging far behind, Max and Judy got lost in the cave.
    Max and Judy, who were lagging far behind, got lost in the cave.
11. Counterpoint, which is a melody added as an accompaniment to another melody, was developed centuries ago.
12. MODEL   Everyone who comes late for dinner will have to go hungry.
13. MODEL   Charlie, who comes late for dinner, usually finds something in the refrigerator.

Unit 38—Avoiding Unnecessary Commas

A: COMMENTARY

In the eighteenth and nineteenth centuries, when reading aloud was a more frequent pastime than it is today, writers punctuated heavily. They tended to insert a comma wherever an oral reader would be likely to pause even momentarily. In the twentieth century we have moved toward a minimum of punctuation, using just enough to make meaning clear to a person reading silently.

To use few punctuation marks, then, is to be modern. This unit illustrates a number of the places in which commas should ordinarily not be placed. These are as follows:

1. between verb and predicate nominative
2. between verb and direct object
3. before a series
4. before *and* or a similar conjunction separating two words or phrases (A series of three or more items does require at least one comma.)
5. after *and* or a similar conjunction separating the two main clauses in a compound sentence

One exception to all five of these instances is that if a nonessential element is inserted, it should be enclosed by commas (see Units 36 and 37).

B: EXERCISES

1 A. **That animal is an antelope.**
  B. **An antelope is a graceful, speedy animal.**
  C. **The truth is that I am an admirer of antelopes.**

Each of the sentences above contains a construction called a *predicate nominative,* which may consist of one word or a number of words. The predicate nominative usually follows one of the *be* verbs (*is, are, was, were, have been,* and so on) and defines or renames the subject. In A the predicate nominative is (What two words?) _____. In B it is (What four words?) _____. In C it is (What seven words?) _____.

2   **S   V   *Predicate Nominative***
His answer was that some mistakes are likely.

The example above, like those in exercise 1, shows that a comma (should/ should not) _____ be placed between a verb and a predicate nominative.

3 A direct object does not follow a *be* verb. It names a person or thing affected by the action of the verb. It typically fills the third slot in a sentence that starts with the subject, continues with a verb showing some sort of action, and then names the person or thing acted upon:

S   V   *Direct Object*
She bought dishes.

In sentence A below, the direct object is (What five words?) _____ _____. In B the direct object is (What four words?)

_____.

A. **She bought a complete set of dishes.**
B. **She bought dishes, glassware, and silver.**

4 **S   V   *Direct Object***
We read *Gulliver's Travels* and *Pilgrim's Progress.*

What does the example above show about punctuation before most direct objects? _____

5 **We read, I believe, *Gulliver's Travels* and *Pilgrim's Progress.***

An exception to the rule illustrated in exercise 4 is shown above. When an interpolated element occurs between verb and direct object, (How many?) _____ comma(s) is (are) used.

6 **This action involves our pride, our reputation, and our honor.**

The sentence above shows that a comma normally (should/should not) _____ be placed before a series.

7 **At stake are, it is reasonable to say, our pride, our reputation, and our honor.**

Explain why commas appear before the series in the sentence above.

_____

_____

8 **Our football offense is equally strong in the air and on the ground.**

Note the lack of a comma before *and*. The sentence illustrates the fact that ordinarily when two phrases or words are joined by *and* (finish the sentence) _____.

9 **The offensive team left the field, and the defensive team loped out to replace them.**

As Unit 35 has shown you, a comma generally precedes a word like *and* in a compound sentence. The example above shows a comma before the *and*, but after the *and* (Finish the sentence) _____.

10 The exercises above do not show, of course, *all* the places where unnecessary commas might slip in, but they do illustrate most of the trouble spots. One summary might be to say that a comma should not be used unless you know why you are using it. Another might be that commas should be used almost entirely just to help the reader. Or (supplying your own summary of this unit) the principle might be stated in this way: _____

_____

C: ASSIGNMENTS

• Look carefully at the use of commas in an article in a magazine of good quality. Can you justify the use of each? Do you find any that are placed where this unit says they should not be?

• The passage below is peppered ridiculously with commas. Some of them should be kept. Others should be deleted. A few would be kept by some editors, deleted by others. Which do you recommend for deletion? Why?

Kit Carson, unlike Paul Bunyan, was an actual person. In fact, Carson City, Nevada, Ft. Carson, Colorado, and Carson Pass, California, are all named, after him.

SEMI (OR) ; / UNIT 39

Christopher, as his parents, called him, was born December 24, 1809, in Madison County, Kentucky. At age fifteen, he ran away, from home, and joined, some traders, on their way, to Santa Fe. As a result, he became a trader, and, a frontiersman, as well as, a fur trapper.

In his thirties, he met John Frémont, who explored widely, in the West. Carson served well, as his guide, and dispatch-bearer, between the West, and Washington, D.,C. He, also, was the, very able, guide, for General Stephen Kearny, who was renowned, as a leader, in the, rather shameful, Mexican War.

After the Mexican War, was over, Carson served, in a different way, as an Indian agent, in Taos. During the Civil War, he became a colonel, in the Union, or Northern, Army. After the war, he took on the really, important position, of Superintendent, of Indian Affairs, for Colorado Territory.

He is, certainly, a true, folk hero, of the United States. He accomplished much, in the service of his country. And, all of this, was done, as well as a volume of memoirs, by a man, who, although it is hard to believe, never even learned, to read and write.

ANSWERS TO SECTION B

1. an antelope   a graceful, speedy animal   that I am an admirer of antelopes
2. should not
3. a complete set of dishes   dishes, glassware, and silver
4. MODEL   There should usually be no punctuation just before a direct object.
5. two
6. should not
7. MODEL   There is an interpolated element between the verb and the series.
8. MODEL   no comma is needed
9. MODEL   no comma should be used
10. Give yourself credit for any statement warning against the use of unnecessary commas.

Unit 39—Using Semicolons and Commas in Combining Sentences

A: COMMENTARY

Sometimes two statements deal with the same topic and can logically be put together as one sentence. For example:

City traffic is still very heavy.
Some controls over it are proving effective.

We can combine the two statements in this way:

City traffic is still very heavy, but some controls are proving effective.

Or in this way:

City traffic is still very heavy; however, some controls are proving effective.

Note that in the first combination we used a comma and *but*. In the second we used a semicolon and *however*.

Section B of this unit emphasizes that when we have *and, but, for, or, nor, yet,* or *so* as a connective, we punctuate with a comma. If no one of these seven coordinating conjunctions (as they are sometimes called) is present, we punctuate with a semicolon.

Professional writers sometimes use a comma where this unit prescribes a semicolon, as in this sentence:

The pumper truck sped down the street, then came the truck with ladders.

They may do so because they are seeking a special stylistic effect. Beginning writers, however, should follow the principles developed in this unit.

One rare use of the semicolon is not considered in Section B. It is illustrated in this sentence:

In the audience were Claude Lest, a congressman; Archer Brand, a poet; Agnes Volty, a dramatist; and Prudence Snaffler, a union organizer.

The semicolons make the list easier to read than commas would. It is not wise, though, to use semicolons instead of commas unless they separate similar parts within a sentence; note that in the example each semicolon separates name and occupation from another name and occupation.

B: EXERCISES

1 **The hotel was built thirty years ago. It is still in good condition.**

Since the two sentences above are closely related, perhaps they should be combined. For example, they could be made into a compound sentence, using a comma and *but*. Write the sentence that would result. _____

_____

_____

2 When we combine two sentences by using *and, but, for, or, nor, yet,* or *so,* we use the punctuation that you used in exercise 1. In other words we use a (what mark? _____. (Unit 35 discusses this kind of punctuation further.)

3 When we combine sentences without using *and, but, for, or, nor, yet,* or *so,* the punctuation is different. Here, for instance, is a second way to combine the sentences in exercise 1:

The hotel was built thirty years ago; however, it is still in good condition.

This time the mark between the two main parts is a _____.

4 **Its business has been uniformly good; last year, for instance, it averaged 90 percent occupancy.**

In exercise 3 we used the connective *however.* In the example above, no connective at all was used between the two main parts of the compound sentence. The punctuation mark used between the parts is once more a

_____.

5 Our examples have shown us that in a compound sentence with the connective *and, but, for, or, nor, yet,* or *so,* we generally place a (what mark?)

_____ between the main parts and that when one of those

seven words is not present we place a (what mark?) _____ between the main parts.

6 Place in each blank the standard punctuation mark.

   A. **The hotel grossed over $400,000 last year _____ and its net profits were close to $50,000.**

   B. **The hotel grossed over $400,000 last year _____ its net profits were close to $50,000.**

7 These two sentences are a little more complicated, but the principles remain the same. Again, insert the standard punctuation mark.

   A. **Although the hotel is now for sale, the price must not be very low _____ for the agent was reluctant to quote a figure.**

   B. **My client will be interested if the price is less than half a million _____ at least that is what he led me to believe.**

8 Let's summarize. When we combine two sentences, we use a comma between the parts if _____

_____.

We use a semicolon between the parts if *and,* _____, _____, _____,

_____, _____, or *so* is not the connective.

9 In exercises 9 and 10 write in the missing punctuation.

    A. I heard the voice of a small child in the garden _____ but it was not Nina's.

    B. I heard the voice of a small child in the garden _____ it was not Nina's, however.

10 A. A few years ago we spent 26 percent of our personal income for food _____ now the percentage is only 19.

    B. It is still true that in many countries over half the personal income is spent for food _____ nevertheless, the proportion is declining in some of them.

11 Write a compound sentence in which you make two related statements about the television industry. Arrange to use *and, but, for, or, nor, yet,* or *so* as a connective. Punctuate in the standard way.

_____

_____

_____

12 Rewrite your sentence for exercise 11 without using a connective such as *and.* Punctuate in the standard way.

_____

_____

_____

C: ASSIGNMENTS

• In another textbook, some other kind of book, or a magazine, find and copy five or more compound sentences. Comment on the punctuation. Does it follow the principles described in this unit?

• Write a compound sentence for each connective: *and, but, for, or, nor, yet,* and *so.* Then rewrite each sentence, omitting the connective. Punctuate in the standard way.

ANSWERS TO SECTION B

1. The hotel was built thirty years ago, but it is still in good condition.
2. comma

3. semicolon
4. semicolon
5. comma   semicolon
6. A. comma   B. semicolon
7. A. comma   B. semicolon
8. the connective *and, but, for, or, nor, yet,* or *so* is used   *but, for, or, nor, yet*
9. A. comma   B. semicolon
10. A. semicolon   B. semicolon
11. MODEL   The television industry suffered a little from the ban on cigarette commercials, but other advertising soon made up for the losses.
12. MODEL   The television industry suffered a little from the ban on cigarette commercials; other advertising, however, soon made up for the losses.

Unit 40—Common Uses of the Colon

A: COMMENTARY

This unit concerns four frequent and three occasional uses of the colon. The frequent uses are these:
1. before a formal quotation
2. before a formal or rather formal list
3. before a list that is an appositive
4. after the salutation of a business letter

Less frequent are these uses:
1. between numbers for a biblical reference
2. between numbers indicating an exact time
3. after a word like *Note*

The following additional comments may be helpful:
1. Sometimes instead of a list, the colon may introduce a single word used as an appositive. Example:

   One emotion conquered all the rest: gratitude.

2. Sometimes a sentence begins with a list, followed by an expression like *these, all these,* or *such qualities.* Example:

   Double-dealing, deceit, and treachery: all these are common in the underworld.

3. Following a colon, the first word of a quoted sentence is capitalized. If the sentence is not quoted, the capital is optional.

   George N. Douglas is responsible for this penetrating observation: "You can tell the ideals of a nation by its advertisements." (*Note the capital.*)
   One thing is certain: If (*or* **if) men do not learn to live together, they will die together.**

B: EXERCISES

1 The quotation in sentence B below is (more/less) _____ formal than the one in A.

   A. Helen said, "Let's take turns reading the parts."
   B. This is what President Grant said on the subject: "I know no method to secure the repeal of bad or obnoxious laws so effective as their stringent execution."

2 Informal quotations, such as that in sentence A in exercise 1, are usually separated by a comma from an introductory expression such as *he said*. Formal quotations, as sentence B illustrates, are usually separated from *he said, she said,* and so on, by a _____.

3 What punctuation differentiates the two sentences below? _____
   A. The European countries from which most persons emigrated to the United States between 1820 and 1910 were the following: Germany, Ireland, Austria, Italy, and Russia.
   B. The European countries from which most persons emigrated to the United States between 1820 and 1910 were Germany, Ireland, Austria, Italy, and Russia.

4 In exercise 3A the use of *the following* suggests that a formal list is being introduced. The two examples in exercise 3 illustrate the fact that when a formal list is introduced by such expressions as *the following* or *as follows*, a (what mark?) _____ usually precedes the list, but when no such expression is used, (finish the sentence) _____.

5 In those years new baseball franchises were established in these cities: Milwaukee, Minneapolis–St. Paul, Los Angeles, Kansas City, and Houston.

Although this example is not very formal, it concludes with a list in apposition to *these cities*. It shows, then, that a list that is an appositive is generally separated from the rest of the sentence by a _____.

6 These are Patrick Henry's most famous words "Give me liberty or give me death!"

Copy the sentence, punctuating properly. (Do likewise in exercises 7, 8, 9.)

7 I make my best grades in these subjects history, biology, and electronics.

_____

_____

8 The subjects in which I make my best grades are history, biology, and electronics.

_____

_____

9 The following are among the best-known figures of speech metaphor, simile, and personification.

_____

_____

10 This exercise has so far illustrated three uses of the colon. What are they?

_____

_____

_____

11 **Dear Sir: Dear Mr. Gilhooley:**

The examples above show salutations of two business letters. If the letters were friendly, personal letters, the punctuation mark after each salutation would be a comma. In a business letter, though, the mark following the salutation is a _____.

12 **Luke 2:7**

This reference is to the seventh verse in the second chapter of Luke, in the New Testament. Between numbers for biblical chapter and verse, it is customary to use a _____.

13 **Guests began arriving at 8:30 P.M.**

Explain the use of the colon illustrated above.

_____

_____

14 **Note: All unused ammunition must be returned to the storehouse.**

After a word such as *note*, which calls particular attention to a following statement, the conventional punctuation is a _____.

15 Exercises 11–14 have illustrated what four miscellaneous uses of the colon?

_____

_____

_____

_____

C: ASSIGNMENTS

• From any available book or magazine choose three quotable passages of two or three lines each. Write some introductory words, such as (*Author*) *has this to say about* (*subject*). Then copy the passage, punctuating with colon and quotation marks.

• Write three sentences in which you use *the following* or *as follows*. Punctuate correctly.

• Write two sentences in which a list or possibly a single word (see the first example in A) serves as an appositive. Punctuate correctly.

• Write two examples of each of the four uses of the colon illustrated in exercises 11–14.

ANSWERS TO SECTION B

1. more
2. colon
3. colon in A
4. colon   there is no punctuation
5. colon
6. These are Patrick Henry's most famous words: "Give me liberty or give me death!"
7. I make my best grades in these subjects: history, biology, and electronics.
8. The subjects in which I make my best grades are history, biology, and electronics.
9. The following are among the best-known figures of speech: metaphor, simile, and personification.
10. MODEL   A colon is generally used before a formal quotation, a formal list, or a list that is an appositive.
11. colon
12. colon
13. MODEL   A colon is used between numbers representing hours and minutes in designations of time.

14. colon
15. MODEL   A colon is used after the salutation of a business letter, between numbers for biblical chapter and verse, between numbers for indicating precise times, and after an introductory word such as *note*.

Unit 41—Apostrophes to Show Possession

A: COMMENTARY

Much omission or misuse of apostrophes results from carelessness. Some persons, though, have never mastered the simple principles presented in Section B:

1. The possessive form of a noun not ending in *s* is written with an apostrophe and *s*.
2. The possessive form of a noun ending in *s* is written with an apostrophe after the *s*.
3. The possessive form of *Jones*, or other proper nouns ending in *s*, may be written with an apostrophe after the *s* or with an apostrophe and another *s*: *Jones'* or *Jones's*. The second form is more frequent.
4. Possessive personal pronouns (*yours, hers, its, ours,* and *theirs*) have no apostrophes.

In item 3, note that the apostrophe alone is generally used when an awkward pronunciation would arise from two *s*'s: *Jesus' last words* (not *Jesus's*); *Socrates' last words* (not *Socrates's*).

The possessive of *somebody else* that is now favored is *somebody else's*.

In writing the possessive of inanimate (nonliving) nouns, some careful writers prefer using *of* rather than an apostrophe or an apostrophe and *s*: *the cover of the book* rather than *the book's cover; the top floor of the building* rather than *the building's top floor*, and so on, because technically the book or the building does not really possess anything. This restriction, though, is less often followed than it once was. Perhaps it is wisest to use whichever form sounds better in a particular sentence.

An expression such as *the man in the next room's umbrella* is obviously awkward, and *the man's in the next room umbrella* is no improvement. Try something like *the umbrella belonging to the man in the next room*.

B: EXERCISES

1 **Kay is a woman. She wears a woman's watch.**

Does the word *woman* end in *s*? _____ According to the example, how do we indicate the possessive form of a noun that does not end in *s*?

2 **Kay and Phyllis are girls. They have girls' watches.**

Does the word *girls* end in *s*? _____ According to the example, how do we indicate the possessive form of a noun that ends in *s*?

_____

3 Exercises 1 and 2 illustrate the two basic principles for writing the possessive forms of nouns. One deals with possessives of nouns not ending in *s*; the second, with possessives of nouns ending in *s*. In your own words, summarize the two principles.

_____

_____

4 **I enjoy Keats' poetry and Dickens' novels.**
I enjoy Keats's poetry and Dickens's novels.

For a proper noun ending in *s*, two acceptable forms exist, as illustrated above. Write the two possible possessive forms for *Jones* and for *Morales*.

_____ _____   _____ _____

5 **We live next door to the Joneses. The Joneses' cars often block our driveway.**

The plural of *Jones* is _____. The possessive of *Joneses* is

_____.

6 **This book is yours. It is ours. It is hers. It is theirs.**
The dog wagged its tail.

Exercises 1–5 concern the possessive forms of nouns. The sentences above contain possessive forms of personal pronouns. According to these examples,

should possessive personal pronouns be written with apostrophes? _____

7 Write the possessive form of each word in exercises 7–9.

snake _____ snakes _____ cowboy _____

cowboys _____ ostrich _____ ostriches _____

8 lizards _____ cow _____ elephants _____

men _____ women _____ ladies _____

9 Adams _____ Adamses _____ Adam _____

Hoskins _____ Smith _____ the Smiths _____

10 Write two possessive forms (for example, *your* and *yours* for *you*) for each of these pronouns:

us ＿＿＿＿ ＿＿＿＿ them ＿＿＿＿ ＿＿＿＿ her ＿＿＿＿ ＿＿＿＿

who (one form) ＿＿＿＿＿＿

11 Write a sentence containing *it's* (meaning "it is") and another containing *its* (possessive). ＿＿＿＿＿＿＿＿＿＿＿＿＿＿＿＿＿＿

＿＿＿＿＿＿＿＿＿＿＿＿＿＿＿＿＿＿＿＿＿＿＿＿＿＿＿＿＿＿

＿＿＿＿＿＿＿＿＿＿＿＿＿＿＿＿＿＿＿＿＿＿＿＿＿＿＿＿＿＿

C: ASSIGNMENTS

• Write the names of ten persons, ten animals, and ten things. Then write the possessive form of each.

• Repeat what you have just done, but this time write the plural forms only. Again write the possessive forms.

• Write several sentences with the possessive forms *yours*, *hers*, *its*, *ours*, *theirs*, *somebody's*, and *somebody else's*. You may use more than one possessive per sentence if you wish.

ANSWERS TO SECTION B

1. No   We use an apostrophe and *s*.
2. Yes   We use an apostrophe only.
3. MODEL   For nouns not ending in *s*, form the possessive by using an apostrophe and *s*. For nouns ending in *s*, form the possessive by using only an apostrophe, which goes after the *s*.
4. Jones' Jones's (*but never* Jone's)   Morales' Morales's (*but never* Morale's)
5. Joneses   Joneses'
6. No
7. snake's   snakes'   cowboy's   cowboys'   ostrich's   ostriches'
8. lizards'   cow's   elephants'   men's   women's   ladies'
9. Adams' *or* Adams's   Adamses'   Adam's   Hoskins' *or* Hoskins's   Smith's   the Smiths'
10. our, ours   their, theirs   her, hers   whose
11. MODELS   It's almost spring already. The dog no longer lies on its warm mat.

Unit 42—Apostrophes to Show Contractions

A: COMMENTARY

This unit concerns the tendency to misplace the apostrophe in words such as *doesn't* and *you're*. Whenever you are in doubt, simply ask yourself what sounds are left out when you pronounce the contracted (shortened) form, and write the apostrophe in the vacated slot.

B: EXERCISES

1 "Well tell him to hurry."
  "Hell hurry if you tell him."

  Careful reading shows that probably *We'll* and *He'll* are intended. Without the apostrophe, *we'll* looks like _____ and *he'll* looks like _____.

2 So apostrophes do have their uses. Without them, *she'd* looks like _____, *she'll* looks like _____, *I'll* looks like _____, and *we'd* looks like _____.

3 Even when a contracted form, such as *doesn't*, is not likely to be confused with another word, present English usage requires an apostrophe. Students often omit it and sometimes put it into the wrong spot. Let's see what the right spot is.
  In *he'll*, the contraction for *he will*, the apostrophe takes the place of the omitted letters _____ (what letters?).

4 Analyze *we'll*, *she'd*, *she'll*, *I'll*, and *doesn't*. Is it true that the apostrophe goes into the slot where letters (or sounds) have been omitted? _____

5 *Won't* and *shan't* are partial exceptions to the principle of putting an apostrophe where letters have been left out. *Woll* is an old form of *will*; *won't* is a contraction of *woll not*. Letters are left out in two places, but only one apostrophe is used. *Shan't* (now rarely used) is a contraction of *shall not*, with *ll* and *o* left out. Write the contractions of *will not* and *shall not*. _____ _____

6 What is the basic principle concerning the place where the apostrophe goes when you write a contraction? _____

7 Write these words as contractions: **do not** _____ **does not** _____ **cannot** _____ **should not** _____ **have not** _____ **has not** _____ **are not** _____ **were not** _____ **is not** _____

8 Write the contractions of these words: **I had** _____ **I have** _____ **you have** _____ **they have** _____ **we have** _____ **he had** _____ **you had** _____ **they had** _____

9 Write the contractions of these words: **I am** _____ **you are** _____ **he is** _____ **she is** _____ **it is** _____ **we are** _____ **they are** _____

10 Write the contractions of *of the clock* (as in "It's ten _____.") and the short form of 1979. _____ _____

C: ASSIGNMENTS

• Make as long a list as you can of contractions with *not* (*don't*, and so on).

• Make a similar list of contractions with *have*, *has*, and *had* (*I've*, and so on).

• Make another list of contractions with *shall* and *will* (*I'll*, and so on).

• Names such as *O'Brien* are contractions of sorts. O' means "descendant of." List several such names. (Note that O. *Henry,* the pseudonym of an author, is not one of these.)

ANSWERS TO SECTION B

1. well, hell
2. shed, shell, Ill, wed
3. wi
4. Yes
5. won't shan't
6. MODEL The apostrophe goes in place of the omitted letters (or sounds).
7. don't doesn't can't shouldn't haven't hasn't aren't weren't isn't
8. I'd I've you've they've we've he'd you'd they'd
9. I'm you're he's she's it's we're they're
10. o'clock '79

Unit 43—Apostrophes in Certain Plurals

A: COMMENTARY

The four uses of the apostrophe treated in this unit are much less important than its use in possessives and contractions. The four items that may be pluralized with an apostrophe and *s* are letters (for example, three *n*'s), words referred to as words (four *moreover*'s), symbols (two ¶'s), and numerals (several 6's).

When no likelihood of misreading exists, the apostrophe is sometimes omitted in these plurals. You may write either *I made two B's and two C's* or *I made two Bs and two Cs.* You may write either *the 1980's* or *the 1980s.* But *There are two is in* eligible is hard to read; change *is* to *i*'s.

Be sure not to pluralize nouns by using apostrophes (unless the nouns happen to be referred to as words). Some sign painters appear to be apostrophe happy, advertising *cucumber's* and *egg's* when they mean *cucumbers* and *eggs.*

B: EXERCISES

1 ***Mississippi* has four *i*'s, four *s*'s, and two *p*'s.**

As you know, most plurals are formed by adding *s* or *es* to the singular. The example above, though, shows that plurals of _____ are formed by adding an apostrophe and *s*.

2 **In two minutes he used eleven *like*'s and nine *you know*'s.**

In the example above, we are writing about *like* and *you know* as words. The plural of a word referred to as a word is formed by _____

_____.

3 **Some companies use &'s as official parts of their names.**

The plurals of symbols such as &, +, >, and < are also formed by _____

_____.

4 **I can't tell which are 2's and which are 5's.**

State the rule illustrated by this example. _____

_____

5 Try, without looking back at exercises 1–4, to list the four kinds of items whose plurals are formed by use of an apostrophe and *s*.

_____

_____

6 Write a sentence in which you use the plural of *t*.

_____

7 Write a sentence in which you use the plural of *too*.

_____

8 Write a sentence in which you use the plural of +.

_____

9 Write a sentence in which you use the plural of 8.

_____

C: ASSIGNMENTS

• Write two sentences to illustrate the formation of the plural of each: letters, words referred to as words, symbols, and numerals.

ANSWERS TO SECTION B

1. letters
2. adding an apostrophe and *s*
3. adding an apostrophe and *s*
4. MODEL Plurals of numbers are indicated by adding an apostrophe and *s*.
5. letters, words referred to as words, numbers, and symbols
6. MODEL *Committee* has two *m*'s, two *t*'s, and two *e*'s.
7. MODEL You use too many *too*'s.
8. MODEL Many typewriters do not have +'s.
9. MODEL Two 8's are 16.

Unit 44—Hyphens in Dividing Words

A: COMMENTARY

Often you will be able to avoid dividing a word at the end of the line, and you should do so if you can. When division is not easily avoidable, you should follow the principles discussed below and in B:

1. A word may be divided only between syllables.
2. A single letter should not be left on either line.
3. A one-syllable word may not be divided.
4. Prefixes and suffixes should not be divided.
5. The endings -*ed* and -*es* should not be separated from the basic word.
6. The hyphen showing division must be placed at the end of the line, not the beginning of the next line.

Here are some additional comments and suggestions:

1. As a rule, do not divide proper names (*Metcalf*), abbreviations or letter words (*WCBS*), and numbers (2,236,482).
2. If a hyphenated word must be divided, make the break at the hyphen (*self-adjusting*, not *self-ad-justing*).
3. *Fall-ing* and *sin-ning* are both correctly divided; the identity of a basic word should be kept if possible.
4. *React* may be divided between *e* and *a*, but *appeal* may not. The reason is that, in *appeal*, *ea* represents a single sound.
5. In *indent* and other words with two consecutive different consonant sounds, divide between the consonants (*in-dent, as-pect*).
6. A consonant usually clings to the following vowel (*so-cial, na-tion, na-ture*). An exception is in a word such as *tapestry* (*tap-es-try*), where the syllable (*tap-*) is accented and has a short vowel sound.

B: EXERCISES

1 "Contrary to male sentimentality and psychology, the con-
frontation of a hostile crowd, by a woman, is like a tonic."
    —W. Bolitho

It is wise to avoid dividing many words at the ends of lines, but sometimes division is necessary. The typesetter has had to divide the word *confronta-tion* above. The syllables of this word are *con fron ta tion*. The typesetter

has divided it between two of its ⎯⎯⎯⎯⎯, putting a ⎯⎯⎯⎯⎯
at the end as a signal.

2 A word may be correctly divided only between syllables. Usually you can tell by pronouncing a word where each syllable ends. If you cannot, your

dictionary will guide you. At what places may each of these words be divided? (Write each word, dividing it into syllables.)

unfortunately _____ **disaster** _____

modification _____

3 Good typists and typesetters follow the rule that a word should not be divided so that only one letter is on either line. (Some printing houses, in fact, object to having only two letters.) If the rule about avoiding single letters is followed, which two of the words below may not be divided?

obey admit harpy catty _____ _____

4 A word, you remember, may be divided only between syllables. May any of these words be divided? _____

room thrush though strength

5 The *-ed* ending on a verb and the *-es* ending on a verb or noun customarily are not separated from the main part of the word. Generally, then, would *skinned, perches,* and *churches* be divided at all? _____

6 Careful typists and typesetters also try to avoid dividing a prefix or a suffix. Thus, though the prefix *ante-* has two syllables, it would not be divided. Neither would the suffix *-able.* In how many places may *hypertension* be legitimately divided? _____

7 Let's summarize. When a word must be divided at the end of a line, the division is made between _____. A single letter (may/may not) _____ be left on either line. A one-syllable word (may/may not) _____ be divided. The endings (which two?) _____ should not be separated from the basic words. The hyphen to indicate the division is placed _____.

8 Underline the words that may not be divided.

convey lumpy strong about asked thought repay exit searches searcher emit meanness meant watched boxes

9 Divide into syllables the five words from exercise 8 that may be divided.

_____ _____ _____ _____ _____

10 Indicate where each of these words may be divided. (Use your dictionary if necessary, but remember prefixes and suffixes.)

intravenous _____ existentialism _____

extraterritoriality _____

C: ASSIGNMENTS

• At which point or points, if any, may each of the following words be divided? Check your dictionary whenever you are in doubt.

across	fatuous
catalog	Herbert
clowned	ignition
clowning	intuition
contend	paraplegic
crouched	pleading
crouches	reagent
discrepancy	spinning
dissatisfied	summation
enough	346,281
ex-President	WKCR

ANSWERS TO SECTION B

1. syllables, hyphen
2. un for tu nate ly   dis as ter   mod i fi ca tion
3. obey   harpy
4. No
5. No
6. Two (after *hyper* or *ten,* but not after *hy*)
7. syllables   may not   may not   *-es* and *-ed*   at the end of the line
8. lumpy strong about asked thought searches emit meant watched boxes
9. con vey   re pay   ex it   search er   mean ness
10. intra ven ous   ex is ten tial ism   extra ter ri to ri al i ty (*Intra* and *extra* are indivisible prefixes.)

Unit 45—Miscellaneous Uses of Hyphens

A: COMMENTARY

Hyphens are the most annoying of punctuation marks, partly because practices in hyphenation change with time. Thus *baseball* was originally *base ball,* then *base-ball,* and finally *baseball.* Hyphens sometimes seem like chameleons: we write *a well-run store* but *the store was well run.*

Despite its vexatiousness, the hyphen performs a number of useful functions, sometimes holding words or parts of words together and sometimes holding them apart. Moreover, the principles illustrated in this unit are fairly consistently observed. In summary, those principles are:

1. Compound numbers (*forty-eight*) are hyphenated. A number such as *three hundred* is not hyphenated.
2. Words used to represent exact fractions (*one-seventh*) are generally hyphenated. If the fraction is only approximate, the hyphen is less likely. In a fraction such as *one twenty-fourth* only one hyphen is used.
3. In titles of relatives, compounds with *in-law* and *great-* are hyphenated.
4. Unusual compounds that might otherwise confuse the reader (*fire-eater*, *troll-like*) are hyphenated.
5. Groups of words used together as a single modifier (*hurry-up-and-wait* tactics, *slow-down* tactics) are ordinarily hyphenated. However, hyphens are not generally used when the modifier follows the word modified (the reprimand was *well deserved*). Also, when an *-ly* adverb comes before an adjective (a *plainly evident* fact), the combination is not hyphenated.
6. Combinations of a number or a letter with something else (*4-inch* gasket, *H-bomb*) are hyphenated.
7. Words such as *re-covered* (meaning "covered again") that might be confused with similar words are hyphenated. (When one is speaking, the two words are given different stress.)
8. Prefixes before proper names (*anti-Castro*) are hyphenated.
9. In indicating letter-by-letter spelling (*t-h-e-i-r*), we use hyphens to separate the letters.
10. In expressions such as *pre- and post-war deficits* a suspension hyphen is used as a signal to the reader that an attachment to the first element is coming later.
11. When in doubt about hyphenation, consult your dictionary, although it will not answer every possible question.
12. The U.S. Government Printing Office *Manual of Style* advises: "In general, omit the hyphen when words appear in regular order and the omission causes no ambiguity in sense or sound."

B: EXERCISES

1 **I bought twenty-seven shares of stock.**
I bought one hundred shares of stock.

The first sentence shows that a compound number, such as *twenty-one* or

ninety-nine, (is/is not) _____ hyphenated. The second sentence shows

that a number such as *one hundred* or *ten million* (is/is not) _____
considered a compound number.

2 **One-fifth of the students made A's.**
About one fifth of the wheat was moldy.

The first sentence shows that when words are used to express exact fractions, a _____ separates the parts. The second sentence shows that when the fraction is only approximate, (a/no) _____ hyphen is used.

3 **My father-in-law and his stepson visited my half brother and me to discuss my great-grandfather's estate.**

In titles of relatives, as the example shows, *in-law* and *great-* compounds are hyphenated. Compounds with *step* and *grand* are closed up. Those with *half* are generally written with two words but are sometimes hyphenated. Make up an original sentence or two containing an *in-law* compound, a *great-* compound, a *grand-* compound, and a compound with *step*. _____

_____

_____

4 **In the sideshow were a fire-eater and a troll-like dwarf.**

Why would *fireeater* and *trolllike* be harder to read than *fire-eater* and *troll-like*? _____

_____

5 On the basis of the answer to exercise 4, write a rule to cover this kind of situation. _____

_____

_____

6 **The fly-now-pay-later plan has led to increased sales of first-class tickets.**

Fly-now-pay-later and *first-class* are groups of words used together as single modifiers. As you notice, such modifiers are usually hyphenated. Make up a sentence in which you use *come-as-you-are* and *high-flying* in this way.

_____

_____

7 **She is a well-known author.**
The author is well known.

In the first sentence *well-known* comes before *author*, the word it modifies. In the second sentence, *well known* follows *author*, the word it modifies.

Write a rule that will cover the principle involved in this distinction.

_____

_____

_____

8 **Bring a 10-inch plank.**
The A-bomb and the X-ray have one thing in common.

Write a rule that will cover the principle involved in the two examples.

_____

_____

9 **I recovered my wits enough to say that the sofa would have to be re-covered.**

Do *recovered* and *re-covered* in the sentence above mean the same thing?

_____ Why is the hyphen desirable in the second one?

_____

10 **Ex-President Cleveland was still pro-Venezuela.**
His ex-fiancée is back in New York.

Prefixes before proper names are always hyphenated, as in the first example. Only a few, such as *ex-*, *self-*, *quasi-*, are generally hyphenated otherwise. (Consult your dictionary when in doubt.) Write another example like

those in the first sentence. _____

_____

11 **The correct spelling is s-u-p-e-r-s-e-d-e.**

Write a rule to cover the principle illustrated above.

_____

_____

12 **Both his pre- and post-war statements were ridiculed.**
The payment was in ten- and twenty-dollar bills.

The hyphens after *pre-* and *ten-* are called suspension hyphens because they suspend the meaning for a while. They make unnecessary the repetition of *war* and *dollar*. Copy the following sentence, punctuating correctly:

Both first and second class passengers are included. _____

_____

C: ASSIGNMENTS

• The expressions below are written without hyphens. Decide which ought to be hyphenated, and rewrite showing the hyphens.

1. The word *deceive* is spelled deceive.
2. a forget me not
3. Y shaped island
4. semiindividualistic
5. belllike
6. recreation (a second creation)
7. ultraatomic
8. motherinlaw
9. stepchild
10. greatgrandfather
11. Chicago Detroit highway
12. a one dish meal
13. smoke resistant fabric
14. The fabric is smoke resistant.
15. a most favored nation treaty
16. shellless
17. a clearly untrue statement
18. Afro American relations
19. elderly shoemaker
20. wooden shoe maker
21. light brown hat (a brown hat light in weight)
22. light brown hat (a hat colored light brown)
23. a two barrel cannon
24. long and short term interest rates
25. 10, 12, and 14 foot boards
26. retreat (to treat again)
27. unionized (not ionized)
28. lost his self control
29. ex vice president
30. unAmerican
31. thirty one
32. thirty second
33. four in hand tie
34. three forty ninths
35. one eighth of the distance
36. about one eighth of the distance
37. a know it all attitude
38. to blue pencil a manuscript
39. Shooting at the target, she hit the bull's eye.
40. The bull's eye was red and inflamed.

ANSWERS TO SECTION B

1. is   is not
2. hyphen   no
3. MODEL   Her mother-in-law, her great-grandmother, and her stepdaughter all live in one unhappy household.
4. MODEL   The *eea* and the *lll* could be momentarily confusing.
5. MODEL   In compound words a hyphen usually separates adjacent repeated vowels or an identical consonant used three times in succession.
6. MODEL   We'll invite all our high-flying friends to a come-as-you-are party.
7. MODEL   When a compound adjective comes before a noun, it is customarily hyphenated, but after the noun it is usually written as two words.
8. MODEL   Compounds made of a numeral plus a word or a letter plus a word should be hyphenated.
9. No   MODEL   It prevents confusion with *recovered*.
10. MODEL   Ex-Governor Rye was accused of being pro-Communist.
11. MODEL   In writing a word to indicate and emphasize its spelling, one customarily uses hyphens between letters.
12. Both first- and second-class passengers are included.

Unit 46—Dashes

A: COMMENTARY

The dash is a relatively informal mark, not often used in formal writing. It is especially useful in reproducing conversation because of the natural tendency of speakers to shift sentence structure or leave sentences unfinished. In formal prose its most common use is to set off inserted elements containing commas, such as the examples in exercises 4 and 5. Excessive use of dashes should be avoided even in informal writing because other marks are often more precise.

Printers call the regular dash the *em-dash*. It is longer than the *en-dash*, used, for example, in 1973–79. Neither of these dashes should be confused with the hyphen, which has other purposes. When you write an em-dash, make it about as long as two hyphens; make the en-dash about as long as one-and-a-half hyphens. Since the standard typewriter keyboard has no dash, use two hyphens for an em-dash and one for an en-dash.

The uses of dashes covered in this unit are the following:

1. to indicate a sudden shift in sentence structure (*I wanted a—you don't really care what I wanted, do you?*)
2. to indicate an interrupted and hence unfinished sentence (*Then I saw—*)
3. to set off an inserted or summarizing element that contains commas (*My*

grandfather—gray, tiny, almost emaciated—will probably not live much longer.)

4. to signal a surprise ending of a sentence (*I climbed, clawed for toeholds, grasped at branches—and slid back fifteen feet.*)

5. to substitute for *to* or *through* in expressions such as *1810–12, Chapters 2–4, pages 7–11, a May–July report.* (The en-dash is used for these.)

In an occasional sentence, especially one introducing a list, either a dash or a colon can be justified. The example in exercise 5, *Let's buy only essential foods—bread, milk, and eggs,* could conceivably use a colon, although the informality of *Let's* suggests that the informal dash is more appropriate. In contrast, because of its formal tone, the following sentence is more likely to require a colon:

Let us struggle to conquer such evils: intolerance, bigotry, and extremes of selfishness.

B: EXERCISES

1 **"Then Mabel began to—oh, perhaps I should say that her eyes looked glazed."**

In the sentence above, the speaker started the sentence in one way and then

_____ .

2 **We ought to buy—what do you think?**

The most common use of the dash is to signal a sudden change in sentence structure. Does the example above, like that in exercise 1, illustrate this use? _____

3 **"After that, we should—"**
"Wait a minute!" Jim interrupted.

The first sentence above is obviously unfinished. Comment on the use of

the punctuation. _____

_____

4 **Thomas Jefferson—President, statesman, architect, farmer, inventor, and philosopher—was one of America's most versatile men.**

In the example, the part within dashes is an inserted element, not part of the basic structure. As a rule, such elements are set off by commas (see Unit 36). Explain why dashes are clearer than commas would be in the

example. _____

_____

5 Let's buy only essential foods—bread, milk, and eggs.
Bread, milk, and eggs—these should be enough.

The examples above are similar to the one in exercise 4. They show that appositives or summarizing words, when commas are included, are often

6 Joey picked up his violin case, grinned goodbye at his proud mother, started off for his lesson—and ended up at the ball park.

Did you expect the sentence above to end as it did? _____ Write a rule to cover this use of the dash. _____

7 pages 42–45   1937–39   Chapters 4–7   a June–August decline

The dashes in the expressions above are shorter than "regular" dashes but are longer than hyphens. What is the purpose of the en-dashes above?

8 The halfback—a handsome boy—took the ball—on a handoff from the quarterback—and started around right end—I believe—and was thrown out of bounds—right at my feet.

The sentence above is intended as a horrible example from which dasho-maniacs (users of excessive dashes) may profit. What is the warning implied by the example? _____

9 Finish the following incomplete sentence. Use a sudden change in sentence form and punctuate correctly. **We were watching a** _____

10 Punctuate the following sentence correctly:

For these reasons economy dependability and durability I believe that Thurston trucks are your best buy.

11 Add a surprise ending to the following sentence, and punctuate appropriately:

I glided gracefully across the ice, saw Donna in the stands, waved to her

12 Write a two-sentence conversation in which the first speaker is interrupted.

_____

_____

C: ASSIGNMENTS

• Illustrate in sentences the five uses of dashes, as listed in Section A.

ANSWERS TO SECTION B

1. MODEL changed to a different statement
2. Yes
3. MODEL A dash signals the interruption of a sentence.
4. MODEL The presence of other commas would make the sentence confusing. (*or: Thomas Jefferson* would seem at first glance to be part of a series.)
5. MODEL set off by dashes
6. No (but don't count *Yes* as wrong) MODEL An unexpected ending for a sentence may be signaled by a dash.
7. MODEL They separate numbers referring to pages or years or chapters, and they separate names of months used as compound modifiers.
8. MODEL Do not use many dashes.
9. MODEL We were watching a—but why bore you with that?
10. For these reasons—economy, dependability, and durability—I believe that Thurston trucks are your best buy.
11. MODEL —and found myself sprawling on my back
12. MODEL "I don't believe—" Herbert began.
    "We want facts, not beliefs!" she snapped.

Unit 47—Parentheses and Brackets

A: COMMENTARY

The singular of *parentheses* is *parenthesis*. The set of two marks ( ) is *parentheses*. They are also sometimes called *curves*, especially in England.

Parentheses, like dashes, are subject to abuse. If you find yourself putting many expressions in parentheses, look at your sentence structure to see whether some of the parenthetical expressions should not be tied in more closely or perhaps not included at all.

Parentheses are like dashes in another way: both set off material that breaks rather abruptly into sentence structure. In some instances either parentheses or dashes can be justified. Parentheses, though, are a little more formal; also, material in parentheses is less emphasized than that between dashes:

> The explanations (there are three of them) are contradictory.
> The explanations—there are three of them—are contradictory.

The second example places more stress on the fact that three explanations exist.

This unit considers three uses of parentheses. The first two, which are rather minor, are to enclose numbers or letters pertaining to items in a sequence and to enclose dates not directly woven into the sentence structure. In the first of these uses, practice varies: (1) is often found but so are 1) and 1. The third use of parentheses is most important—to enclose material only loosely related to the rest of the sentence and often not connected grammatically in any obvious way. Entire sentences may be parenthetical if their relationship to the rest of the paragraph is rather loose. On rare occasions, even an entire paragraph may be in parentheses.

Parenthetical elements do not greatly affect the other marks of punctuation, as this example shows:

> When the battle finally ended (about six in the evening, most historians say), the losses on each side exceeded a thousand.

The comma after the second parenthesis would normally come after *ended* but is delayed by the parenthetical remark.

Brackets have fewer uses than most other punctuation marks. Except for certain technical uses that need not concern us, brackets are used *within a quotation* for the insertion of a correction, comment, or added information.

On very rare occasions a parenthetical element may have another such element inside it. Brackets may then be used for the inner element:

> The Germans use the word *Vorstufe* (literally "forestage" [a misleading term in English]) to designate the developments preceding the real beginning of anything.

B: EXERCISES

1 Parentheses may be used (1) to enclose numbers or letters pertaining to items in a sequence, (2) to enclose certain dates, and (3) to enclose additional comments only loosely related to the rest of the sentence.

The sentence above summarizes the first half of this exercise and also illustrates one use of parentheses. What use is illustrated, (1), (2), or (3)?

---

2 Composer Edward MacDowell (1861–1908) is best remembered for his *Woodland Sketches.*

The July Revolution (1830) deposed Charles X.

These two examples show that when dates are not directly woven into the sentence structure, (finish the sentence) _____

_____.

3 **The stock market crash of 1929 (there has never been another so severe) drove many millionaires to bankruptcy and even to suicide.**

Although the material in parentheses is related to the general topic of the sentence, the logical connection is only loose and the grammatical connection nonexistent. For the insertion of such material, (finish the sentence)

_____.

4 **These statistics (Table 2) show the relative increase of purchasing power. No other World Series (with the possible exception of that in 1926) was ever so dramatic.**

Write a sentence of your own, modeled on either of the examples above, containing a similar parenthetical expression.

5 **"Three of Ernst Hoffmann's tales provided the basis for the [Offenbach] opera *Tales of Hoffmann*."**

Note that the sentence above is quoted. The word *Offenbach* did not appear in the original quotation but was inserted by the person using the quotation.

The brackets are used, then, to show _____.

6 **"Paul Gauguin turned from a successful career in law [actually in banking] to an even more successful career in art."**

Once more an insertion, this time a correction, has been made within quoted material. The punctuation marks conventionally used for inserting any kind of comment or correction within a quotation are _____.

7 **"His repreive [*sic*] was short."**

In quoting, one must quote exactly, even including errors. The Latin *sic*, meaning "thus" or "that's the way it really is," is placed in brackets to show that the mistake was in the original material. In the example above, the error to which [*sic*] calls attention is _____.

C: ASSIGNMENTS

• Write sentences in which each of the following items might appropriately be enclosed in parentheses:

1. See Plate X
2. 1914–18 (dates of World War I)
3. 1564–1616 (dates of Shakespeare's birth and death)
4. the losing candidate was Stevenson
5. 1   2   3
6. a memento of his father
7. Gerald R. Ford

• Write sentences in which each of the following items might appropriately be placed in brackets.

1. *sic*
2. actually 1976
3. Thomas

ANSWERS TO SECTION B

1. (1)
2. MODEL   they are customarily enclosed in parentheses.
3. MODEL   parentheses are customarily used.
4. MODEL   The statistics (see the chart on the next page) are impressive.
5. MODEL   the insertion of added material within a quotation.
6. brackets
7. the misspelling of *reprieve*.

Unit 48—Quotation Marks
with Direct Quotations

A: COMMENTARY

The principles presented in this unit are the following:

1. Direct quotations, which give the exact words of a speaker or writer, are placed in quotation marks. Indirect quotations, which merely summarize what someone said, should not be placed in quotation marks.
2. A fragment of a direct quotation is punctuated in the same way as a complete direct quotation.

3. Single quotation marks enclose a quotation within a quotation.

Although a few writers, such as William Saroyan, seldom or never employ quotation marks, the marks are helpful to readers and for that reason will be required of you in the above circumstances. One type of quotation in which they should ordinarily be omitted, though, occurs in term papers or other writing: a *long* quotation is usually indented extra spaces and single-spaced. The indention and the spacing signify that the material is quoted.

In England, single quotation marks are used where Americans generally use double, and vice versa. Some American and Canadian publications also follow this practice, but it is certainly not general in the United States.

Remember that quotation marks are always used in pairs. Avoid careless omission of the second quote.

B: EXERCISES

1 A direct quotation is one in which the exact words of a speaker or writer are

quoted. Which is a direct quotation, A or B? _____

A. Jack said, "I'd like to ride the horse."
B. Jack said that he'd like to ride the horse.

2 According to the example in exercise 1, (a direct quotation/an indirect quo-

tation) _____ is enclosed in quotation marks.

3 Jack said "that he would like to ride the horse."

Explain why the punctuation in the sentence above is incorrect.

_____

_____

4 Clayton said that my accusation was "completely ridiculous."

Note that only part of Clayton's words are quoted directly and that therefore no capital letter is used. Is the punctuation of a quoted fragment the

same as with a quoted complete sentence? _____

5 Marvin announced, The next dance will be a polka.
Marvin announced that the next dance would be a polka.

Copy the sentence that contains a direct quotation. Add the necessary quo-

tation marks. _____

_____

6 Lois asked, "Was it Emerson who said, 'To be great is to be misunderstood'?"

Notice that in this example we have a quotation within a quotation. What punctuation marks are used for this purpose? _____

_____

7 Bulwer-Lytton once wrote, "Fate laughs at probabilities.

What correction should be made in the sentence above? _____

_____

8 "Fate," Bulwer-Lytton wrote, laughs at probabilities."

What correction should be made in the sentence above? _____

_____

9 Helena remarked, I believe that Bulwer-Lytton once said, Fate laughs at probabilities.

Copy the sentence above, punctuating it as needed with double and single quotation marks. _____

_____

_____

C: ASSIGNMENTS

• Write five pairs of sentences. In the first sentence of each pair use a direct quotation from a speaker or a writer. In the second sentence rewrite the first, changing the direct quotation to an indirect one.

• Write two sentences in which you include a fragment of a direct quotation.

• Write three sentences in which you include a quotation within a quotation.

ANSWERS TO SECTION B

1. A
2. a direct quotation
3. MODEL The part of the sentence in quotation marks is not a direct quotation, so no marks should be used.
4. Yes
5. Marvin announced, "The next dance will be a polka."
6. single quotation marks

7. Add quotation marks at the end.
8. Add quotation marks before *laughs*.
9. Helena remarked, "I believe that Bulwer-Lytton once said, 'Fate laughs at probabilities.' "

Unit 49—Other Punctuation with Quotation Marks

A: COMMENTARY

The placement of other punctuation with closing quotation marks is not universally agreed upon. British preferences disagree in a number of ways with American, and not all American editors agree completely among themselves. The recommendations in this unit are based on the most common practice of American editors.

The comma and period customarily go inside the closing quotes; the semicolon and colon go outside.

The placement of the question mark and exclamation mark, since it may be either inside or outside the closing quotes, is perhaps most confusing. The principle is that the mark goes inside the quotes if the quotation itself is a question or an exclamation; otherwise it goes outside. In the case of a double question, the question mark goes inside:

"Did she ask, 'What's your hurry?' "

The dash, which is not considered in the exercises in Section B, goes inside in the case of an unfinished sentence:

"Nell, I—" he began.

Otherwise it goes outside:

The beets next go to a "deracinator"—a vicious-looking assortment of whirling knives.

The same principles apply to placement of marks with single quotes as with double quotes:

"Has he sung 'Night and Day'?" I asked.
"No, but he sang 'When You and I Were Young, Maggie.' "

B: EXERCISES

1 **Dora said quietly, "The next day the diamond disappeared."**

Unit 40 treats the comma or colon *before* quoted material. Here we are concerned with the location of punctuation with *closing* quotation marks (the second in the pair). According to the example above, a period with closing quotes is placed (inside/outside) _____ the quotation marks.

2 "A grass snake," said the professor, "is actually a legless lizard."

According to the example above, a comma with closing quotes is placed

_____

3 "Hurry!" he begged.
   "Why should I?" I retorted.

Note that the quoted material in the first sentence is exclamatory and that the quoted material in the second sentence asks a question. When this is true, the exclamation mark or question mark is placed _____

_____

4 Imagine his telling us, "Germany really won the war"!
   Did he say, "Germany really won the war"?

Note that this time the quoted material is not exclamatory or interrogative. The whole of the first sentence, though, is exclamatory, and the whole of the second sentence is interrogative. Such sentences are rare, but when they do occur, the exclamation mark or question mark is placed _____

_____

5 "History repeats itself"; true, but with countless variations.
   "History repeats itself": this is not a completely true statement.

Only infrequently does a semicolon or a colon appear with closing quotation marks. When it does, according to the examples, it is placed _____

_____

6 Which of the following three sets of examples summarizes most accurately what has been said in this unit? (There's only one set in which *all* the examples are right.) _____

A	B	C
"I slept".	"I slept."	"I slept."
"Come," she said.	"Come," she said.	"Come", she said.
"Where?" I asked.	"Where?" I asked.	"Where"? I asked.
"Run"! I shouted.	"Run!" I shouted.	"Run"! I shouted.
"Bells"; I hear the poem yet.	"Bells"; I hear the poem yet.	"Bells;" I hear the poem yet.
"Forlorn:" a sad word.	"Forlorn": a sad word.	"Forlorn": a sad word.

7 Insert the indicated punctuation where needed, placing it correctly in relation to the closing quotation marks.

A. "Rhodes" said Professor Teak, "was once a commercial power" (comma, period)
B. "What a liar" exclaimed Rhonda. (exclamation mark)
C. What a time to recite "Trees" (exclamation mark)
D. "Where is Rice Institute" she asked naively. (question mark)
E. Have you read Frost's "Birches" (question mark)
F. I sang "Die Lorelei" no one applauded. (semicolon)
G. This, then, was the source of "Venus and Adonis" Ovid's *Metamorphoses.* (colon)

C: ASSIGNMENTS

• Here are several patterns of sentences with some of the words given. Fill in words to complete the patterns, and punctuate correctly.

1. "(*Statement*)" she said, "but (*Statement*)"
2. "(*Exclamation*)" he shouted.
3. She asked, "(*Question*)"
4. Did he say, "(*Statement*)"
5. Oh, no, he must not read "(*Title*)" (The whole sentence is exclamatory.)
6. I heard her lecture called "(*Title*)" it was inspiring.
7. Tell me this about "(*Title*)" is it based on fact?
8. "(*Statement*) '(*Title*)'"
9. "(*Question*) '(*Title*)'"
10. "(*Question*) '(*Question*)'"

ANSWERS TO SECTION B

1. inside
2. inside the closing quotation marks.
3. inside the closing quotation marks.
4. outside the closing quotation marks.
5. outside the closing quotation marks.
6. B
7. A. "Rhodes,"   power."   B. liar!"   C. "Trees"!   D. Institute?"
   E. "Birches"?   F. "Die Lorelei";   G. Adonis":

Unit 50—Quotation Marks with Titles; Other Uses of Quotation Marks

A: COMMENTARY

The most important point discussed in this unit is that titles of short works (specifically, poems, articles or essays, chapters, lectures, and songs or other short musical selections) are customarily enclosed in quotation marks. Unit 52 treats the italicizing (underlining) of titles of longer works.

Quotation marks are less frequently used now than they have been previously to enclose technical terms, words referred to as words, definitions (except when directly quoted), slang words, and nicknames. Sometimes, when a technical term is first introduced, it is quoted or italicized, but the quotes or italics are dropped thereafter. Italics are now more common than quotes to indicate words referred to as words. In informal context no reason exists for putting quotation marks around slang terms and nicknames, and in formal context perhaps the slang is not appropriate.

Readers find annoying an excessive use of quotation marks for miscellaneous purposes. Here is an example:

> "Cracking" is the "breaking down" of "molecular" structure of "crude" oil and the "regrouping" of molecules after the "cracking process" has knocked "hell" out of the "raw crude."

In the sentence above none of the quotes are justified, with the possible exception of the first pair. Since the reference to *hell* is inappropriate in this context, a substitute expression should be found.

British publications and those few American publications that prefer single quotation marks would use those marks instead of the double ones recommended in this unit.

B: EXERCISES

1 I still remember Poe's poem "The Raven" and his short story "The Gold Bug."

The sentence above shows that quotation marks are placed around the titles of _____ and _____.

2 An article entitled "The Future of Ballet" appeared in the April *Harper's*.

Note that names of magazines (like names of books) are customarily italicized (underlined in writing). Titles of articles or essays, however, are punctuated with _____.

3 Chapter II of *The Origin of Species* is entitled "Variation Under Nature."
What does the example above show about the use of quotation marks?

_____

_____

4 Dr. Levin's lecture, "The New World of the Trilobite," will be postponed.
Lecture titles are enclosed in _____.

5 Offenbach's "Barcarolle" is one of my favorite melodies.
Titles of songs and short musical selections are enclosed in _____

_____.

6 Summarize the points so far covered in this exercise, emphasizing the difference in treatment of titles of short works and long works.

_____

_____

7 The reaction between sulfur chloride and vegetable oils is known as "vulcanization."
Technical names, this example reminds us, are often enclosed in _____

_____. (This practice is less common, though, than it once was.)

8 "Demagogue" historically means "leader of the people."
In the example above, the first word is referred to as a word, and the last four words are a quoted definition. Alternatively, *Demagogue* and *leader of the people* may be italicized. Or *Demagogue* may be italicized and "leader of the people" quoted. There (is/is not) _____, then, complete consistency in usage here.

9 His friends consider him a "turkey."
Slang terms in the past were usually enclosed in quotation marks. Today we reason that if the context is very informal, the quotation marks are not needed because slang is informal, too, and if the context is formal, the slang term should probably be replaced. In other words, quotation marks around slang terms now seem (hard/easy) _____ to justify.

10 **"Iron Man" Lou Gehrig could certainly "swat that 'apple.' "**

Avoid excessive use of quotation marks, especially those that call attention to the writer's choice of words. If the example above appeared on a sports page, which is generally informal, no apologetic quotation marks are needed. If the writer were writing for a more formal publication, he or she probably

should _____

_____.

C: ASSIGNMENTS

• Compose several sentences in which you include titles of poems, short stories, essays or articles, lectures, chapters, and songs.

• Skim the pages of a reputable magazine, noting the instances in which quotation marks are used in nonfiction material. Comment on the frequency or infrequency of such marks for purposes other than reporting of conversation or indicating of titles. Although you may not find many uses other than the basic two, comment on the purpose and necessity of any that you do find.

ANSWERS TO SECTION B

1. poems, short stories
2. quotation marks
3. MODEL Titles of chapters (or other sections of books) are enclosed in quotation marks.
4. quotation marks
5. quotation marks
6. MODEL Titles of short works—poems, short stories, articles, essays, chapters, lectures, or brief musical compositions—are placed in quotation marks, but titles of long works are italicized (underlined).
7. quotation marks
8. is not
9. hard
10. MODEL substitute other words for *swat that apple*. (The quotation marks around *Iron Man* would probably be kept, although editorial practice varies.)

Unit 51—Paragraphing of Conversation

A: COMMENTARY

The paragraphing of conversation is one of the many helps that a writer supplies to the reader. It enables the reader to realize almost automatically that a second person has begun speaking. In addition, it can reduce the necessity for repetitive *she said, he said,* and so on. In a long conversation, it is true, the reader needs an occasional *Tom asked* or the like as a reminder, but not every paragraph requires one. The paragraphing, the quotation marks, and possibly the content or the speech mannerisms are often clues enough.

The basic principle of paragraphing of conversation illustrated in this unit is that a different paragraph is used for each speaker. A rare exception to this principle is the babbling of overlapping remarks from a group, where it doesn't really matter who says what.

The second principle is that if one person speaks two or more consecutive paragraphs, quotation marks are used at the beginning of each paragraph but not at the end—except for the conclusion of the speaker's whole statement. Of course, if the speech is interrupted by *he said* or other material, the usual rules for quotation marks apply.

B: EXERCISES

1   Charles asked, "What changes does the new copyright law contain?"
       "They are very substantial," Opal began.

The example above shows the basic principles for paragraphing conversation. Each person's words are in quotation marks. Also, the change to a

different speaker requires that a new _____ be started.

2   "One of the changes is in the duration of copyright, which is now considerably longer than the former renewable twenty-eight-year period.
       "A second change," Opal continued, "is in the attention given to television performances and other technological developments."

This example differs from that in exercise 1. Here the same person speaks two consecutive paragraphs. Why, in your opinion, are there no quotation

marks at the end of the first paragraph? _____

_____

3 Look again at the example in exercise 2. Note that quotation marks begin the second paragraph. In your opinion, why is this practice followed?

_____

_____

4 **Students were shouting encouragement. "Hold on!" "We'll get you down!" "Somebody's getting a ladder!" "Don't let go!"**

Occasionally, as in the chorus of shouts above, no need exists to identify specific speakers. In such a case, the words spoken by different speakers are often placed _____.

5 In exercises 5–7 imagine that each short line represents a whole *paragraph* of speaking. Insert quotation marks and a paragraph sign (¶) where needed.

Clay said, _____. _____, she replied.

6 **Melvin began to explain. _____. _____, he concluded.**

7 **_____? asked George. _____, Susan told him. _____? he persisted.**

8 Write two short paragraphs of conversation, involving two speakers. Use quotation marks as needed.

_____

_____

_____

9 Write two short paragraphs in which the same person speaks without interruption. Use quotation marks as needed.

_____

_____

_____

10 Write a short paragraph with several persons speaking almost together. (See exercise 4 as an example.) Use quotation marks as needed.

_____

_____

C: ASSIGNMENTS

• Glance through two or three novels or short stories that you have available (preferably not in the same book or magazine). Note whether the principles of using paragraphs and quotation marks are the same as those discussed in this unit. If variations exist, try to decide whether or not the task of the reader is made easier because of those variations.

• Write about a page of conversation between yourself and one or two of your friends. Choose any topic of interest to you. Confine the conversation to short speeches. Paragraph and use quotation marks in the ways presented in this unit.

ANSWERS TO SECTION B

1. paragraph
2. MODEL They would make it appear that the speaker had concluded whatever she was going to say at that time.
3. MODEL They serve as a reminder that someone is being quoted.
4. in the same paragraph

5. ¶ Clay said, "_____."

   ¶ "_____," she replied.

6. Melvin began to explain. "_____.

   ¶ "_____," he concluded.

7. ¶ "_____?" asked George.

   ¶ "_____," Susan told him.

   ¶ "_____?" he persisted.

8. MODEL Walker asked her, with concern in his voice, "Did you get to sleep last night?"
   "Yes," she said, "but not until very late."
9. MODEL Grandad told us, "Picket fences were once much more common than they are now.
   "They usually had sharp points at the top. I suspect that those were to discourage small children from climbing over."
10. MODEL All the children began shouting at the teacher. "Miss Lyon!"

"Read us a story!" "Story!" "No story!" "Puzzles!" "Let's do puzzles!" "Story!" "Puzzles!" "Miss Lyon!"

Unit 52—Underlining (Italics)

A: COMMENTARY

Some publications, especially newspapers and a number of magazines, use little or no italic type, preferring quotation marks or capital letters or some other device instead. The practices described in this unit are those followed by the majority of book editors and some magazine editors, and recommended by most teachers.

As Section B shows, titles of books, magazines, newspapers, and long musical compositions are italicized. Full-length plays (not usually one-act plays) may be added to this list. A few publications also italicize names of works of art and names of ships, trains, and planes, but this practice is much less frequent than it once was.

B: EXERCISES

1 **His book *Ragtime* was favorably reviewed in *Saturday Review*.**

Unit 50 shows that titles of short literary works are customarily enclosed in quotation marks. The example above shows that printers ordinarily set titles

of _____ and _____ in italic type.

2 Since you cannot write or type italics (unless you have a special typewriter), you need to use a substitute—underlining. If you gave a manuscript to a printer, underlined portions would be set in italic type. Copy the example

from exercise 1, underlining appropriately. _____

_____.

3 **The *Daily Tribune* published an ecstatic review of her singing in *Aïda*.**

The example shows that titles of _____ and _____ are also ordinarily set in italic type.

4 **Being lazy, I am attracted by the philosophy of *mañana*.**
She was guilty of an astonishing *faux pas*.

What conclusion about italics can you draw from these two examples?

_____

_____

5 Footnote to exercise 4: Some foreign expressions have been used often enough in English that they no longer seem foreign. Your dictionary may help you when you are in doubt. Words such as *bona fide* and *debutante* are examples. In World War II *blitzkrieg* "lightning war" was used so widely that it was treated as an English word instead of German. Any very widely used foreign word is not italicized in ordinary use. Should *ensemble* and *apropos* be italicized? _____

6 **There are three *l*'s in *parallel*.**

When letters are referred to as letters or words are referred to as words, they are _____. (Note: Quotation marks are often used for this purpose, but are considered less formal. "l"'s, "l" 's, and "l's" all look awkward.)

7 **You have no alternative. You *must* resign.**

Don't use italics for emphasis very often, because emphasis on large numbers of words results in almost no emphasis at all. In the sentence above, *must* has been italicized because _____

_____.

8 Summarize this exercise by filling in this list of uses of italics (underlining):

   A. titles of _____, _____, _____, and _____

   B. (what kind of?) _____ words

   C. letters referred to as _____, and words referred to as _____

   D. rarely, for purposes of _____

9 In writing or typing we use _____ as a substitute for italic type.

C: ASSIGNMENTS

• Write two examples of each of the eight uses of italics mentioned in exercise 8.

• Check a textbook or a good magazine to note its use of italics. Are italics used in the ways recommended in this unit? Do you find italics used at any time for any other purpose?

ANSWERS TO SECTION B

1. books, magazines
2. His book <u>Ragtime</u> was favorably reviewed in <u>Saturday Review.</u>
3. newspapers, operas (*or* long musical works)
4. MODEL   Foreign words used in English are customarily underlined (italicized).
5. No
6. underlined (italicized)
7. MODEL   the writer wanted to emphasize it
8. A. books, magazines, newspapers, operas   B. foreign   C. letters, words D. emphasis
9. underlining

Unit 53—Capitalization in Sentences and in Formal Parts of Letters

A: COMMENTARY

The principles of capitalization treated in this unit are as follows. Capitalize:
1. the first word of a sentence
2. the first word of a quoted complete sentence or a quoted group of words equivalent to a sentence but not a word or group of words taken out of sentence context
3. a direct question within a longer sentence (optional), but not an indirect question
4. a complete sentence within parentheses if it is not part of another sentence and, optionally, if the complete sentence is part of another sentence
5. as a rule, a complete sentence following a colon but not a partial sentence
6. lines of poetry, unless they are not capitalized in the original
7. in the salutation of a letter, the first word and the word that stands for the person being addressed
8. in a complimentary close, only the first word

B: EXERCISES

1 **The study of geology occupies much of her time.**

The preceding sentence illustrates what may be the first thing you ever learned about capitalization. What is this principle?

_____

2 **George remarked, "She goes on field trips every week."**

In this example a complete sentence is quoted as part of a longer sentence. Write a rule to cover the capitalization of *She* and other words at the start of a quoted sentence.

_____

_____

3 **"She picks up dozens of stones," he said, "and classifies them carefully."**

Explain why *and* is not capitalized. _____

_____

4 **He added that the intensity of her interest was "amazing." As an after-thought he said, "In fact, unbelievable!"**

In both sentences above, a fragment of a sentence is enclosed in quotation marks, yet only one is capitalized. In the first sentence the fragment has presumably been taken from a sentence. In the second the fragment is the equivalent of a complete sentence even though it lacks some of the usual parts. The quoted equivalent of a complete sentence (should/should not)

_____ begin with a capital letter.

5 **The question is: Can a better solution be found?**
The question is whether a better solution can be found.

The first sentence contains a direct question; the second, an indirect question. Note the differences in wording. Within a longer sentence, which may

be capitalized—a direct or an indirect question? _____

6 **His statement (See the enclosure) is concise.**
His statement (see the enclosure) is concise.
His statement (enclosed) is concise.
His statement is concise. (See the enclosure.)

The first two sentences show that when a *complete* sentence is enclosed in parentheses within another sentence, a capital letter is optional. The third sentence shows that when a *part* of a sentence is enclosed in parentheses,

(a capital letter/no capital letter) _____ is used. The fourth sentence shows that when a complete sentence in parentheses is not part of another sentence, (a capital letter/no capital letter) _____

_____ is required.

7 **This was what the patrolman reported: Two automobiles had sideswiped.**
This was what the patrolman reported: two wrecked automobiles.

The first sentence shows that when a complete sentence follows a colon, it

is customary to use _____ (although some editors prefer
a small letter). The second sentence shows that when only a part of a sen-

tence follows a colon, it is customary to use _____ .

8 **My heart leaps up when I behold**
A rainbow in the sky. —Wordsworth

This example shows that in writing or quoting poetry (finish the sentence)

_____

_____

9 **Dear Mr. Green:**   **Dear Sam,**
  Dear Madam: **Dear old Sam,**
  Gentlemen:

Write a rule that will cover the capitalization in these salutations of letters,
including the lack of a capital letter in *old*.

_____

_____

10 **Yours truly,**
  Yours sincerely,
  Very truly yours,

What rule of capitalization applies to complimentary closes of letters?

_____

_____

C: ASSIGNMENTS

• Write three original sentences to illustrate Rule 2 in Section A (one for
each part of the rule), two for Rule 3, two for 4, two for 5, one for 7, and one
for 8.

ANSWERS TO SECTION B

1. MODEL   The first word of a sentence is capitalized.
2. MODEL   Capitalize the first word of a quoted complete sentence.
3. MODEL   The words starting with *and* are not a complete sentence.
4. should
5. a direct question
6. no capital letter   a capital letter
7. a capital letter   a small letter
8. MODEL   it is customary to capitalize the first word of each line (unless, of course, the original author did not do so).
9. MODEL   In the salutation of a letter, capitalize only the first word and the word or words that indicate the receiver of the letter.
10. MODEL   In the complimentary close of a letter, capitalize only the first word.

Unit 54—Capitalization of School Subjects, Titles of Relatives, Other Titles

A: COMMENTARY

The principles of capitalization developed in this unit are these:

1. Names of school subjects are capitalized if they are proper nouns (such as *German*) or if they are accompanied by a letter or number to indicate a specific course (such as *Psychology 1A*).
2. Titles of relatives and military and other titles are capitalized if followed by the person's name, or if they serve as substitutes for a person's name (*Lieutenant Smedley; Will that be all, Lieutenant?*).

   Publishing houses are not completely uniform in their policies for capitalizing titles such as those discussed in this unit. Newspaper editors generally favor fewer capitals than do editors of magazines and books. The practices recommended here are those most commonly followed in magazine and book publishing.

B: EXERCISES

1 **Jeri is majoring in history and minoring in French.**

   The two school subjects mentioned in the example above are _____

   and _____.

2 *French,* like *English* and *Spanish,* is the name of a language. It is the name of a specific language. In traditional grammar it is called a *proper noun,* like *Gerald R. Ford* or *Taj Mahal.* On the basis of this clue explain why *French* is capitalized in exercise 1 and *history* is not. _____

3 It is possible, though, to make *history* part of a proper noun:

Jeri is taking History 128.

Now we are referring to a specific history course, a particular thing. So *History 128* or *History 5A* or the like is a proper noun. Write a sentence in which you make *chemical engineering* part of a proper noun. _____

4 Examples A, B, and C below illustrate the three basic principles involved in capitalizing titles of relatives. Example A shows that when signal words such as *my, his, your, the,* or *a* are used, a common noun is likely to follow and that in this case the title of the relative (is/is not) _____ capitalized.

A. **Sometimes my cousin annoys me.**
B. **Sometimes Cousin Egbert annoys me.**
C. **Sometimes you annoy me, Cousin.**

5 Sentence B in exercise 4 shows that when the name of the relative is used with the title, the combination is treated as a proper noun. Should *aunt* in *aunt Emma* and *uncle* in *uncle Benjamin* be capitalized? _____

6 A footnote to exercise 5: Editors normally prefer *my Cousin Egbert,* with *Cousin* capitalized despite the signal word *my.* But if *Egbert* were set off by commas, they usually would recommend *my cousin, Egbert.* Following these principles, you would write (*his aunt Ethelberta/his Aunt Ethelberta*) _____; (*his aunt, Ethelberta/his Aunt, Ethelberta*)

_____.

7 Sentence C in exercise 4 shows a second occasion for capitalizing the name of a relative. Note that the title *Cousin* is used as a substitute for a proper name: *Sometimes you annoy me, Egbert.*

A. **Then grandfather started up the stairs.**
B. **Don't go upstairs, grandfather.**

Should grandfather be capitalized in both A and B, in either A or B, or in neither? _____

8 Sometimes the captain annoys me.
Sometimes Captain Edgerton annoys me.
Sometimes you annoy me, Captain.

Compare the sentences above with those in exercise 4. Do the same principles of capitalization seem to apply to titles of relatives and to other titles,

such as military? _____

9 The principles illustrated in exercises 4 and 8 apply to titles other than
those of relatives and military personnel. For example, they apply to
political figures and professors. Underline the correct expression in each
group below.

A. The professor came *or* The Professor came
B. Yes, professor *or* Yes, Professor
C. Then Professor Roberts spoke *or* Then professor Roberts spoke

10 You would normally write *the president of the company* (small *p*). However, out of respect for the office, it is customary to write *the President of
the United States*. Also, within a given organization or company the employees are often asked to capitalize the titles of officers of that organization
or company, writing *the Grand Potentate of the Mystic Order*, for example,
or *the Governor has decided*. . . . So, if you are Miss Rogers, secretary to
Vice-President Smith, you probably will be expected to type *the* (*vice-*

president/Vice-President) _____ has decided. . . .

11 For exercises 11–13 write the letters representing groups of words that are
correctly capitalized.

A. a geology course	B. a Geology course	_____
A. geology 101	B. Geology 101	_____
A. studying greek	B. studying Greek	_____

12 | | | |
|---|---|---|
| A. my grandmother said | B. my Grandmother said | _____ |
| A. This way, dad. | B. This way, Dad. | _____ |
| A. uncle Horace | B. Uncle Horace | _____ |
| A. my uncle Horace | B. my Uncle Horace | _____ |
| A. my uncle, Horace | B. my Uncle, Horace | _____ |

13 | | | |
|---|---|---|
| A. the sergeant in front | B. the Sergeant in front | _____ |
| A. the treasurer of a firm | B. the Treasurer of a firm | _____ |
| A. I agree, major. | B. I agree, Major. | _____ |
| A. ensign Burch | B. Ensign Burch | _____ |

C: ASSIGNMENTS

• Make up two examples of your own similar to each of those in exercises 1, 4, and 8 (a total of fourteen sentences).

• What words in the following paragraphs should be capitalized?

Saturday mornings go like this. Grandad and grandma rise early. My sister, who is the student in our family, is up not much later to study her geography, german, or her hardest course, physics 39. Then mother and dad get up, unless dad, who is a colonel in the Pentagon, had late duty the previous night. I am the last to crawl out of bed.

The phone usually starts ringing about eight o'clock. Typically, aunt Clarissa calls at an ungodly hour to check on mother's plans for the day. Then dad gets a call. "Oh, is this general Botts? I'll check it at once, sir. Goodbye, general." Mother is president of the Science Club and the vice-president and the program chairman need some help. I get a call or two, usually from my cousin, Clarence, or my uncle Ray. Then my oldest sister's friends start ringing. "Oh, I met the nicest corporal last night. He's going to be an actor when he gets out—studied theater, you know." More of the same for hours, and my own calls don't get through. "Gosh sake, mom, dad, sis, let somebody else use the phone once in a while. I need to call professor Sikes about some work he wants me to do in chem lab." What were Saturday mornings like before the telephone was invented?

ANSWERS TO SECTION B

1. history, French
2. MODEL Proper nouns are capitalized. *French* is a proper noun, but *history* is not and is therefore not capitalized.
3. MODEL Chemical Engineering 203 is what I must take next year.
4. is not
5. Yes
6. his Aunt Ethelberta   his aunt, Ethelberta
7. both A and B
8. Yes
9. A. The professor came   B. Yes, Professor   C. Then Professor Roberts spoke
10. Vice-President
11. A B B
12. A B B B A
13. A A B B

Unit 55—Capitalization of Proper Names and Miscellaneous Items

A: COMMENTARY

A basic principle of capitalization is that names of general classes of things are not capitalized but that names of particular, individual things are. Thus *woman* is not capitalized but *Sylvia Plath* is.

Some differences exist in the interpretation of this basic principle. Each large publishing house has its own style manual that establishes a house policy in controversial matters, such as *Red River* versus *Red river*. Newspapers tend to use fewer capitals than do magazines and books; specifically, newspapers tend to capitalize only the identifying word in names such as *Red river*, *Grand avenue*, or *Roosevelt university*.

Other principles covered in this Unit are the following:

1. In literary titles the first word and all other important words are capitalized. Prepositions and conjunctions are unlikely to be capitalized unless they come first or are more than four letters long; *the*, *a*, and *an* are capitalized only if they come first.
2. Names of sacred writings and of the Deity and his Son are capitalized. Pronouns that refer to God, such as *He* and *Him*, are capitalized less often than they once were.
3. Names of seasons are generally capitalized only if personified. (*Personification* is treating an abstract thing as if it were human: *Old Man Winter*.)
4. Names of directions are generally capitalized only when they refer to sections of the country.
5. Nouns that are strongly personified are capitalized: *the messenger of Death himself*. Modern writers only occasionally personify. If the personification is mild, as in *then death brought him peace*, no capital letter is used.
6. Nicknames that substitute for proper names are capitalized.
7. Both parts of a hyphenated word such as *Star-Telegram* are capitalized, but a word such as *Forty-second* (in *Forty-second Street*) requires only one capital.
8. Style manuals are inconsistent in treatment of terms such as *plaster of Paris* (or *paris*) and *Bessemer steel* (or *bessemer*). A good rule to follow is to use a small letter if the term is no longer associated with the place or person. Thousands of English words (*volt*, *dahlia*, *hector*) are based on proper names but are no longer capitalized.
9. In each point in an outline the first word is customarily capitalized.

B: EXERCISES

1 **The day was Saturday, and the month was June.**

Day and *month* are general words, but *Saturday* names a particular day and *June* names a particular month. The principle involved in these simple examples is a basic one in capitalization. Words that name (What kind of?) _____ things are not capitalized, but those that name _____ things are capitalized.

2 **a street**   **Vine Street**
a river   **Missouri River**
some mountains   **Rocky Mountains**

Do the examples above illustrate the principle established in exercise 1?

_____ The capitals in the column at the right represent the formal practice of most book and magazine publishers; most newspapers would not capitalize Street, River, Mountain, and other similar parts of compound proper names. A book editor would be likely to prefer (*Baltic sea/Baltic Sea*) _____.

3 **a holiday**   **Thanksgiving Day**
a period in history   **the Middle Ages**

A newspaper reporter would probably write *Thanksgiving day,* but would capitalize both words in *Middle Ages.* The examples above (illustrate/do not illustrate) _____ the same principles as in exercises 1 and 2.

4 Write the names of a college, a high school, a company, and a building. Capitalize in formal style.

_____   _____

_____   _____

5 Write the names of an organization, a lake, a commercial product (that is, a brand name), and a variety of airplane. Capitalize in formal style.

_____   _____

_____   _____

6 *Native Son*
Murder in the Cathedral
The Education of Henry Adams
A Man for All Seasons
The Land That Time Forgot

Using the literary titles above as a basis, construct a rule for capitalization of such titles. Your rule should not neglect at least indirect reference to words like *a* and *the*.

_____

_____

7 **We read Genesis in the Old Testament and the Fatiha in the Koran to compare their views of God.**

The example above shows that names of sacred writings and of the Deity

(finish the sentence) _____.

8 **The spring and summer were both unusually hot.**
Songs, Spring thought perfection,
Summer criticizes.   —Browning

In the first example the names of seasons are referred to merely as names of seasons. In the second example they are personified—given human qualities; that is, Spring is able to think and Summer is able to criticize. On the basis of these examples, write a rule about capitalizing names of seasons.

_____

_____

9 **Go west one mile.**
She lives in the West.

The examples above show that names of directions are capitalized only when

_____.

10 **Hushed in the alabaster arms of Death**
Our young Marcellus sleeps.   —J. R. Randall

Ordinarily words like *death, love, mercy* would not be capitalized. Why is

Death capitalized in the example? _____

11 **Paul (Big Poison) Waner was the older of two famous Pittsburgh out-fielders who were brothers. Lloyd was Little Poison.**

What does the example show about capitalization of nicknames of proper

names? _____

12 **I bought a *Courier-Journal* on Thirty-third Street.**

Comment on the capitalization in the two hyphenated words; try to state

the principle. _____

_____

13 **lives in Morocco**
bound in morocco leather

Many words that were once proper names have lost their original association. Thus morocco leather now usually does not come from Morocco, nor
is paris green (an insecticide) associated with Paris or china dishes with

China. The modern tendency is to use (capital/small) _____
letters in such derivatives.

14 **I. Ancient instruments for telling time**
    A. Clepsydras
    B. Hour-glasses

The first word in a topic listed in an outline, this example shows, is ordi-

narily (capitalized/not capitalized) _____.

15 **Write *T* or *F* (for *True* or *False*) after each statement.**

  A. As a rule, names of general classes of things are capitalized. _____

  B. *Basin Street* illustrates formal style in capitalization. _____
  C. Book editors prefer *Dark Ages* (the name of a period in history), but

    newspaper reporters prefer *Dark ages.* _____
  D. The title *The Importance Of Being Earnest* is correctly capitalized.

    _____

  E. It is correct to write *the God of the Bible* and *pagan gods.* _____

  F. *Winter* should always be capitalized. _____
  G. The Yankee outfielder was known as *Joltin' Joe Dimaggio.* This capi-

    talization is correct. _____
  H. It is customary to capitalize the first word in each point in an out-

    line. _____

C: ASSIGNMENTS

• Decide whether each italicized letter should or should not be capitalized,
and give your reason. Assume a formal context.

1. On the third *s*unday in the *f*all, the freshmen at *c*entral *c*ollege gathered and
walked *e*ast along *p*enn *s*treet.
2. Kelly celebrated *n*ew *y*ear's *e*ve by reading. He became engrossed in a story
called "*t*ravels *w*ith *a m*onkey."
3. "This *d*ocument is our *m*agna *c*harta," said the leader of the *u*nion. "The
*c*lovis *c*orporation will never again be able to browbeat its workers."

4. We can only pray to god and to our savior that the blindfold will be ripped from the eyes of justice.
5. "The type face named gothic has no serifs," explained Bill Thorne, whose nickname was printer's ink.

• Examine a page of a daily newspaper and one nonfiction article in a magazine of good quality. Make notes on differences and similarities in their capitalization.

ANSWERS TO SECTION B

1. general, particular
2. Yes   Baltic Sea
3. illustrate
4. MODEL   Monmouth College   Shelby High School   the Magnavox Corporation   the Prudential Building
5. MODELS   the Kiwanis Club   Lake Superior   Rice Krispies   Douglas DC-3
6. MODEL   In literary titles capitalize the first word, the last word, and all other important words.
7. are capitalized
8. MODEL   Capitalize names of seasons only if the seasons are personified.
9. MODEL   they refer to parts of the country
10. It is personified.
11. MODEL   Nicknames of proper names are capitalized.
12. MODEL   Compound proper names and compound proper adjectives are capitalized.
13. small
14. capitalized
15. A. F   B. T   C. F   D. F   E. T   F. F   G. T   H. T

Unit 56—Using Numbers

A: COMMENTARY

Many newspapers have a rule that figures rather than words should be used for any number above nine or ten or twelve or some other arbitrarily chosen number. Book and magazine publishers, though, generally use figures only for any number that would require more than two words to express. Thus they would prefer *one million* but *1,300,000; twenty-six* but *126.*

As Section B points out, both newspaper and other publishers uniformly use figures for numbers representing pages, chapters, addresses, measurements, telephones, rooms, dates, percentages, scores, and Social Security numbers. This is true even when the number could be expressed in one or two words.

In street names that are ordinal numbers *Sixth* or any other one-word number is customarily spelled out, but compound numbers take any of three forms: *Twenty-first, 21st,* or *21,* with the version in words being most common. However, if the number is large, such as *132nd* or *132 Street,* spelling out is too cumbersome. (Be sure to space carefully: *21132nd Street* could be either 21 132nd Street or 211 32nd Street.)

It is considered stylistically poor to start a sentence with a figure or to mix figures and words (representing numbers) in the same sentence. Ideally, they should not be mixed in the same paragraph, but if greater awkwardness would result, some mixing is permissible to prevent it.

In plays, parts are generally designated like this: *Act I, Scene i, lines 1–3,* which may be shortened to *I, i, 1–3* or *I.i.1–3.*

In designations of time, words are used with *o'clock,* but figures are more usual with A.M. and P.M.

Most large numbers are marked off by commas, which separate groups of three digits, starting the count from the right. Exceptions are Social Security and other serial numbers, telephone numbers, years, and address numbers.

A number, unlike a word, should not be divided at the end of a line. The reason is illustrated by the difficulty of reading 1,363,- on one line and 467 on the next.

B: EXERCISES

1 **ten helmets**
   one hundred helmets
   116 helmets

   Should figures or words be used to indicate numbers? The answer given by most publishers of books and magazines is illustrated above. If the number

   can be stated in no more than (How many?) _____ words, the words are preferred.

2 **page 24   Chapter 6 (or VI)   813 Main Street   a 1 by 10″ board**
   telephone 898-1472   Room 121   April 1, 1922   5 percent
   a 32–28 victory   320-19-6241 (Social Security number)

   Some of the items above represent possible exceptions to the principle described in exercise 1. On the basis of these examples you would conclude that

   figures are used for numbers that indicate what ten kinds of things? _____

   _____ _____ _____ _____ _____ _____

   _____ _____ _____

3 419 East Tenth Street   620 Thirty-ninth Street
                          or 620 39 Street
                          or 620 39th Street

A one-word street name (such as *Tenth*) is ordinarily spelled out. When a compound number is used as the street name, though, three possibilities exist. Look at the examples, and name the possibilities.

_____   _____

_____

4 *Poor:* 263 hogs were inoculated.
  Better: The veterinarian inoculated 263 hogs.

In the "better" sentence the writer has avoided beginning a sentence with a

_____.

5 Besides the 263 hogs, he treated 37 cattle and 10 sheep.

Normally, as exercise 1 indicated, 37 and 10 would be spelled out. Then why, in your opinion, is it considered desirable to use figures in the sentence above?

_____

_____

6 Turn to Act III, Scene iii, lines 14–21.

The most usual manner of designating passages in a play is illustrated above. Tell what that manner is.

_____

_____

7 four o'clock   4:20 P.M.

With *o'clock* it is customary to use (words/figures) _____.

With A.M. or P.M. it is customary to use (words/figures) _____.

8 2,867   42,448   4,874,216

Explain the principle governing placement of the commas in the numbers

above. _____

9 Social Security No. 372-84-1495   telephone 847-9621
  the year 1977   1429 North Clancy Street

The items above are (illustrations of/exceptions to) _____
the principle you wrote for exercise 8.

C: ASSIGNMENTS

• All numbers below are stated in figures. If you were the editor of a book or
magazine, which ones would you change to words? What other changes would
you make in some?

8 o'clock	3333333	Act 2
9" by 3'	3,914 8th Street	Scene 3
a score of 10 to 9	2:42 P.M.	line 14
telephone No. 3,386,249	$500	416 pairs
9 pairs	500 pens	Room 7
1000000	1000001	Chapter 14
26 students are in this class.		377 cars and 10 trucks

ANSWERS TO SECTION B

1. two
2. pages, chapters, street addresses, dimensions, telephones, rooms, dates, percentages, scores (in athletics or other competition), Social Security numbers
3. MODELS Write it out as an ordinal number (like *Thirty-ninth*). Use a cardinal number (like 39). Use an ordinal numeral (like 39*th*).
4. figure
5. MODEL It is preferable to avoid mixing, in the same sentence or paragraph, numerals and words representing numerals.
6. MODEL Use capitalized Roman numerals for the acts, small Roman numerals for the scenes, and Arabic numerals for the lines.
7. words   figures
8. MODEL In writing large numbers, ordinarily set them off with commas in groups of three, starting at the right.
9. exceptions to

PART FIVE

USAGE

"Me and him done real good."

"He and I did very well."

Since the two sentences above are equally clear, does it really matter which sentence you write or say? A great many people believe that it does matter. They realize that success in professional and personal life comes a little more easily for those who do not offend by using what many believe to be sloppy language. And they know that although what they say is undeniably of great importance, how they say it influences the way other people react.

Most units in this section concern the few pronouns, like *he* versus *him*, and the few verbs, like *did* versus *done* or *was* versus *were*, that many people use as indicators of good or bad usage. Other units treat adjectives, adverbs, intensifiers, and abbreviations.

Unit 57—Personal Pronouns as Subjects and Objects

A: COMMENTARY

Some pronouns may be used almost anywhere in a sentence that a noun may be used. Some of these pronouns are *this, that, these, those, anyone, anybody, everything, anything, all, one, mine, yours, his, hers, theirs, its, ours, you,* and *it.*

> EXAMPLES: **Everything** is lost. (subject)
> **We lost** *everything.* (direct object)
> **He gives** *everything* **else the blame.** (indirect object)
> **That is** *everything.* (subjective complement; also called predicate nominative)
> **Save us from** *everything* **hostile.** (object of preposition)

Other pronouns, however, are less versatile. The pronoun *he,* for instance, may be used as a subject or as a subjective complement but not as an object. We can say *He saw the sunrise* or *It was he* but not *Mack saw he in the park.*

Pronouns of this type can be divided into two groups, which in traditional grammar are said to be in the nominative and objective cases. (Some newer grammars say merely that the pronouns fit into different slots in a sentence.)

Nominative Case	*Objective Case*
I, he, she, we, they	**me, him, her, us, them**

Pronouns in the nominative case are most frequently used (in standard English) in one of these positions:

1. Subject: *He* is here.
2. Subjective complement (after *be, being, been, am, is, are, was, were*): It is *she* (or *he, I, they, we*). (Informal: It is *her, him, me, them, us.*)

Pronouns in the objective case are most frequently used (in standard English) in one of these positions:

1. Direct object: The jury acquitted *him.*
2. Indirect object: We gave *her* the keys.
3. Object of a preposition: The policeman stepped between *them.*

Probably none of the example sentences would give you trouble. You would never say, for instance, *Him is here,* or *The jury acquitted he.* However, a personal pronoun sometimes causes trouble when used with another pronoun or a noun. So you may occasionally have a problem choosing the standard pronoun in sentences such as these:

The jury acquitted Ralph and (*he, him*).

The policeman stepped between Sandra and (*she, her*).

Remember this rule: *Use the same pronoun in the compound element that you would use alone.*

EXAMPLE: **This package is for her and (*I, me*).**

Here you should cross out *her and* and read the sentence again. You would not say *This package is for I.* You would say *This package is for me.* So you should say *This package is for her and me.*

B: EXERCISES

1 *She* **waited in the lobby for Jim.**
Does the italicized personal pronoun in the sentence above sound right?

―――――

2 *Her* **waited in the lobby for Jim.**

Does the italicized personal pronoun in the sentence above sound right?

―――――

3 Judging from exercises 1 and 2, you should say:

Gordon and (she, her) ――――――― **waited in the lobby for Jim.**

4 ――――― **wanted student representation on the committee.**

Which five of the following pronouns sound right in the blank?

I, me, he, him, she, her, we, us, they, them ―― ―― ―― ―― ――

5 The pronouns that you listed in exercise 4 may be used as subjects. Do any of the five (*I, he, she, we, they*) fit in the blank in the following sentence? ―――――

The pantomime amused ―――――**.**

6 Copy from exercise 4 the five pronouns that could be used as the objects in the example in exercise 5. ―― ―― ―― ―― ――

7 Could the pronouns *you* and *it* fit in the blanks in both exercises 4 and 5?

―――――

8 On the basis of exercises 4–7, complete the following sentences:

A. **These five personal pronouns may be used as subjects:** ―― ――

―― ―― ――

B. These five personal pronouns may be used as objects: _____ _____ _____

_____ _____

C. These two personal pronouns may be used as either subjects or objects:

_____ _____

9 This sentence is correct:

He rowed the boat over to the island.

Suppose we revise the subject to include another rower, like this:

Marge and he rowed the boat over to the island.

How do you know that *he*, rather than *him*, is correct?

_____

_____

10 If a pronoun were substituted for *Marge* in exercise 9, should it be *she* or

her? _____

11 The instructor excused Janet from the test.
The instructor excused him from the test.

Combine the two sentences above, showing that two persons were excused.

_____

Why did you use *him* rather than *he*? _____

_____

12 This sentence contains a compound subject:

Marge and he rowed the boat over to the island.

This sentence contains a compound object:

The instructor excused *Janet and him* from the test.

Does the presence of the extra part of the subject or object (*Marge* and

Janet) affect the choice of pronoun? _____

13 In other words, in a compound subject or a compound object we use (the

same pronoun as/a different pronoun from) _____
the one we would use if the subject or object were simple. The presence of

the extra part of the subject or object makes (a/no) _____ difference.

14 The package is for my brother.
The package is for me.

Combine the two sentences above, showing that the package is for two persons.

_____

_____

15 The word *for* in your sentence for exercise 14 is a preposition. The words *my brother and me* form a compound object of a preposition. As is true of other compound objects, the presence of another noun or pronoun makes

(a/no) _____ difference in the choice of pronoun.

16 If you do not know whether to use a subject pronoun or an object pronoun in an object construction, try using the pronoun by itself, without the rest of the compound construction. For instance, suppose that you wonder whether the pronoun *her* is correct in this sentence:

To Geraldine and *her*, fat people are always a subject of ridicule.

Rewrite the sentence, omitting *Geraldine and*.

_____

_____

17 Does the sentence you wrote for exercise 16 appear correct? _____ Then is the original sentence correct? _____

18 Using the same system, decide whether the italicized parts of the following sentences are correct. Rephrase any pronouns that are wrong.

A. *Ralph and him* were stopped by a policeman.

_____

B. After the duet there was scattered applause for *Tillie and her*.

_____

C. The coach praised *Bob and I* for footwork.

_____

19 Choose the correct pronouns in these sentences.

A. (They/Them) _____ and (we/us) _____ studied in the library.

B. The students selected (she/her) _____ and (he/him) _____.

C. Al wrote a story about Emil and (they/them) _____.

20 Write sentences as follows:

A. A party was given for a man and a woman. Use pronouns instead of the

two names. _____

_____

B. You and someone else attended a convention. (As a matter of courtesy, refer to the other person first.) Use pronouns instead of names.

_____

_____

C. Mr. Sams and a group of other people (represented by a plural personal pronoun) were given smallpox vaccinations.

_____

_____

C: ASSIGNMENTS

• Rewrite each sentence according to directions. Many revisions will involve a change in one or more of the pronouns. Do not change pronouns to nouns.

EXAMPLE: The game was won in the last inning by Ron and me. (Make *the game* the object.) *Ron and I won the game in the last inning.*

1. The room was straightened up by my wife and me. (Start with *My wife and.*)
2. She likes you and him. (Change so that the boy likes the girl.)
3. The contest was between Jane and Kenneth. (Change *Jane* and *Kenneth* to pronouns.)
4. Arthur will be helped by Ted and Jeanne. (Make *Ted* and *Jeanne* the subject, and substitute a pronoun for each.)
5. Sally and I beat Hilda and him. (Make Hilda and her partner the winners.)
6. Sally and I beat Hilda and him at tennis. (Make Hilda and her partner the subject. Use *were beaten* as the verb.)
7. Gordon and Jane are in love. (Substitute a pronoun for *Jane.*)
8. Mark and I gave our address to them. (Change the sentence so that *they* did the giving.)
9. Vera and they escorted the war heroes. (Make *the war heroes* the subject.)
10. Dad, Louise, and I started across the room toward Barnard and him. (Let Barnard and his companion do the walking.)

• Construct sentences as follows:

1. Use two personal pronouns as the compound subject of a sentence.
2. Tell by whom something was done. The object of *by* should be compound and should contain at least one personal pronoun.
3. Use two personal pronouns as the compound object of the verb *shoved.*

Note: If you cannot automatically choose the standard pronouns in compound subjects and objects, you need more practice. Make up several sentences like those in this exercise, and practice saying them over and over, both silently and aloud, until they sound natural to you.

ANSWERS TO SECTION B

1. Yes
2. No
3. she
4. I, he, she, we, they
5. No
6. me, him, her, us, them
7. Yes
8. A. I, he, she, we, they   B. me, him, her, us, them   C. you, it
9. MODEL   *He* is the pronoun that would be used if *Marge* were not in the sentence.
10. she
11. The instructor excused Janet and him from the test.   MODEL   *Him* would be used here if there were no other object.
12. No
13. the same pronoun as   no
14. The package is for my brother and me.
15. no
16. To her, fat people are always a subject of ridicule.
17. Yes   Yes
18. A. Ralph and he were stopped by a policeman.
    B. Correct
    C. The coach praised Bob and me for footwork.
19. A. They, we   B. her, him   C. them
20. MODELS   A. A party was given for him and her. (Object pronouns must be used.)
             B. She and I attended a convention. (Subject pronouns must be used.)
             C. Mr. Sams and they were given smallpox vaccinations. (*They* must be used.)

Unit 58—Pronoun Case: In Predicate Nominatives, in Appositives, and Before Gerunds

A: COMMENTARY

This unit covers three problems in case. The first is that of the pronoun in a sentence like this:

This is he (she, we, they).

Within a few decades *him* (*her, us, them*) may completely replace *he* (*she, we, they*) in such sentences. At present, however, especially in your formal writing and speaking, you are less likely to be criticized if you use the forms *he, she, we, they.*

The second item considered is the case of pronouns in appositive (literally "placed beside") constructions. In all carefully edited work a pronoun in apposition is in the same case as the word with which it is in apposition. Thus we say:

Subject *Appositive*
Our family, Mother and Dad and I, often argue about politics.

Because *family* is used as the subject, its appositive must consist of a word or words that can be used as subjects. In contrast, consider:

Obj. Prep. *Appositive*
The present was for the whole family, Mother and Dad and me.

Here *family* is an object, and the words that are in apposition must also be the kind that can be used as objects.

A special kind of appositive is the construction like *we students* or *us students*. If you do not know whether to say *we* or *us* in a particular sentence, use the form you would use if the word *students* were not present: *We* (*students*) *have our rights. Congressional actions affect us* (*students*).

The case of a noun or pronoun before an *-ing* word depends on meaning. Two sentences from Section B may help to clarify the basic point:

    A. **I like the nurse caring for me.**
    B. **I like the nurse's caring for me.**

In A, I like the nurse who is caring for me. In B, I may not like the nurse at all, but I do like her taking care of me. (Grammatically, it may be noted, the sentences are different. In A the direct object is *nurse*; in B it is *caring*.)

The pronouns *that* and *this* have no possessive, so of course we say *I had not thought of that* (not *that's*) *occurring.*

269

Because of awkwardness the possessive is not used in a sentence such as *Imagine the president of the university upholding such a measure.* Contrast that sentence with *Imagine his upholding such a measure,* where the possessive is probable in formal context.

B: EXERCISES

       S   be   PN
1 **The victor was Hans Lieder.**
       S   be PN
  The victor was he.

In the sentences above, note the pattern S-*be*-PN. The predicate nominative names the subject in a different way; it is in a sense equivalent to the subject. The verb is a form of *be: am, is, are, was, were, may be, could be, must have been,* and so on. In the second sentence of the example the predicate nominative is (the same pronoun as/a different pronoun from)

_____ the one that would be used as a subject.

2 **Yes, this is she.**
  It was they who wrote the script.
  Is it we who will be accused?
  It may have been he who found the stylus.

The four pronouns used here as predicate nominatives are _____, _____, _____, and _____. Could each of these pronouns also be used as the subject of a sentence? _____

3 In summary, in a sentence following the **S-*be*-PN** pattern, a pronoun used as the **PN** is the same as _____

_____.

4 **Both quarterbacks, Tom and he, were injured.**

The subject of the sentence above is *quarterbacks. Tom and he* is an appositive; it is placed beside the subject and renames the subject. The pronoun *he* is used because it does rename the subject and could be a subject. Should *she* or *her* be used in the blank below?

The two sisters, Helen and _____, became singers.

5 **Injuries hampered both quarterbacks, Tom and him.**

In the sentence above, *quarterbacks* is no longer the subject. Instead, it is an object. Anything in apposition to *quarterbacks* must therefore be a word that can be used as an object. For that reason *him* is correct. Should *she* or *her* be used in the blank below?

We applauded the two sisters, Helen and _____.

6 **Both of us, John and me, were relieved.**

This sentence is tricky. *John and me* is in apposition to *us*. *Us* is the object of a preposition. *Me* is used in the appositive here instead of *I* because

_____

7 **(We, Us) girls wanted to take a cab.**

Students sometimes do not know whether to say *we girls* or *us girls*, *we students* or *us students*. The solution is simple. In the example above, if *girls* were not included, would you say **We** or **Us?** _____

8 **A cab stopped for (we, us) girls.**

In the sentence above, if *girls* were not included, would you say *we* or *us*?

_____

9 On the basis of exercises 7 and 8, finish this sentence:

If I am uncertain about whether to say *we students* or *us students*, I should use _____

_____

10 Explain the difference in meaning in these two sentences:

A. **I like the nurse caring for me.**
B. **I like the nurse's caring for me.**

_____

_____

11 In sentences A and B below is it Fred or his playing that is too loud?

_____

In sentences C and D do I enjoy him or the playing? _____

A. **Fred's playing was unnecessarily loud.**
B. **His playing was unnecessarily loud.**
C. **I enjoy his playing the trumpet.**
D. **I enjoy hearing his playing.**

12 **I saw Fred playing a trumpet.**
I saw him playing a trumpet.

In the two sentences above, are we trying to say that we saw the playing or

that we saw Fred (him)? _____

13 In exercises 10–12 we have seen that before an *-ing* word we sometimes in formal context use a possessive like *nurse's*, *Fred's*, or *his*, and sometimes we do not. We use the possessive unless we are referring directly to the nurse, Fred, him, and so on. That is, we use the possessive if it is the caring, the playing, and so on, that we are talking about. So we say:

A. **I had not thought of (his/him)** _____ **accepting a bribe.**

B. **We noticed (their/them)** _____ **lying beside the road.**

C. **Imagine (their/them)** _____ **being able to sleep through all that noise!**

D. **Picture (their/them)** _____ **living in luxury and wearing diamond-studded belts.**

14 Assuming a formal context, choose the preferable word for each blank.

A. **It was (they/them)** _____ **who reacted first.**

B. **Could this indeed be (he/him)** _____?

C. **The referees, Earl and (I/me)** _____, **were booed constantly.**

D. **The crowd constantly booed the referees, Earl and (I/me)** _____.

E. **(We/Us)** _____ **children were sent to bed.**

F. **Our parents sent (we/us)** _____ **children to bed.**

G. **(Him/His)** _____ **departing so suddenly was a tactical error.**

C: COMMENTARY

• Make notes over a day or so on each pronoun that you hear or read in sentences of the *This is he* (or *him*) type. Include the other possible pronouns (*I, me, she, her, we, us, they, them*). Do you observe differences between usage in printed and in spoken material? Does the formality of the situation or the prestige of the speaker or writer make any difference?

• Write five sentences in each of which a pronoun is used in an appositive construction with a noun also in apposition. (Review exercises 4 and 5 if necessary.)

• Write sentences with these words: *we parents, us children, we farmers, us secretaries, we mechanics.*

• Write a sentence requiring a pronoun or a noun before each of these *-ing* words (five sentences in all): *working, crying, shouting, flying, arguing.*

ANSWERS TO SECTION B

1. the same pronoun as
2. she, they, we, he   Yes
3. one used as a subject
4. she
5. her
6. MODEL   it means the same thing as an object
7. We
8. us
9. MODEL   the form I would use if *students* were not there
10. MODEL   In A I like the nurse. In B I like the way she cares for me.
11. his playing   the playing
12. Fred (him)
13. A. his   B. them   C. their   D. them
14. A. they   B. he   C. I   D. me   E. We   F. us   G. His

Unit 59—Reference of Pronouns

A: COMMENTARY

The pronouns *he, she, it, him, her, they, them, that, this,* and *which* are among the most useful words in the English language. We often use one of them so that we will not have to keep repeating *Helen, General Washington, the tennis champions, the defeat of the invaders,* or some other word or group of words. A pronoun gives us a short way of saying the same thing.

But if our listener or reader does not know what a certain pronoun stands for, we fail to communicate. For example:

Hugh told Ralph that he had done something foolish.

Who is *he?* The reader can't be sure whether Hugh or Ralph performed the foolish act. In other words, the reference of the pronoun *he* is not clear.

This, that, and *which* are especially tricky. Sometimes, especially in informal or semiformal communication, *this, that,* or *which* can refer to a whole idea rather than to a specific person or thing:

Our team was ten points behind, but this did not discourage our coach.

It is necessary to be sure, though, that the meaning of *this*, *that*, or *which* is not misleading. The word *which* proved confusing when one student wrote:

In these factories workers make shoes, which cover several hundred thousand square feet.

B: EXERCISES

1 A. **Tom told his brother that he might be falling in love.**
  B. **When you have taken the old coat from the box, throw it into the alley.**

  Are you positive that you know what *he* means in A? _____

  Are you positive that you know what *it* means in B? _____

2 Let's rewrite the sentences in exercise 1 to make the meanings clear.

  A. **Tom said to his brother, "**_____

  _____**.**"

  B. **When you have taken the old coat from the box, throw** _____

  _____.

3 Not all pronouns cause problems of reference. The following ones often do: *he, she, it, him, her, they, them, that, this,* and *which* (as well as possessive forms like *his* or *theirs*). A good rule to follow, each time you use one of these words, is to make sure that your reader or listener cannot

  possibly _____

  _____.

4 A. **I bought an ancient car, which proved within a few days to be completely dependable.**
  B. **I bought an ancient car, which proved within a few days to have been a mistake.**

  Since *which* is close to *car*, we assume that it refers to *car*. In (A or B?)

  _____, however, *which* does not really refer to *car*.

5 In exercise 4, A is clear because the writer is referring to a car that proved dependable. In B, though, the car did not prove to be a mistake. What was

  it that proved to be a mistake? _____

6 Rewrite 4B in order to make the meaning perfectly clear. (Hint: You may want to start with *Buying*.)

_____

_____

7 I enjoyed *Crime and Punishment*. He provides remarkable insights into the human mind.

After you read the sentence above, you have to pause for a moment to figure out who *He* is. Who do you suppose is meant by *He*? _____

_____

8 Dostoyevsky's *Crime and Punishment* is psychologically penetrating, yet he wrote it before the days of much psychological research.
In conversation no one would object to the sentence above. In formal writing, however, careful writers avoid having a pronoun refer to a possessive (*Dostoyevsky's* in our sentence). They might write the sentence like this:

_____

_____

(Hint: If you are stuck, try starting with the title.)

9 The word *astronomy* has always fascinated me. I expect to make a career in it.

Does the writer mean that he expects to make a career in a word? _____
Rewrite the sentence so that the reference of *it* is clear.

_____

_____

10 They say that the forest fire may endanger our village.

In conversation all of us sometimes use *they* when we don't want to bother to identify precisely, or when we do not know exactly who "they" are. But careful writers generally avoid an indefinite *they*. Rewrite the sentence above, substituting something definite for *they*.

_____

_____

11 The instructors try to be fair to the students, but they sometimes complain that they grade too harshly.

After careful reading you decide that the first *they* refers to _____ and the second *they* to _____. You might revise the sentence like this, omitting both *they*'s:

_____

_____

12 The point of this exercise is that when you use pronouns, (finish the sentence) _____

_____

_____.

C: ASSIGNMENTS

• In formal writing, how might each of the following sentences be revised to correct faulty pronoun reference? (Often there is more than one possible meaning, and two or more revisions may be possible.)

1. Mrs. Brett was angry with Mrs. Clark at first, but she finally apologized for her behavior.
2. They say that an influenza epidemic is probable this year.
3. A Democrat won the Senate seat and a Republican won the governorship, which surprised the experts.
4. Andrews and Kosnikoff played two chess games to a stalemate, but he won the third one.
5. I like *For Whom the Bell Tolls*; he certainly holds your interest.
6. The instructor told Roger that he could no longer be with the class.
7. A mangy dog came over into our yard and dug up our sweet peas, which I did not like at all.
8. The Kneirs and the Farrs quarreled. They said that they had planted bushes on what was really their land.
9. Mr. Craig decided in favor of the station wagon. This, as it turned out later after he had used it to haul many large loads, was wise.
10. Before feeding the dog, Charlie put on his pointed hat and made him do a few tricks.
11. Students enjoyed finding examples of unclear thinking, which the teacher encouraged.

ANSWERS TO SECTION B

1. Both answers are no.
2. A. MODEL You (*or* I) may be falling in love   B. MODEL   the box (*or* the coat) into the alley

3. MODEL   misunderstand
4. B
5. MODEL   buying an ancient car
6. Buying an ancient car proved within a few days to have been a mistake.
7. the author (*or Dostoyevsky*)
8. MODEL   *Crime and Punishment* is psychologically penetrating, yet Dostoyevsky wrote it before the days of much psychological research.
9. No   MODEL   . . . I expect to make a career in astronomy.
10. MODEL   The rangers say that the forest fire may endanger our village.
11. students, instructors
    MODEL   The instructors try to be fair, although students complain about too harsh grading.
12. MODEL   you should be positive that your reader or listener will understand the meaning of each pronoun

Unit 60—Consistency in Pronouns

A: COMMENTARY

This unit concerns consistency in person and number of pronouns. Personal pronouns are frequently classified in this way:

FIRST PERSON: **I, me, my, mine, we, us, our, ours**
SECOND PERSON: **you, your, yours**
THIRD PERSON: **he, him, she, her, it, his, hers, its, they, them, their, theirs**

Also treated as third person are indefinite pronouns, such as *anyone, one,* or *each,* and all nouns, such as *Thomas, a dog, a person.*
    This unit illustrates these principles:

1. Unnecessary shifts from one person to another should be avoided. Not *When you get a leg cramp, a person should* . . . but *When you get a leg cramp, you should.* . . . If two different people are being considered, then of course a shift is justified: *I suggested, and you agreed.*
2. *One* and *one's* may be shifted to *he* and *his* and *she* and *her.* (The British, however, ordinarily avoid this shift.)
3. Unnecessary shifts of pronoun number should be avoided—that is, shifts between singular and plural. For example, *he* or *his* should not shift without reason to *they* or *their.*
4. To avoid sexism, one should show discretion in using masculine pronouns to refer to both males and females.

    Something special needs to be said about the fourth point. In recent years many people have come to realize that masculine pronouns are too often used when both sexes are meant. The language needs a pronoun that means "either he or she." (Many alternatives have been suggested, for example, *heshe, himer,* and *hiser* to mean "he or she," "him or her," and "his or her," but none of the suggestions have received universal acclaim.) We tend to say *The typical worker looks forward to his week-ends for relaxation,* ignoring the huge number of typical workers who are female. Often we can find a way to avoid the apparent bias:

> **Typical workers look forward to their week-ends as times for relaxation.**
> **The typical worker looks forward to week-ends as times for relaxation.**
> **The typical worker looks forward to his or her week-ends as times for relaxation. (Perhaps slightly awkward)**

This problem of bias occurs most often when a singular indefinite pronoun occurs earlier in the sentence: *anybody, anyone, each, everybody, everyone, nobody, no one, somebody, someone.* You can clearly see that these words are singular, because you say, for example, "Everybody is here," not "Everybody are here." So a following pronoun that means the same thing should also be singular: *If anybody wants a ticket, he should call me* (not . . . *they should call me*). But *he* seems biased, even though the writer intends no discrimination. *He or she should call me* is possible, and so is *She or he should call me.* Rewording is also possible: *Anyone who wants a ticket should call me.* But occasionally, especially when *he or she* or *she or he* would have to be repeated two or three times in a short space, just the one word *he* (or just the one word *she*) may need to be used to prevent awkwardness.

Either and *neither* are almost always singular. (For an exception, see Unit 66.) Therefore *he* and *his* (or *she* and *her*) rather than *they* and *their* are standard formal English to refer to these words.

B: EXERCISES

1 POOR: **If a person has an opportunity to travel, you must take it, or they will always be sorry.**

Pronouns in the sentence above shift in every clause. The sentence begins with *a person,* then switches without any reason to the pronoun *you,* and suddenly changes over to (what pronoun?) _____.

2 In exercise 1, *you* and *they* could be replaced by the masculine pronoun _____ or by the feminine pronoun _____.

3 Try to think of a way to rewrite exercise 1 without using either of its two troublesome pronouns. (One possibility is to start with *A person who has an opportunity to travel* . . .)

4 Sometimes a shift from *he* to *you,* or from some other pronoun to still another, is justified and necessary:

He caught a train, but I decided to fly.

The shift above is of course acceptable because the sentence concerns (how

many?) _____ different persons.

5 Another kind of acceptable shift is from *one* or *one's* to *he* (*him, his*) or *she* (*her, hers*):

When one is unable to go to sleep, he (or *she,* or *he or she*) is likely to try one expedient after another in the pursuit of Morpheus.

Without such a shift, repeated *one's* could become awkward. One could

keep using *one* until _____ could wonder where _____ might ever end

with _____'s use of _____!

6 On the other hand, a single repetition of *one* can sometimes eliminate both inconsistency and the sexist dilemma:

A. **When you first see the Jefferson Memorial, one is struck by its exquisitely graceful use of curved lines.**
B. **When one first sees the Jefferson Memorial, one is struck by its exquisitely graceful use of curved lines.**

Which sentence is better? _____ Why? _____

_____

7 POOR: **If a person is fond of buttermilk, they should buy some at the Crossroad Dairy.**

The sentence above shows another undesirable shift. Is *a person* singular

or plural? _____ Is *they* singular or plural? _____

Is there any reason for shifting from the singular to the plural? _____

8 What change should be made to correct the poor sentence in exercise 7?

_____

9 **Each does the work as well as he can.**
Each does the work as well as they can.
Each does the work as well as possible.

Does *each* refer to one person or more than one person? _____

Should the pronoun that refers to *each* be singular or plural? _____

Which sentence is grammatically standard, the first or the second? _____
Which sentence avoids a possible appearance of bias, the first or the third?

_____

10 **Someone has dropped her pliers.**
Someone has dropped their pliers.

Does *someone* refer to one woman or more than one? _____
Should the pronoun that refers to *someone* be singular or plural?

_____

Is the first or the second the better sentence? _____

11 anybody   anyone   each   everybody   everyone
   nobody   no one   one   somebody   someone

The pronouns listed above are all singular. This is shown by the fact that
you would use *is* or *was* with each of them rather than *are* or *were*. Since
the pronouns are singular, it is consistent to use (*singular* or *plural?*)

_____ pronouns in referring to them.

12 **Neither of the girls found what she had dreamed about.**
Did either of the girls find what she had dreamed about?

Neither and *either*, with rare exceptions, are also singular. They mean
"neither one" and "either one." In the sentences above, therefore, the

singular pronoun _____ is used rather than the plural *they*.

13 Write in each blank the letter corresponding to the best description of the
sentence.

_____ Each of the girls should bring her own equipment.

_____ Each of the students should bring his or her own equipment.

_____ Each of the students should bring their own equipment.

_____ Each of the students should bring his own equipment.

_____ All students should bring their own equipment.

A. This sentence is suitable for a mixed group but is a little awkward.
B. This sentence is nonstandard in its usage.
C. This sentence is suitable for an all-female group.
D. This sentence is standard and unbiased.
E. This sentence is standard but may appear biased unless all members of
    the group are male.

C: ASSIGNMENTS

• Start sentences in the ways indicated below, and finish each in such a way that a pronoun is needed to refer to the italicized word.

> EXAMPLE: **If a** *person* **orders a five-dollar meal,**
> **If a person orders a five-dollar meal, he** (or *she*, or *he or she*)
> **is exceeding the office limit for a lunch.** (*He* **or either of the other choices refers to** *person*.)

1. If a *person* buys ham these days,
2. After *one* has solved the puzzle,
3. First *you* loosen the brackets, and
4. *Each* may do whatever
5. Does *everyone* have
6. *Someone* failed to remove
7. If *anybody* opens this door,
8. *Each* of the women should
9. *Each* of my twelve cousins
10. *Neither* of the players
11. Has *either* of these playwrights
12. Until *you* have seen Paris,
13. *Nobody* should enter the room until
14. *One* may enter the room if
15. Whenever a *person* loses

ANSWERS TO SECTION B

1. they
2. he, she
3. MODEL   A person who has an opportunity to travel must take it or run the risk of always being sorry.
4. two
5. one, one, one, one
6. B   MODEL   Sentence A shifts from *you* to *one*, but B is consistent.
7. singular   plural   No
8. MODEL   Change *they* to *he, she,* or *he or she,* or rewrite to avoid the personal pronoun.
9. one   singular   first   third
10. one   singular   first
11. singular
12. she
13. C   A   B   E   D

Unit 61—Irregular Plurals

A: COMMENTARY

In English we write *one cat, two cats, a sermon, many sermons,* and so on. That is, we just add an *s* to show that most nouns are plural.

We have inherited a few unusual plurals from the way the language was spoken over a thousand years ago. That is why we say *feet, geese, lice, men, mice, teeth,* and *women,* as well as *children* and *oxen* and the old-fashioned plurals *brethren* and *kine* (cattle).

A few plurals are just like the singulars. These are most often names of animals, but not always. Some of them are *bass, deer, fish, grouse, salmon,* and *sheep.* So we say "I saw two deer," not "deers."

A few other words have two plurals, with different meanings: *cloths* and *clothes, dies* and *dice, geniuses* and *genii, shot* and *shots.*

Most of Section B concerns foreign nouns widely used in English. There are many such words. When you are in doubt about a plural not discussed here, refer to your dictionary.

B: EXERCISES

1 How many syllables does *boy* have? _____ How many does *boys* have?

_____

How many does *bush* have? _____ How many does *bushes* have? _____
On the basis of these examples (and many more that you can think of), it

may be said that *es* is used in a plural if there (is/is not) _____ one more syllable in the plural than in the singular.

2 Which four of these words need *es* in the plural? *church, drama, latch,*

grass, clock, sex, window _____ _____ _____ _____ Now

write those four plurals. _____ _____ _____ _____

3 In *lady* note that the last two letters are a consonant and *y*. In words like that we change the *y* to an *i* and add *es* to make a plural. Write the plurals

of *lady, baby, army, navy,* and *kitty.* _____ _____ _____

_____ _____ (Exceptions to this rule are people's names, like
Mary or *O'Grady,* where the *y* is kept: two *Marys,* the *O'Gradys.*)

4 Words like *toy* and *monkey* end in a vowel and *y*. So they aren't pluralized like *lady.* All we do is add *s: toys.* Write the plurals of *key, monkey, turkey,*

282

valley, volley. _____ _____ _____ _____

_____

5 In some words ending with *f* or *fe*, the last sound in the singular is /f/, but when we say the plural, the corresponding sound changes to /v/. So we write *knife* but *knives*, *calf* but *calves*. Write the plurals of these words:

loaf _____ self _____ half _____ leaf _____

life _____ elf _____ shelf _____ thief _____

wolf _____

6 Words that end in *o*, like *echo*, cause trouble because some of their plurals end in *s* and some in *es* and still others in either *s* or *es*. It's hard to remember which is which. The easiest solution is to memorize the following plurals with *es* endings and write all the rest with *s*:

echoes   embargoes   heroes   potatoes
tomatoes   torpedoes   vetoes

Copy and memorize these seven words.

_____ _____ _____ _____

_____ _____ _____

7 We pluralize the main noun in words with *in-law*: my two *sisters-in-law*. Write the plurals of *brother-in-law*, *father-in-law*, *mother-in-law*.

_____ _____ _____

8 Some foreign words may be pluralized in either of two ways. For example, the Romans pluralized *index* as *indices*, and we may write either *indexes* or *indices*. (Often in such cases the Anglicized forms eventually replace the older forms. For example, very few people any longer say *stadia* and *gymnasia*.)

The foreign plurals are still almost always used in some other words, though. Two of these are *criteria* (the plural of the Greek *criterion*) and *phenomena* (from *phenomenon*). So we should write:

One crit _____ **is** . . .   **Two of the crit** _____ **are** . . .

this phen _____   **these phen** _____

9 A male graduate is an *alumnus*; the plural is *alumni*. A female graduate is an *alumna*; the plural is *alumnae*. All graduates as a group (male and female together) are *alumni*.

Choose two of those words and write sentences that show you understand the difference.

_____

_____

10 Some Greek nouns ending in *is* have plurals in *es*. For example, the plural of *axis* is *axes*. Write the plurals of these words:

basis _____ crisis _____ diagnosis _____

emphasis _____ neurosis _____ oasis _____

synopsis _____ synthesis _____ thesis _____

C: ASSIGNMENTS

• Check your dictionary to see what plural or plurals are listed for each of the following words.

alga	cactus	ellipsis	gladiolus	poet laureate
amoeba	campus	esophagus	hippopotamus	radius
antenna	cherub	focus	larva	stimulus
apex	concerto	formula	medium	tempo
appendix	editor-in-chief	fungus	passerby	vertebra

ANSWERS TO SECTION B

1. one   one   one   two   is
2. church, latch, grass, sex   churches, latches, grasses, sexes
3. ladies, babies, armies, navies, kitties
4. keys, monkeys, turkeys, valleys, volleys
5. loaves, selves, halves, leaves, lives, elves, shelves, thieves, wolves
6. echoes embargoes heroes potatoes   tomatoes torpedoes vetoes
7. brothers-in-law   fathers-in-law   mothers-in-law
8. criterion   criteria   phenomenon   phenomena
9. MODEL The two alumni were wearing tuxedos, and their wives, the alumnae, were also dressed very formally.
10. bases, crises, diagnoses, emphases, neuroses, oases, synopses, syntheses, theses

Unit 62—Adjectives and Adverbs

A: COMMENTARY

This unit discusses two situations in which adjectives and adverbs are sometimes confused.

One of the situations is in a sentence like this:

My sister answered (quick/quickly).

Here the adverb *quickly* is needed because we are describing not my sister (a noun) but rather the way she answered (a verb).

The other situation is in a sentence like this:

The pears taste (sweet/sweetly).

This time the adjective *sweet* is needed because it is the pears that we are describing, not the way somebody performs the act of tasting.

Since *good* and *well* are more often confused than any other adjective and adverb, the differences between these two words will be emphasized in Section B.

B: EXERCISES

1 The sentences below illustrate three uses of the adjective *good*. In sentence

A, *good* modifies (describes)_____.

    Adj   S
A. Good canaries have purple toenails.

          S   be Adj
B. These canaries are good.

          S   LV Adj
C. These canaries taste good.

2 In sentence B in exercise 1 the verb is a form of *be* (*is, was, are*, etc.). Does

good modify *are,* or does it tell about the canaries? _____

3 In sentence C in exercise 1 the verb is a linking verb meaning somewhat the same thing as "seem to be," and similar to such other linking verbs as *feel, sound, look,* or *smell.* Does *good* tell how the act of tasting is performed, or

does it again modify *canaries?* _____

4   **S   V**
    These canaries sing _____.

In this sentence the verb does not merely link, as *are* and *taste* do in exercise 1. Instead, *sing* names an action that the canaries perform. The word that follows will tell how the action was performed; it will not describe the canaries. That is, this sentence requires an adverb (a word *added* to the *verb*), not an adjective. It is different in pattern from the sentences in

exercise 1. Therefore the adverb (*beautiful*/*beautifully*) _____ is a good way to complete the sentence.

5 The word *good* is normally an adjective and *well* is normally an adverb.

Should you use *good* or *well* to complete the example in exercise 4? _____

6 Is *good* or *well* preferable in each of these sentences?

    A. **The maps were** _____.

    B. **He drew** _____ **maps.**

    C. **He drew maps** _____.

    D. **He drew** _____.

    E. **He drew very** _____.

    F. **Did he draw** _____ **maps?**

    G. **Did he draw** _____?

    H. **Did he draw maps** _____?

7 Tell why *well* is needed in sentences G and H in exercise 6.

_____

_____

8 Is *good* or *well* preferable in each of these sentences?

    A. **He plays the bassoon** _____.

    B. **Joanna punts very** _____ **for a girl.**

    C. **My handwriting isn't as** _____ **as it once was.**

    D. **If everything goes** _____, **I'll be home by three.**

    E. **I never did learn** _____ **study habits.**

    F. **I never did learn to study** _____.

    G. **I never did learn very** _____.

9 The same principle applies to the choice between other adjectives and adverbs. In the sentence *His words were very sincere*, you know that *sincere* is used instead of *sincerely* because _____

_____

10 In the sentence *He spoke very sincerely*, you know that *sincerely* is needed instead of *sincere* because _____

_____

11 In exercises 1 and 3 we looked at the sentence *These canaries taste good*. Other linking verbs, like *taste*, are the other verbs of the senses: *smell, sound, feel, look*. So we would write:

These canaries smell (good/well) _____.

These canaries sound (good/well) _____.

These canaries feel (good/well) _____.

These canaries look (good/well) _____.

(In the last sentence, actually either *good* or *well* may be used, with different meanings. The canaries look *good* if they look attractive. They look *well* if they appear to be healthy. After one of the verbs of the senses, if it makes sense to substitute *seem* or *seems*, an adjective is needed. In the rare instances when *seem* or *seems* does not make sense, use an adverb: *He tasted the mixture fearfully*.)

12 Write two sentences in each of which the adjective *good* is needed.

_____

_____

13 Write two sentences in which the adverb *well* is needed.

_____

_____

C: ASSIGNMENTS

• Compose ten sentences, each of which corresponds roughly to one or the other of the patterns below. (You may use other adjectives and adverbs besides *good* and *well* if you wish.)

> **A good lawyer speaks well.**
> **The good angels carry their messages very well.**

• Which word would you use in the following sentences?

1. Your pipe smells (delightful/delightfully) this morning.
2. The captain's voice sounded (calm/calmly).
3. I felt (cautious/cautiously).
4. I felt my way (cautious/cautiously) through the darkness. (Why is this different from 3?)
5. She looked (angry/angrily).
6. She looked (angry/angrily) at her tormentor.
7. The pie tastes (good/well).
8. The king's taster tastes (suspicious/suspiciously).

ANSWERS TO SECTION B

1. canaries
2. canaries
3. canaries
4. beautifully
5. well
6. A. good   B. good   C. well   D. well   E. well   F. good   G. well   H. well
7. MODEL   It explains how the act of drawing was performed.
8. A. well   B. well   C. good   D. well   E. good   F. well   G. well
9. MODEL   the words are being described
10. MODEL   the act of speaking is being described
11. good (in each example)
12. MODELS   The chili was (or tasted) very good.
            Our team played a good game.
13. MODELS   Julie makes chili very well.
            Our team played well.

Unit 63—Comparison of Adjectives and Adverbs

A: COMMENTARY

Adjectives and adverbs, which are words often used in comparisons, exist in three "degrees":

POSITIVE	COMPARATIVE	SUPERLATIVE
small	smaller (less small)	smallest (least small)
remarkable	more (less) remarkable	most (least) remarkable
quickly	more (less) quickly	most (least) quickly

The exercises in Section B present a conservative point of view about what is "correct" in expressing comparisons with adjectives and adverbs. You will find that some effective speakers and writers disregard, or sometimes disregard, one or more of the four conservative rules below:

1. In comparing two things, use the comparative degree of adjectives and adverbs (*the taller of the two* rather than *the tallest of the two*).
2. With adjectives of two syllables or more, especially if they end in *-able, -al, -ed, -en, -ful, -ic, -id, -ile, -ive, -ose, -ous, -que,* or *-ure,* use *more* and *most* for the comparative and superlative degrees, not *-er* and *-est.*
3. Do not compare words that cannot logically be compared, like *square, vertical, complete, perfect,* or *unique.* (Square is square; if something is square, nothing else can be "more square.")
4. Avoid double comparatives and double superlatives. (It is enough to say *colder* and *coldest; more colder* and *most coldest* are redundant.)

B: EXERCISES

1　A. **Jack is stronger than his brother.**
　　B. **Of the two brothers, Jack is the stronger.**

Do sentences A and B mean the same thing? _____ Since they do mean the same thing, does it make sense to use the same comparative word (*stronger*) in both? _____

2　In exercise 1, sentence A, would it be good English to use *strongest* instead of *stronger*? _____ Since B is only another way of expressing A, would it be good English to use *strongest* in B? _____

3　A word such as *stronger* is conventionally used in comparing two things. It is in the comparative degree. A word such as *strongest,* in the superlative degree, is used in comparing three or more things. Therefore we should say:

This is the (larger/largest) _____ *of the two melons* and *This is the (larger/largest)* _____ *of the three melons.*

4　A number of adjectives form the comparative and superlative with *more* and *most* rather than with *-er* and *-est.* These ordinarily are words of three syllables or more but include some two-syllable words. They often end in *-able, -al, -ed, -en, -ful, -ic, -id, -ile, -ive, -ose, -ous, -que,* or *-ure.* Try to list one adjective for five of these endings. _____ _____ _____

_____ _____

5　As we saw in exercises 1–3, meticulous speakers and writers use the comparative degree of such words as *strong* and *large* when they are comparing only two things. Similarly they use the comparative degree of the words discussed in exercise 4 when they are comparing only two things. So they

say *Mr. Crowder is the (more/most)* _____ *candid of the two speakers.*

6 Meticulous speakers and writers also say:

   A. **Mr. Crowder was the (less/least)** _____ **verbose of the two speakers.**

   B. **Mr. Crowder was the (less/least)** _____ **argumentative of the five speakers.**

   C. **Mr. Crowder was the (more tactful/most tactful/tactfuler/ tactfulest)**

   _____ **of the two speakers.**

7 A number of adjectives, at least in theory, represent absolute qualities. For example, if a geometrical figure is circular, no other figure can be more circular. If a line is vertical, no other line can be more vertical. Logically, then, words such as *circular* and *vertical* (can/cannot) _____ be compared.

8 Other words in the same general category as *circular* and *vertical* include *perfect, full, empty, equal, complete, true, false.* The word *unique,* which by strict definition means "the only one of its kind," belongs here too. Is it then logical to say that one flower is *more unique* than another or that a scarf is *very unique?* _____

9. A. Explain why a person cannot logically say that one jar is *fuller* than another. _____

   _____

   B. Can one jar be *more nearly full* than another? _____

10 A. **This was the unkindest cut of all.**
   B. **This was the most unkind cut of all.**
   C. **This was the most unkindest cut of all.**

   Shakespeare wrote C, which was "correct" in his time, but today we argue that since *most* and *-est* mean the same thing, there is no need to repeat. Therefore we would say either A or B. Similarly, the two of the following

   sentences that we would consider standard today are _____ and _____.

   A. **She is even happier than she was before.**
   B. **She is even more happier than she was before.**
   C. **She is even more happy than she was before.**

11 Adverbs, like adjectives, have comparative and superlative degrees, and their use is traditionally guided by rules like those we have looked at for adjectives. For example, we should write *Of the two marksmen, he usually shoots more accurately* (not *most accurately*). For another example, we (should/ should not) _____ write *When Fred and Harry raced, Harry ran fastest.*

12 A number of adverbs correspond to such adjectives as *square* or *complete*: *squarely, completely, vertically, fully, perfectly,* and so on. From the standpoint of the conservative, should we write *The little town was more completely engulfed by floodwaters than it had ever been before?* _____

C: ASSIGNMENTS

• List fifteen words (excluding those listed in the answer to exercise 4) that should ordinarily be compared with *more* and *most* rather than with *-er* and *-est.* Try to find words with several different endings.

• Try to think of at least five adjectives that cannot logically be compared. Do not include words mentioned in Sections A and B.

• Choose the conservative form in each of these sentences.

1. Glenn's response was the (quicker/quickest) of the two.
2. Lena is definitely the (more/most) graceful of the two skaters.
3. This two-cent piece is (rarer/more rarer) than that one.
4. My line is (more/more nearly) horizontal than yours.
5. The floor is (more/more nearly) level on this side of the room.
6. Of the two sisters, Grace has the (better/best) mind.
7. The (commonest/most commonest) complaint is that taxes are too high.
8. Have you ever seen a more (unique/unusual) sugar bowl?
9. The subway trains are much (rapider/more rapid) than the buses.
10. The subway trains are the (more/most) rapid of the two means of travel.
11. The subway trains are the (most rapid/most rapidest) of all the vehicles.
12. The subway trains are the (most rapid/more rapid) of all the vehicles.
13. Our fuel tank was (emptier/more empty/more nearly empty) than ever.
14. Today is (peacefuler/more peaceful) than yesterday was.
15. Jane had the (highest/most perfect) score in the class.

ANSWERS TO SECTION B

1. Yes   Yes
2. No   No
3. larger, largest

4. MODELS   lovable, casual, treasured, forsaken, resentful, frantic, candid, fragile, pensive, verbose, nervous, antique, mature
5. more
6. A. less   B. least   C. more tactful
7. cannot
8. No
9. A. MODEL   If a jar is full, no other jar can be more full, since *full* means that no more can be put in.   B. Yes
10. A   C
11. should not
12. No

Unit 64—Prepositions

A: COMMENTARY

A prepositional phrase consists of a preposition plus its object and possibly modifiers of the object. Some of the common prepositions, with examples of phrases, are the following:

about	(about the house)
above	(above the stadium)
after	(after the party)
among	(among the guests)
around	(around the roadblock)
at	(at the museum; *but never* where at)
before	(before noon)
beside	(sitting beside Muriel)
besides	(no one besides Tim is coming)
between	(between you and me)
by	(by the stream)
concerning	(concerning your question)
down	(down the gutter)
during	(during the storm)
for	(for Maureen)
from	(from the president)
in	(reading in the library; *but* going into the library)
in front of	(in front of an audience)
inside	(inside the oven)
into	(stepping into the elevator; *not* stepping in the elevator)
like	(like Jim)
of	(of the hill)
off	(fell off the table; *not* fell off of the table)

over	(over the bump)
through	(through the crowd)
to	(to a meeting; *but never* where to)
together with	(together with a lieutenant)
toward	(toward the flag)
under	(under the sofa)
until	(until the intermission)
with	(with the class)

Prepositions usually cause great difficulty to persons learning English as a second language. It is easy to see why. You live *in* America or *in* Canada but *on* the land, *on* the farm but *in* the city, *on* earth but *in* the world. You may be a secretary *to* the manager or *of* the manager. You may go *up*town or *down*town without regard to the elevation of the land, and once you get there you may be *on* the town (although apparently no one has ever been *on* the city). You may be *in* bed or *on* the couch but seldom *in* the bed and never *on* couch. You may be interested *in* music but have no aptitude *for* music.

There is not any logic in our use of prepositional phrases. Fortunately, if we speak the language from childhood we learn without effort to use these words—or most of them. There are, however, a few very common problems in the use of prepositional phrases.

1. One problem involves the use of one preposition with more than one object. As you know from your own use, one preposition may introduce several objects.

    EXAMPLE: We work *during* rain, sleet, or hail.

This example has one preposition but three objects. This is all right whenever the preposition really fits with all three. But consider this sentence:

    POOR: He likes living on the farm rather than the city.

In this sentence the word *on* belongs with *farm* but not with *city*: one doesn't live *on* a city.

    BETTER: He likes living on the farm rather than in the city.

When you use a preposition with more than one object, be sure that it is normally used with each one.

2. Another problem involves the use of more than one preposition with a single object; two or more prepositions can refer to a single object.

    EXAMPLE: He is upset about and suspicious of Harvey's actions.

Also, a preposition may be used twice to refer to one object.

    EXAMPLE: Cheryl is contented *with*, even delighted *with*, her job.

When a preposition is used twice to refer to one object, the first occurrence can usually be deleted:

    EXAMPLE: Cheryl is contented, even happy, with her job.

The trouble is that certain verbs, modifiers, and nouns are associated with certain prepositions but not with others. For instance, a person may be

interested in . . .   *but not*   interested of . . .
a proponent of . . .   a proponent in . . .
contented with . . .   contented against . . .

and so on. The problem comes in a sentence like this:

FAULTY: He is interested but suspicious of the new approach.

It's all right to be *suspicious of* but a person isn't *interested of.*

BETTER: He is interested in but suspicious of the new approach.

3. Still another problem with prepositions is their idiomatic use. No one questions *in front of*, but some editors and teachers don't like *in back of*. (They prefer *back of* or *behind*.) *Off of* and *where at* and *where to* make use of an unnecessary word.

The words *whom* and *which* seem to attract an unnecessarily repeated preposition:

FAULTY: She is the girl with whom he went with.
            This is the principle for which I stand for.
CORRECT: She is the girl whom he went with. (*or* with whom he went)
            This is the principle which I stand for. (*or* for which I stand)
CORRECT: She is the girl he went with.
            This is the principle I stand for.

B: EXERCISES

1 **This dress can be worn in summer and in winter.**

In the example above there are two prepositional phrases, *in summer* and *in winter*. Are both phrases introduced by the same preposition? _____

2 Since the same preposition introduces the two prepositional phrases, one of the prepositions might be eliminated, as follows:

This dress can be worn in summer and winter.

In this sentence the preposition *in* has two objects, *summer* and _____.

3 **Jack Benny starred on radio and television.**

The two objects of the preposition *on* in the example are _____ and _____.

4 Sometimes prepositions are *wrongly* used to refer to more than one object in a sentence:

Their forces were supreme in the air and the land.
Military forces may be supreme *in* the air, but it would be better to say

that they are supreme _____ the land.

5 Usually the choice of preposition to be used with an object depends on the words used along with the preposition. For instance, we say:

He is interested *in* bowling.
He is a proponent *of* bowling.
He talked *on* (or *about*) bowling.
He refrained *from* bowling.
He is disgusted *with* bowling.

If we want to get two of the above ideas into the same sentence, we may be tempted to say *He is interested and a proponent of bowling*. The italicized sentence is incorrect because we do not say *interested of* but *inter-*

ested _____.

6 Here is another problem that sometimes crops up. It is correct to say:

He is the man *with* whom I fought.
                    and
He is the man whom I fought *with*.

Is it correct to say: *He is the man with whom I fought with?* _____

Why or why not? _____

7 Cross out the unnecessary preposition in each of these sentences:

   A. **Keep off of the grass.**
   B. **Where is he at?**
   C. **Where did she go to?**
   D. **I am parked in back of the auditorium.**

8 Which one of the following sentences is wrong?

   A. **We moved off the freeway.**
   B. **Where is the key at?**
   C. **Put the typewriter back of the desk.**

9 Write a sentence in which you state that you prefer the farm as a place to live rather than the village. Use the words *on the farm* in the sentence.

_____

10 Write a sentence in which you state that somebody is a relative of **young**

Tom Foresman and is proud of him. Use the words *is related to* in your sentence. The words *young Tom Foresman* should end the sentence.

_____

_____

C: ASSIGNMENTS

• Rewrite the following sentences correctly.

1. There is no society in heaven or earth such as he envisions.
2. Max spends most of his time in the clubhouse or the beach. Right now, I don't know where he's at.
3. We saw the picture of the fugitive in the paper and television.
4. Do you know with whom he went with to the theater?
5. She is interested but seldom refers to her new friend.
6. Look in back of the sofa for your ball.
7. Do you know where Sue went to?
8. The cat jumped off of the porch.
9. I am disgusted and suspicious of Mr. Carter.
10. He will arrive on the bus or private car.

ANSWERS TO SECTION B

1. Yes
2. winter
3. radio, television
4. on
5. in
6. No MODEL One *with* is enough.
7. of   at   to   in
8. B
9. MODEL   I would rather live on the farm than in the village.
10. MODEL   Max is related to and is proud of young Tom Foresman.

Unit 65—Intensifiers

A: COMMENTARY

It would be easy to say to students, "Never use *sort of, sure, terribly,* and so on, as intensifiers." That, however, would be a dishonest approach. Matters of usage are seldom so clear-cut. Following the findings of scholars who study modern usage, I have attempted to show that "correct" and "incorrect" represent oversimplification in judging the appropriateness of a given intensifier. I have presented evidence on which you may base your own practice, perhaps guided somewhat by your own preferences and somewhat by the preferences of your instructors or other persons with whom you work. If, for instance, you sometime have a conservative employer who insists upon his or her own version of English and who abhors an expression like *terribly late, sort of late*, common sense dictates that you will avoid offending him or her unnecessarily.

Section B divides intensifiers into three groups, while insisting upon the possibility of upward movement from one group to another.

GROUP 1: unquestioned in either formal or informal contexts: *very, certainly, surely, really, extremely, intensely, quite, rather, somewhat, fairly*

GROUP 2: questioned by some people, especially in formal contexts: *terribly, awfully, mighty, pretty*

GROUP 3: questioned by many people, especially in formal contexts: *some* (for *somewhat*), *sort of, kind of, sure* (for *surely*), *real* (for *really*), *awful, terrible,* and *powerful*

Needless to say, these words are listed only as intensifiers. In other uses (for example, *he is a powerful man*) no one would raise a question. When you are in doubt as to whether a word is used as an intensifier, test it by seeing whether *very* could be substituted for it in your sentence.

The intensifier *quite* should be used with some caution because it may be ambiguous. For instance, if someone says *Glenn does his work quite well, quite* may be intended to mean "extremely," but a slightly different tone of voice may give the word the meaning "rather." The written version of the sentence does not distinguish these meanings. A further complication is that *quite* may also mean "completely," as in *He has quite recovered from his illness.*

B: EXERCISES

1 Words such as *very* or *rather* are often called adverbs. They are not used in sentences, however, in the ways that most adverbs are. For instance, you may say *she talks rapidly*, using the adverb *rapidly*. But may you say *she talks very?* _____ Or you may say *I tried hard*, with the adverb *hard*, but may you say *I tried rather?* _____

2 Since words such as *very* and *rather* differ from ordinary adverbs, some modern grammarians put them into a separate group, called *intensifiers*. That name is appropriate. If you say, for instance, *Millicent is very intelligent*, the word *very* is intended to strengthen the intensity of your statement about the girl: she is not merely *intelligent*, but *very intelligent*. If you say *Millicent is*

rather intelligent, you are suggesting a (higher/lower) _____
degree of intelligence.

3 Intensifiers in English are in short supply. As a consequence we tend to
overwork the few we have. We also occasionally use other words as intensifiers, often distorting the usual meanings of those words. For instance, in the
eighteenth century *vastly* was used with great frequency: *vastly strong, vastly
large, vastly tired,* even *vastly small.* Why is *vastly small* an odd expression?

_____

_____

4 We tend to use some intensifiers in both formal and informal situations,
others largely in informal contexts. The line, however, is indistinct. Which

of the two following sentences do you consider more formal? _____

   A. **They are very late.**
   B. **They are terribly late.**

5 Despite the fact that *terribly* in the sense of *very* probably seems informal
to you, or maybe even incorrect, *Webster's Third New International Dictionary* considers it a synonym for *extremely* and *intensely* and cites evidence
of this use from Professor Gilbert Highet, novelist Mary McCarthy, and
British poet and critic Herbert Read. In other words, the statement sometimes made that *terribly* should not be used as an intensifier is (true/an

oversimplification) _____.

6 Among the intensifiers that almost everyone agrees are suitable in both
formal and informal contexts are *very, certainly, surely, really, extremely,
intensely, quite, rather, somewhat,* and *fairly.* Would such words be equally
appropriate for use in conversation with friends and in an honors thesis?

_____

7 As exercises 4 and 5 indicate, *terribly* is regarded by some people as an incorrect intensifier or at best as informal. In the same category come *awfully*
(as in *awfully late*), *mighty* (*mighty late*), and *pretty* (*pretty late*). The
advice in this book is not that you should never employ those expressions
but rather that you should realize that some people may question your use
of English if you do. That is, unlike the intensifiers in exercise 6, these are

looked upon by some people with (pleasure/disdain) _____.

8 In a still different category come *some* (as in *He is some late*), *sort of* and
kind of (as in *sort of late*), *awful* (*awful late*), *real* (*real late*), *sure* (*sure
late*), *terrible* (*terrible late*), and the obsolete or dialectal *powerful* (*power-*

ful late). These are generally regarded as informal at best. You would be (likely/unlikely) _____ to find them in an article written by one of your professors.

9 Intensifiers, then, fall roughly into three categories, although the boundary lines are not solid or distinct. In your own words, name the three categories.

A. _____

B. _____

C. _____

C: ASSIGNMENTS

• In addition to the intensifiers listed in Section A, try to think of a few others (possibly slang or even mild profanity).

• Listen for a few minutes to a conversation and a few minutes to a lecture, paying careful attention to the use of intensifiers. Take notes. Comment on any differences you observe in the use of intensifiers in these two situations.

• Copy in list form the intensifiers in Groups 1, 2, and 3, and put the word *late* or *tired* or *happy* after each. Ask yourself, one or two friends, and if convenient a professor or other professional person, whether he or she uses each of the expressions and whether the circumstances of use vary. Make a tally of the results.

ANSWERS TO SECTION B

1. No   No
2. lower
3. MODEL   Since *vastly* refers to great size, it contradicts *small*.
4. Probably A
5. an oversimplification
6. Yes
7. disdain
8. unlikely
9. MODELS   A. those suitable for both formal and informal use
   B. those questioned by some people, especially when used formally
   C. those considered informal at best

Unit 66—Verb Agreement When Subject and Verb Are Separated

A: COMMENTARY

In most sentences verb agreement causes no problems. Most past tense verbs have a common form, such as *walked* or *brought,* that is used with both singular and plural subjects. Trouble arises, though, when we need to choose between *is* and *are, was* and *were,* or *has* and *have,* and also when we need to decide whether *sing* or *sings* (or any comparable verb) is needed with a third-person subject.

A singular subject requires a singular verb, and a plural subject requires a plural verb. Even when words come between the subject and the verb the principle holds true. But sentences like this sometimes confuse people:

John's plan for the festivities _____ well received.

There, the plural *festivities* makes one think that a plural verb should be used. A moment's thought or a moment's grammatical analysis, however, shows that the *festivities* were not well received; the *plan* was. *Plan* is the subject, a singular noun requiring a singular verb such as *was* or *is* or a common form such as *will be.*

Most teachers and textbooks assert that in sentences with *as well as, together with,* and the like, the interrupter should be ignored in choosing the verb. Thus *Mr. Katz, as well as his wife, was injured* means the same thing as *Mr. Katz was injured, as well as his wife.* Some people argue, though, that the sentence means that two people were injured and that therefore *were* is preferable. These people receive support from Bergen Evans and Cornelia Evans (*A Dictionary of Contemporary American Usage*), who in effect say "Take your choice." If you are addressing a conservative reader or audience, however, you will probably want to play safe and choose the form that agrees with the subject.

Exercise 3 uses as one example *The reason for the decisions was the strong arguments of Gray and Bolling.* That kind of sentence sometimes causes difficulty even without a phrase such as *for the decisions.* Consider *The reason was the strong arguments. . . .* Some people, thinking ahead to the plural *arguments,* incorrectly would use *were. Was* is correct because the subject *reason,* not the predicate nominative *arguments,* determines the number of the verb.

Sentences such as *Some of the hash (apples) was (were) eaten* are oddities. When in doubt about the verb to choose, note whether the noun (*hash, apples*) refers to something that can be counted. If it cannot (you can't count hash!), it is a mass noun and requires a singular verb; if it can be counted, as apples and sacks of sugar can, it takes a plural verb.

All usually takes a plural verb, but in a sentence involving a mass noun, as *All the sand was spilled* or *All her hair was on the floor,* it takes a singular.

(Note that *of* is often not needed after *all*: *all of them*, but either *all the children* or *all of the children*.)

When *each, everybody, everyone, nobody, anybody*, or *anyone* is used as a subject, the verb is singular. This is true even when words come between subject and verb: *Each of the deserters was questioned separately*.

Either and *neither* usually require singular verbs. However, on the rare occasions when their antecedents are plural, these words take plural verbs. In informal use the plural is increasing in frequency: *Neither of the twins were chosen*. No doubt this occurs because of the attraction of the plural noun, such as *twins*. In formal writing the example would require a singular verb.

None may take either a singular or a plural verb. Earlier in this century only the singular was regarded as standard, but the recent tendency has been toward the plural. The reason that *none* may be considered either singular or plural is that its meaning may be either *not one* or *not any*; *not one* would take a singular verb, but *not any* would usually take a plural verb.

Both requires a plural verb.

B: EXERCISES

S   V
1 **The reason is clear.**

As you probably learned years ago, a verb "agrees" with its subject. That is, a singular verb is used with a subject that refers to only one thing, and a plural verb is used with a subject that refers to more than one thing. In

the example above, the subject *reason* is (singular/plural) _____

and the verb *is* is (singular/plural) _____.

2 **The reason for these decisions is clear.**

Writers and speakers are often confused when other words come between the subject and the verb. Actually, with a couple of possible exceptions to be noted later, the intervening words should not affect the choice of verb.

In the example above, the subject _____, being singular, necessarily takes the singular verb _____.

3 Which verb is needed in each sentence?

   A. **The reasons for the decision (is/are)** _____ **clear.**
   B. **The reason for the decisions, which required much contemplation and**

       debate, (is/are) _____ **clear.**

   C. **The reason for the decisions (was/were)** _____ **the strong arguments of Gray and Bolling.**

4   *S   v   **V***

Melissa is coming later.

*S   v   **V***

Melissa, as well as her sisters, is coming later.

Many sentences include, between the subject and the verb, a group of words introduced by *as well as, together with, including, in addition to, along with, no less than, especially,* or similar expressions. The examples above show that such an interpolation (changes /does not affect) _____

_____ the choice of the verb.

5 Which verb is needed in each sentence?

    A. **My brother, in addition to my cousins, (was/were)** _____ **in favor of the plan.**

    B. **Mr. Reese, no less than Mr. Ward and Dr. Lott, (has/have)** _____ **to assume responsibility.**

    C. **My mother, as well as her sisters, (sings/sing)** _____ **beautifully.**

6 **The labor, not the materials, is overpriced.**
The materials, not the labor, are overpriced.

Each sentence above begins with the subject followed by a contrasting negative expression. In such a sentence, judging from the examples, does the negative expression affect the choice of verb? _____

7 **Some of the hash was eaten.**
Some of the apples were eaten.

One example of the few places in which an intervening phrase does affect the choice of verb is shown above. The reason is that we would say *Some hash was eaten* but *Some apples* _____.

8 Similarly we would say:

    A. **All of the flour (was/were)** _____ **stolen.**

    B. **All of the sacks of flour (was/were)** _____ **stolen.**

    C. **Half of the answers (is/are)** _____ **correct.**

    D. **Half of the gravel (is/are)** _____ **still here.**

9 **Each one is gray.**
Each is gray.

Do the two sentences above mean the same thing? _____ When the subject is *each one* or *each*, the verb should be (singular/plural) _____.

10 **Each one of the kittens is gray.**
Each of the kittens is gray.

When a phrase such as *of the kittens* comes between subject and verb, does it affect the choice of verb? _____

11 **Neither one of your two answers is correct.**
Neither of your two answers is correct.

Do the two sentences above mean the same thing? _____ Since *neither* in the second sentence means *neither one*, it takes a (singular/plural) _____ verb.

12 The subject *neither* nearly always requires a singular verb. However, consider this infrequent kind of exception:

Scotsmen and Englishmen were constantly bickering, and neither were willing to concede the smallest point.

Explain why *were* is used here with *neither*.

_____

_____

13 **Either of the girls is a likely choice.**

Either ordinarily means "either one." The verb, then, is usually (singular/plural) _____. (The only exception would be one comparable to the *neither* sentence in exercise 12.)

14 **Everybody was at his best.**
Everyone was at her best.
Nobody was at his best.
Is anybody at her best?
Is anyone at his best?
Everyone in the five tenements was at her best.

The examples above show that the pronouns _____, _____, _____, _____, and _____ take singular verbs even when a phrase intervenes between subject and verb.

15 **None of the casualties were civilians.**
None of the casualties was a civilian.

Either a singular or a plural verb is acceptable with *none*. Present usage generally favors the plural. However, when the intent is to emphasize *not a single one*, the singular is used. Also, sometimes the presence of a following singular noun, such as _____ in the second sentence, may suggest the need for a singular verb.

16 **Both of the boys were soaking wet.**

The sentence above shows that *both* takes a (singular/plural) _____ verb.

17 Supply an appropriate singular or plural verb for each sentence.

A. **Each of the traitors** _____ **hanged.**

B. **Both of the traitors** _____ **hanged.**

C. **All the traitors** _____ **hanged.**

D. **Neither of the traitors** _____ **hanged.**

E. _____ **either of the traitors likely to be hanged?**

F. **Both the two traitors and the two loyalists were criticized, but neither** _____ **hanged.**

G. **Everybody else** _____ **hanged.**

H. **Everybody in the third and fourth cells** _____ **hanged.**

C: ASSIGNMENTS

• Write eight sentences. Construct the first with *as well as my mother* after the subject, the second with *including the peanuts* after the subject, and the others with these phrases:

besides the inconveniences	in addition to the Joneses
along with Sherry and Jerry	no less than the President
especially pecans	not the radishes

Each time force yourself to choose between a singular and a plural verb. Do not evade the issue by choosing a common-form verb such as *talked, must, went,* and so on.

• Is a singular or a plural verb needed in each sentence?

1. About a third of the coffee _____ sold.

2. About a third of the sofas _____ sold.

3. The man with the white shoes _____ reluctant to walk in the street.

4. The man in the white sports car _____ speeding.

5. The heat combined with the gnats and mosquitoes _____ unbearable.

6. My daughters but not my wife _____ fond of opera.

7. A low sound, perhaps only the hum of bees, _____ becoming audible.

8. The most recent address of the Flanagan brothers _____ been lost.

9. The most recent addresses of Mr. Flanagan _____ been lost.

10. A person who wears a puce shirt and teal trousers _____ probably colorblind.

• Use each of these nine words as a subject in a complete sentence:

    each   everybody   everyone   anybody   either   neither   none   both   all

Choose verbs that are clearly singular or clearly plural. In several of the sentences place a phrase between the subject and the verb.

ANSWERS TO SECTION B

1. singular, singular
2. reason, is
3. A. are B. is C. was
4. does not affect
5. A. was B. has C. sings
6. No
7. were eaten
8. A. was B. were C. are D. is
9. Yes singular
10. No
11. Yes singular
12. MODEL Here, *neither* refers to *Scotsmen* or *Englishmen*, both of which are plural words.
13. singular
14. everybody, everyone, nobody, anybody, anyone
15. civilian
16. plural
17. A. was (or another singular)   B. were (or another plural)
    C. were (or another plural)   D. was (or another singular)
    E. Is (or another singular)   F. were (or another plural)
    G. was (or another singular)   H. was (or another singular)

Unit 67—Verb Agreement in Inverted Sentences

A: COMMENTARY

An inverted sentence is one in which the main parts are not in the usual order. Most English sentences move along in a regular fashion from subject to verb to direct object (or some other completer). But fairly often we have sentences like these:

V   **S**

There are still some plums on the tree.

      V   **S**

In the nest were three speckled eggs.

V   **S**

Are Tom and Frieda here?

In the examples, as you see, the verb comes before the subject.

Inverted sentences are often useful (although *there-sentences* are sometimes a trifle wordy). A sentence such as *On the table are some oranges* may break the monotony of a string of subject-verb sentences. Or *Here are some oranges* may in some circumstances be a more suitable sentence than *Some oranges are here*. Many sentences require inverted word order because they are questions: *Are Tom and Frieda here?*, through its word order, sends the reader or listener a signal that says "This is a question."

The purpose of this unit is to combat the tendency to write sentences such as *There is still some plums on the tree* or *In the nest was three speckled eggs*. If you realize that *plums* and *eggs* are the subjects (not *there* and *nest*), you will be more likely to use the needed plural verb, *are* or *were*.

The same principles that apply to verbs in statements also apply to verbs in questions. *Were two cows in the pasture?* is only a question form of *Two cows were in the pasture* and requires the same verb.

B: EXERCISES

    S   **V**

1 **A cow was in the pasture.**

In most English sentences the subject is the first basic part. In the example above, the subject is ⸻.

      V   **S**

2 **There was a cow in the pasture.**

Sometimes sentences are transformed. For instance, the sentence in exercise 1 can be transformed into the question *Was a cow in the pasture?* Or it can be transformed into the sentence at the top of this exercise. Note that in this transformation we begin with *there*. Does the subject still precede the verb? _____ Is the verb still the same as in exercise 1? _____

3 **Two cows were in the pasture.**

Write the *there*-transformation of the example.

_____

_____

4 In the example at the top of exercise 3 the subject is _____ and the verb is _____. In your *there*-transformation of the sentence the subject is still _____ and the verb is still _____.

5 In the *there*-transformation the subject and verb are inverted. That is, the verb comes before the subject, and *there* occupies as a dummy the place of the subject. Is the verb still the same as in the untransformed sentence?

_____

6 *Here* also often appears in sentences with inverted word order. For instance, *A cat is in the basket* may be transformed into *Here is a cat in the basket*.

Or *Five cats are in the basket* may be transformed into _____

_____.

7 A few other words and countless phrases may enter into similar transformations. For instance, *A dog is near the door* may be transformed into *Near the door is a dog*. Or *Some dogs are near the door* may be transformed into

_____.

8 Explain why you used the verb *are* in your answer to exercise 7.

_____.

9 **About two hundred pigeons are housed in that cote.**

Write a transformation of the sentence above. Start with *In that cote*, and end with *pigeons*. Do not use *there*.

_____.

10 Write a *there*-transformation of the example in exercise 9. Start with *In that cote*. Omit *housed*.

_____.

11 **Some pigeons are still in the cote.**

Note in the example the plural verb *are*, which agrees with *pigeons*. Now let's turn the statement into a question:

———— some pigeons still in the cote?

12 **There are still some pigeons in the cote.**

Let's change that statement also into a question:

———— there still some pigeons in the cote?

13 **In the cote there are still some pigeons.**

Back to the pigeons for the last time. Again change the statement into a question.

In the cote ————————————————————————?

14 The conclusion to be drawn from this unit is that ————————————

——————————————————————————————————————

————————————————————————————————————.

C: ASSIGNMENTS

• Write a sentence beginning with each word or phrase in the following list. Restrict your verbs to those that are clearly singular or plural, such as *is, are, was, were, has, have, has been, have been.*

At the end of the rainbow	Near Mrs. Roscoe's house
On the mantel	Seldom
Beside the garage	Never
Constantly	Across the bridge
Here	There

• Write a transformation, using *here* or *there*, for each of these sentences.

1. My best necktie is lying on the floor.
2. My best neckties are lying on the floor.
3. Grating sounds are coming from the dungeon.
4. Some walnuts were still clinging to the branches.
5. Many linguists are in attendance.
6. A dog is in the barn.
7. Two kittens are in the barn.
8. A dog and two kittens are in the barn.
9. A huge throng was in the street.
10. Three aces were still left in the deck.

• Turn into a question each of the sentences in the exercise above.

ANSWERS TO SECTION B

1. cow
2. No   Yes
3. There were two cows in the pasture.
4. cows, were   cows, were
5. Yes
6. Here are five cats in the basket (A plural verb is necessary.)
7. Near the door are some dogs (A plural verb is necessary.)
8. MODEL   It agrees with the plural subject, *dogs.*
9. In that cote are housed about two hundred pigeons.
10. In that cote there are about two hundred pigeons. (A plural verb is necessary.)
11. Are (A plural verb is necessary.)
12. Are (A plural verb is necessary.)
13. In the cote are there still some pigeons? (A plural verb is necessary.)
14. MODEL   even when a verb comes before its subject, it still agrees with the subject.

Unit 68—Verb Agreement with Compound Subjects

A: COMMENTARY

Compound subjects consist of two or more nouns or noun equivalents: *Rex* and *Bertha, Tom* and his *horse, he* or *I, earth* nor *sky,* and so on.

The principles presented in this unit are simple:

1. When the parts of a compound subject are connected by *and,* the verb is plural.
2. When the parts are connected by *or* or *nor,* the verb agrees with the nearer part.

The two principles apply especially to formal usage. In informal situations the present tendency is toward regular use of the plural verb with the connective *nor* as well as *and: neither he nor I were,* for example. When the connective is *or,* the tendency is less toward this variation, although it does exist. In formal writing it is advisable for you to conform to the principles as stated.

B: EXERCISES

       S
1 The two boys are inseparable.
 S   S
Joe and Frank are inseparable.

In the first sentence the basic subject consists of (How many?) _____

word(s). In the second sentence it consists of (How many?) _____ word(s).

2 When two or more words, such as *Joe* and *Frank*, constitute the basic subject, the subject is said to be compound. In each of the following sentences underline the words that constitute the compound subject.

A. **Melba and her brothers were hurrying to the game.**
B. **Oats, peas, beans, and barley grow.**

3 Note that in the examples in exercises 1 and 2 the parts of the compound subject are joined by *and*. For that reason, these compound subjects are clearly plural and require a plural verb. In the second sentence in exercise

1 the verb is _____. In sentence A in exercise 2 the two-word verb is

_____. In sentence B in exercise 2 the verb is

_____.

4 When the parts of a compound subject are joined by *and*, the verb is

always (singular/plural) _____.

5   S   S
Either Helen or Martha is sure to call.

According to the sentence above, the number of persons sure to call is

_____.

6 In exercise 5, since only one person is sure to call, the verb is (singular/

plural) _____.

7   S   S
Either Helen or her parents are sure to call.

In this sentence, as in exercise 5, the connective is *or*. However, this time the part of the compound subject nearer the verb is (singular/plural)

_____.

8 **Either her parents or Helen is sure to call.**

This sentence reverses the order of *Helen* and *parents* in exercise 7. This time the singular part of the compound subject is nearer the verb. The verb is (singular/plural) _____.

9 Exercises 5–8 show that when the parts of a compound subject are joined by *or*, the verb is singular if the nearer part is (singular/plural) _____ and plural if the nearer part is (singular/plural) _____.

10 **Neither Helen nor Martha is likely to call.**
Neither Helen nor her parents are likely to call.
Neither her parents nor Helen is likely to call.

The connective in the sentences above is *nor*. These sentences illustrate the fact that when *nor* connects the parts of a compound subject in formal writing or speaking, the principle governing verb choice is (the same as/ different from) _____ the principle when *or* is the connective.

11 Choose the appropriate verb for each sentence.

A. **Luigi and Giuseppe (was/were)** _____ **renowned for storytelling.**

B. **Luigi or Giuseppe (is/are)** _____ **renowned for storytelling.**

C. **Luigi or his brothers (is/are)** _____ **likely to tell us some stories.**

D. **His brothers or Luigi (is/are)** _____ **likely to tell us some stories.**

C: ASSIGNMENTS

• Compose sentences with the following compound subjects. Use *is* or *are*, *was* or *were*, or *has been* or *have been* as the verb or helping verb. Assume a formal context.

Mr. Ryan and Mr. O'Hara	Mr. Ryan or Mr. O'Hara
the rural area or the cities	the cities or the rural area
the publisher and his authors	the publisher or his authors
the authors or their publisher	neither the authors nor their publisher
neither the publishers nor the authors	oats, peas, beans, or barley

ANSWERS TO SECTION B

1. one   two
2. Melba (and her) brothers   Oats, peas, beans, (and) barley

3. are   were hurrying   grow
4. plural
5. one
6. singular
7. plural
8. singular
9. singular, plural
10. the same as
11. A. were   B. is   C. are   D. is

Unit 69—Verbs and Pronouns with Collective Nouns

A: COMMENTARY

Here is a list of some of the words used as collective nouns: *band, bevy, class, committee, council, covey, group, herd, jury, swarm, team.* Each such word, though singular in form, refers to a collection of individuals.

The points made in this unit are as follows:

1. When a collective noun used as a subject refers to the unit acting as a unit (as it generally does), the verb is singular: *The covey takes off with a startling whir of wings.*

2. When the collective noun refers to individual action, the verb is plural: *The covey take shelter under trees, in hedgerows, and beneath clumps of grass.* (Also possible: *The birds in the covey take shelter. . . .*)

3. Subjects such as *remainder, total,* or *number* take singular verbs when they refer to a single thing: *The remainder of the term is only three weeks.* They take plural verbs when they refer to a number of countable items: *The remainder of the students are being sent to Room 72.* (As a rule, *the number* requires a singular verb and *a number,* a plural verb.)

4. Possessive words and pronouns used to refer to collective nouns should be singular if the verb is singular, plural if the verb is plural: *The band enters and begins its first number. The band enter and make their way to their seats.* (Also possible: *The band members enter. . . .*)

5. When a term such as *ten minutes, seven dollars, two hundred words,* or *eight miles* is used to refer to a unit, it takes a singular verb: *Ten minutes is the maximum time allowed.*

Note also that the following nouns, although they end in *s,* usually take singular verbs: *physics, economics, mathematics, measles, mumps, news.*

These nouns with *s,* however, conventionally take plural verbs: *gymnastics, riches, scissors, trousers.*

A few nouns with *s* may take either singular or plural verbs: *headquarters, means. Acoustics, athletics, ethics,* and *politics* usually take plural verbs but are considered singular when referring to a science, art, or profession: *Acoustics is a still-developing field of study.*

B: EXERCISES

1 Words such as *class, band,* and *bevy* refer to a collection or group of persons or things. They are called collective nouns. The collective noun used in the sentences below is _____.

    A. **The basketball team is having a good season.**
    B. **The basketball team are removing their warm-up jackets.**

2 Notice that in sentence A in exercise 1 the singular verb is used but that the verb in B is *are*. In which sentence is the team thought of as a unit? _____ Is a singular or a plural verb used when the collective noun subject is thought of as a unit? _____

3 In sentence B in exercise 1 the team members function as individuals rather than as a unit. That is, they remove their jackets individually, not in unison as a team. When a collective noun is used in a sentence that implies action by individuals rather than the group, a (singular/plural) _____ verb is customary.

4 In light of exercises 1–3, what verb is needed in each of these sentences?

    A. **The band (was/were) _____ starting to play "Auld Lang Syne."**

    B. **The class (is/are) _____ working in the laboratory on their various projects.**

    C. **Our committee (is/are) _____ going to meet on Friday afternoon.**

    D. **The jury (has/have) _____ diverse backgrounds.**

5 Some words not usually thought of as collective nouns may also take either singular or plural verbs, depending on meaning.

    A. **The remainder of the course is concerned with problems of immigrants.**
    B. **The remainder of the test booklets were destroyed.**

In A, *remainder* refers to a single thing, an amount of time. In B, *remainder* refers to a number of countable things, test booklets. This distinction explains the difference in verbs. Understanding the distinction helps you to choose the appropriate verb in this sentence: *A total of four hundred soldiers* (*is/are*) _____ *affected.*

6 The number of displaced persons is large.
A number of displaced persons are being retrained.

In the first sentence we are talking about *the number* as a number: it is a large number; therefore the number *is* large. But in the second example, a number is not being retrained; rather, displaced persons are being retrained.

Similarly we would say *A number of television sets* (*was/were*) _____ *stolen* and *The number of color television sets* (*has/have*) _____ *grown rapidly.*

7 INCONSISTENT: The class straggles in and takes their seats. It talks noisily until the bell rings.

CONSISTENT: The class straggle in and take their seats. They talk noisily until the bell rings.

In the inconsistent example *class* starts out as a singular, as the verbs *straggles* and *takes* reveal. Then it becomes plural, in *their seats.* Once more it changes—back to singular—in *It talks.* In the consistent example *class* is treated throughout as a plural. Besides the plural verbs, the possessive word

_____ and the pronoun _____ are also plural.
     Note: Some persons say that expressions like *The class are* or *The band enter* are awkward. It is perfectly satisfactory, of course, to substitute *The members of the class are* or *The band members enter.*

8 **If the committee is too large, they will waste much of their time in discussing irrelevant issues.**

How should the sentence above be revised to make it consistent in the collective noun, the verb, the pronoun, and the possessive?

_____

_____

9 Ten minutes is not very long.
Seven dollars is a low price for a watch.
Two hundred words is the average length.
Eight miles is not too far to walk.

In the four examples above, the subjects each appear to be plural. However, *ten minutes* is thought of as a unit of time, *seven dollars* as a unit of money, and so on. When an apparently plural subject refers to something conceived of as a unit, the verb is _____.

C: ASSIGNMENTS

• Make up two sentences using each of these words as subjects: *band, class, committee, herd, jury, team*. One of the sentences in each pair should be written so that a singular verb is required and one so that a plural verb is required.

• Make up sentences in which *remainder, total,* and *number* are used first as singular subjects and then as plural subjects.

• Make up sentences using each of these expressions as a subject: *two hours, four yards, fifty words, nine years.*

ANSWERS TO SECTION B

1. team
2. A singular
3. plural
4. A. was   B. are   C. is   D. have
5. are
6. were, has
7. their, They
8. If the committee is too large, it will waste much of its time in discussing irrelevant issues.
9. singular

Unit 70—Troublesome Verbs: *drive, eat, ride, shake, take, write*

A: COMMENTARY

The *-en* forms *driven, eaten, ridden, shaken, spoken, taken,* and *written,* when used as main verbs, require a helper such as *has, have, had, having, is, are, was, were, being,* or *been.*

The corresponding past tense forms *drove, ate, rode, shook, spoke, took,* and *wrote* are not used, in standard English, with auxiliaries (also called helpers). The major problem that people encounter with the verbs treated in this unit is the tendency to use helpers with verbs that do not need them. Thus we should say *had written,* not *had wrote, have eaten,* not *have ate.* In England the past tense of *eat* is spelled either *ate* or *eat* and is pronounced *et. Eaten,* however, is now the past participle in both England and America.

Rid was once a standard past tense and past participle of *ride: He rid the horse. He had rid all night.* Today that form is archaic or dialectal.

Have shook was once on the verge of becoming standard, but *have shaken* is the modern usage. A similar comment applies to *took* and *wrote:* with the helper we now use *taken* and *written.*

When the past participle is not a main verb, it does not need an auxiliary, as these parts of sentences illustrate:

> Gray's "Elegy *Written* in a Country Churchyard" . . .
> *Driven* from their homes, they . . .
> *Shaken* by their testimony, the defendant . . .
> The accused man, *taken* into custody, demanded . . .

Such uses seldom cause trouble. In a sense, an auxiliary is implied in each: *Elegy That Was Written, having been driven,* and so on.

Other *-en* verbs that are like those treated in this unit are *break, broke, broken; choose, chose, chosen; fall, fell, fallen; freeze, froze, frozen;* and *steal, stole, stolen.*

B: EXERCISES

1 | PRESENT | PAST | PAST PARTICIPLE |
|---|---|---|
| drive | drove | (have) driven |
| eat | ate | (have) eaten |
| ride | rode | (have) ridden |
| shake | shook | (have) shaken |
| speak | spoke | (have) spoken |
| take | took | (have) taken |
| write | wrote | (have) written |

The third column in the table above shows the common element that makes it possible to treat these seven verbs together. All these past participles end in _____.

2 The purpose of this exercise is to combat such nonstandard expressions as *had drove* and the regional *He taken her to the dance.* As you note in the third column, the *-en* forms require the use of an auxiliary (helping) verb such as *have.* Is this true of the forms in the second column? _____

3 Suppose that you do not know whether *ate* or *eaten* is needed in a particular sentence. Exercise 2 has given you the necessary clue. How will you make the decision? _____

_____

4 Suppose now that you have started a sentence like this: *I had already* . . .
The next word is to be a form of *write*. What word do you choose, and why?

_____

_____

5 In exercises 5–11 you will observe several verbs in parentheses, followed by a
sentence or a part of a sentence. For each of the verbs given, you are to
write the past tense or the past participle, whichever is appropriate within
the context.

(*drive, ride, write*)   had _____ home

had _____ home

had _____ home

6 (*shake, take*)   he _____ my hand

he _____ my hand

7 (*shake, take*)   having _____ my hand

having _____ my hand

8 (*drive, ride,*   we _____ to the sheriff

speak, write)   we _____ to the sheriff

we _____ to the sheriff

we _____ to the sheriff

9 (*eat, take*)   I have _____ my lunch

I have _____ my lunch

10 (*drive, eat,*   was being _____

ride, shake,   was being _____

speak, take,   are being _____

write)   were being _____

may have been _____

was already _____

will have been _____

11 (*break, choose, fall,*   The lock was _____.

freeze, steal)   The cast was _____.

The barometer has _____.

No ice had _____.

My watch was _____.

C: ASSIGNMENTS

• Make up one sentence each with *drove, driven, ate, eaten, rode, ridden, shook, shaken, spoke, spoken, took, taken, wrote, written, broke, broken, chose, chosen, fell, fallen, stole, stolen.*

• Become a specialist on one of the seven verbs emphasized in Section B. For example, attune your ear to every use of *shake, shakes, shaking, shook, shaken* for a period of a week. Keep notes and write several paragraphs on your findings. Include variants such as *all shook up*. Comment on the circumstances in which each form appears, especially the past tense and the past participle.

ANSWERS TO SECTION B

1. -en
2. No
3. MODEL If an auxiliary verb is used, the *-en* form is needed, but not otherwise.
4. MODEL I choose *written* because of the auxiliary *had.*
5. driven, ridden, written
6. shook, took
7. shaken, taken
8. drove, rode, spoke, wrote
9. eaten, taken
10. driven, eaten, ridden, shaken, spoken, taken, written
11. broken, chosen, fallen, frozen, stolen

Unit 71—Troublesome Verbs: *begin, drink, ring, sing, sink, swim*

A: COMMENTARY

This unit specifically concerns the verbs *begin, drink, ring, sing, sink,* and *swim.* Their past tense forms are *began, drank, rang, sang, sank,* and *swam.* Their past participles are *begun, drunk, rung, sung, sunk,* and *swum.*

The past tense (*a*-forms) are used when no helping verb (auxiliary) is present: *I began work, I drank some coffee,* and so on.

The past participles (*u*-forms) are used when an auxiliary is present. Auxiliaries are generally *have, has, had, having, is, are, was, were, being, been,* or *having been.*

At one time *begun, rung,* and *swum* were used in standard English without an auxiliary, but that is now seldom if ever true.

Had drank is often used informally but is not standard throughout the United States. *Drunken* was formerly the past participle: *had drunken his ale.* Today *drunken* is only a modifier: *a drunken patron* (or *a drunk patron*).

Section B considers the status of *sang* and *sank.* In the nineteenth century *She sung a solo* was the preferred form, but today *She sang a solo* is more frequent in printed materials. Both *sang* and *sung,* though, are recognized by dictionaries and students of usage as past tense forms in reputable use. The same comment applies to *sank* and *sunk.* In case lifted eyebrows worry you, however, you will see none if you say *She sang a solo* and *She sank the ship,* but you may see some if you use *sung* and *sunk* in those sentences.

The past participle functions in one way without a helper, as in these examples:

Drunk with his own wit, Fritz continued his clowning.
The aria, sung with pensive wistfulness, was delightful.

This kind of usage seldom causes trouble. No one would, for instance, be tempted to say *drank* in the first example.

B: EXERCISES

1

PRESENT	PAST	PAST PARTICIPLE
beg *i* n	beg *a* n	(have) beg *u* n
dr *i* nk	dr *a* nk	(have) dr *u* nk
r *i* ng	r *a* ng	(have) r *u* ng
s *i* ng	s *a* ng	(have) s *u* ng
s *i* nk	s *a* nk	(have) s *u* nk
sw *i* m	sw *a* m	(have) sw *u* m

The table above shows why these six verbs are discussed together. What is the reason? _____

2 The chief problem in these verbs arises from confusion of the past tense and the past participle. The past tense of each verb contains the vowel _____, and the past participle contains the vowel _____.

3 In the third column in exercise 1 note the *have* before each verb. This means that the forms with *u* should be employed as main verbs only when an auxiliary (helping) verb such as *have* is present. Is it desirable, then, to write

I begun studying at eight o'clock? _____

4 In the second column in exercise 1 note that no word such as *have* is included. Simple past tense verbs use no auxiliaries. Is it desirable, then, to write *I had swam for an hour?* _____

5 In summary, we should use the *a*-forms of these six verbs when (an/no) _____ auxiliary is present. We should use the *u*-forms when (an/no) _____ auxiliary is present.

6 In exercises 6–8 for each verb in parentheses choose either the past tense or past participle.

   A. (*swim*) I had _____ for an hour.

   B. (*swim*) I _____ across the lake.

   C. (*sink*) The ship _____ without a trace.

   D. (*sink*) The ship was _____ by an enemy submarine.

   E. (*sing*) She _____ an aria from *Carmen*.

   F. (*sing*) She has always _____ beautifully.

7 A. (*ring*) Have you _____ the bell?

   B. (*ring*) We _____ out the old year.

   C. (*drink*) The baby _____ her milk greedily.

   D. (*drink*) The baby has _____ her milk.

   E. (*begin*) The concert will have _____ before we arrive.

   F. (*begin*) Children _____ crying.

8 A. (*drink*) Has all the wine been _____?

   B. (*begin*) After the concert ended, Jerome _____ to criticize.

   C. (*swim*) This channel has never been _____.

   D. (*sing*) Some popular songs suffer from being _____ too often.

   E. (*sink*) The barge having been _____, the crew had to go home.

   F. (*ring*) Has the bell been _____ yet?

C: ASSIGNMENTS

Compose two sentences each with *drank, drunk, began, begun, rang, rung, sang, sung, sank, sunk, swam, swum.* Check each time on the presence or absence of an auxiliary.

ANSWERS TO SECTION B

1. MODEL   They all use *i* in the present tense, *a* in the past tense, and *u* in the past participle.
2. a, u
3. No
4. No
5. no   an
6. A. swum   B. swam   C. sank   D. sunk   E. sang   F. sung
7. A. rung   B. rang   C. drank   D. drunk   E. begun   F. began
8. A. drunk   B. began   C. swum   D. sung   E. sunk   F. rung

Unit 72—Other Troublesome Verbs

A: COMMENTARY

This unit concerns fifteen verbs that have little in common except that they pose much difficulty for users of English. They are among the most frequently used verbs in the language.

　　The basic principle is that the past tense verbs are used without a helper, but the past participles, when employed as main verbs, each take a helper.

B: EXERCISES

The exercise that follows pertains to the verbs in this list:

PRESENT	PAST	PAST PARTICIPLE
blow	blew	(have) blown
burst	burst	(have) burst
come	came	(have) come
do	did	(have) done
drag	dragged	(have) dragged
draw	drew	(have) drawn
fly	flew	(have) flown
go	went	(have) gone

grow	grew	(have) grown
know	knew	(have) known
run	ran	(have) run
see	saw	(have) seen
tear	tore	(have) torn
throw	threw	(have) thrown
wear	wore	(have) worn

1 Which verb in the list uses the same form throughout? _____

2 What five verbs in the list use -ew in the past tense and -own as the past

participle? _____ _____ _____ _____ _____

3 Notice that the verb forms in the third column are used with auxiliaries (helpers) such as *have, having, was,* or *are.* You should say:

A. **I have (threw/throwed/thrown)** _____ **the ball.**

B. **The birds have (flew/flown)** _____ **south.**

C. **How that child has (grew/growed/grown)** _____!

D. **Had he (knew/knowed/known)** _____ **that before?**

E. **Was the whistle (blew/blowed/blown)** _____?

4 Note that the past tense and the past participle of *drag* are both *dragged.* Make up a sentence with the past tense.

_____

5 *Tear* and *wear,* you notice, are similar in their principal parts. Write a sentence using the past participle of *tear.*

_____

6 Write a sentence using the past participle of *wear.*

_____

7 Write a sentence using the past tense of *come.*

_____

8 Write a sentence using the past participle of *come.*

_____

9 Write a sentence using the past participle of *go.*

_____

10 Write a sentence using the past tense of *run*.

_____

11 Write a sentence using the past participle of *run*.

_____

12 Write a sentence using the past tense of *see*.

_____

13 In exercises 13–17 you will see several verbs in parentheses, followed by a sentence. For each of the verbs given, you are to write the past tense or the past participle, whichever is appropriate in the context.

(*drag, draw, fly,*   We _____ the kite.

see, tear)   _____

                         _____

                         _____

                         _____

14 (*drag, draw, fly,*   We had _____ the kite.

see, tear)   _____

                         _____

                         _____

                         _____

15 (*burst, come, go, run*)   It had _____ immediately.

                         _____

                         _____

                         _____

16 (*do, know, see*)   We _____ the work.

                         _____

                         _____

17 (*blow, burst, come,* It _____ across the snow.

fly, go, run, tear,   _____

throw)   _____

—————————
—————————
—————————
—————————
—————————

C: ASSIGNMENTS

• If any of the verbs in this unit give you trouble, try making up a number of sentences with them, especially the past tense and past participial forms. After checking your sentences for accuracy, practice saying them aloud until the correct forms sound natural to you. Such oral practice, continued for as long as necessary, is the very best way to master bothersome verb forms.

• Compose a sentence with the past tense and another with the past participle of each of the verbs in this unit (thirty sentences in all).

ANSWERS TO SECTION B

1. burst
2. blow, fly, grow, know, throw
3. A. thrown   B. flown   C. grown   D. known   E. blown
4. MODEL   The dog dragged the dirty sack across the lawn.
5. MODEL   She had torn her slacks.
6. MODEL   Have you ever worn culottes?
7. MODEL   The visiting team never came very close.
8. MODEL   You've come a long way, Jack.
9. MODEL   My brothers had gone swimming.
10. MODEL   Grant ran the mile in 4:20.
11. MODEL   He had never run so fast before.
12. MODEL   We saw several meteors last night.
13. dragged, drew, flew, saw, tore
14. dragged, drawn, flown, seen, torn
15. burst, come, gone, run
16. did, knew, saw
17. blew, burst, came, flew, went, ran, tore, threw

Unit 73—*Lay* Versus *Lie*

A: COMMENTARY

Lie and *lay* are often confused with each other. The most common mistake is to use a form of *lay* when a form of *lie* is intended.

This unit suggests that when you are in doubt about the form to choose, you first consider meaning. If the meaning is "to place," you will use *lay, lays, laying,* or *laid*. If the meaning is "to recline," you will use *lie, lies, lying, lay* (past tense), or (have) *lain*.

As a second test, you may note whether your sentence tells about placing *something,* as in *She lays the papers on the desk.* If so, a form of *lay* is needed. Otherwise, a form of *lie* is required, as in *She lies on the couch.*

One source of confusion is that the present tense of *lay* is the same as the past tense of *lie: I lay the papers on the desk* (present tense) and *I lay in bed yesterday until noon* (past tense).

Somewhere some persons have acquired the misinformation that people *lie* and animals or things *lay*. This is completely untrue. People *lie* in bed, dogs *lie* beside the porch, stones *lie* on the ground.

B: EXERCISES

1 **lay   lays   laying   laid**

   The words above are all the forms of *lay,* meaning "to place." Note the spelling of *laid,* which is the past tense and past participle. Which of the four forms would you use in each of these sentences?

   A. _____ the package on the shelf.

   B. She is _____ the package on the shelf.

   C. She _____ the package on the shelf yesterday.

   D. She _____ packages on the shelf whenever she can.

2 Look again at the sentence examples in exercise 1. Is it true that in each sentence the verb means "to place" ("places," "placed," "placing")?

   _____ Is it also true that in each instance the sentence refers to

   placing something? _____

3 In summary, a form of *lay* may be used when the meaning is _____

   _____ and when we are talking about placing _____.

4 lie   lies   lying   lay   (have) lain

The words above are all the forms of *lie*, meaning "to recline" (not to be confused with *lie*, meaning "to tell a falsehood"). Which form would you use in each of these sentences?

A. I enjoy _____ in the sun.

B. I _____ in the sun whenever I can.

C. She _____ in the sun whenever she can.

D. I _____ in the sun all day yesterday.

E. He has _____ in the sun for an hour.

5 Look again at the sentences in exercise 4. Is it true that in each the verb means "to recline" ("reclines," "reclining," "reclined")? _____ Is it also true that in each sentence nothing is placed other than the person who does the reclining? _____

6 In summary, a form of *lie* may be used when the meaning is _____ _____ and when we are not talking about _____ something.

7 To decide, then, whether a form of *lay* or a form of *lie* is needed in a particular sentence, we may note first whether the meaning is "to place" or "to recline." If the meaning is "to place," a form of _____ is required. If the meaning is "to recline," a form of _____ is required.

8 As a second test (if needed), we may note whether the sentence in effect says that something is placed by someone. If it does, a form of _____ is required. If it does not, a form of _____ is required.

9 Underline the proper form in each sentence.

A. I like to (lay/lie) on the beach.
B. Please (lay/lie) the blanket here.
C. I was (laying/lying) there last night.
D. Have you (laid/lain) on this mattress?
E. Have you (laid/lain) anything on this mattress?

10 Again, underline the proper form.

A. He (laid/lay) there last night.
B. Jack (lays/lies) in bed until nine.
C. Don't (lay/lie) there.

  D. **Don't (lay/lie) it there.**
  E. **She has (lain/laid) here for an hour.**

C: ASSIGNMENTS

• If *lie* and *lay* trouble you, oral practice is the best way to gain accuracy and confidence. Make up and say to yourself two or three dozen sentences similar to those in exercises 9 and 10. (In some school and adult classes, the group repeats in unison a number of practice sentences.)

ANSWERS TO SECTION B

  1. A. Lay   B. laying   C. laid   D. lays
  2. Yes   Yes
  3. "to place"   something
  4. A. lying   B. lie   C. lies   D. lay   E. lain
  5. Yes   Yes
  6. "to recline"   placing
  7. lay   lie
  8. lay   lie
  9. A. lie   B. lay   C. lying   D. lain   E. laid
  10. A. lay   B. lies   C. lie   D. lay   E. lain

Unit 74—Set, Sit; Raise, Rise

A: COMMENTARY

Set and *raise* ordinarily mean "to place" and "to lift," so the sentences in which they are used refer to placing or lifting something. In contrast, *sit* and *rise* mean "to take a sitting position" and "to ascend," and the sentences in which they appear do not refer to placing or lifting something.

  One exception to the rule is that you may *sit* a person (or possibly *seat* a person), but you *set a sack* on the table.

  Set and *raise* have a number of less frequently used meanings. In such sentences, though, something still receives an action; for example, *to set a hen, to set a clock, to raise* (or *rear*) *a family, to raise your voice.*

B: EXERCISES

1 **Please set the box here.**
 He sets the package down.
 I am setting the cans on the shelf.

 In each sentence above, the verb means ("to place"/"to take a sitting position") _____.

2 In each sentence in exercise 1 the verb refers to placing a thing. (true/false)

 _____

3 The forms of *set* are *set, sets,* and *setting.* This verb is used when the
 meaning is _____ and when it refers to _____.

4 **I sit here frequently.**
 Grandpa sits here every day.
 Eileen sat on the bench.
 Who was sitting beside her?

 In each sentence above, the verb means ("to place"/"to take a sitting position") _____.

5 In each sentence in exercise 4 the verb refers to placing a thing. (true/
 false) _____

6 The forms of *sit* are *sit, sits, sat,* and *sitting.* One of these forms is used
 when the verb means _____ and when it does not refer to

 _____.

7 When you are uncertain whether to use a form of *set* or a form of *sit,* you
 may apply either or both of two tests. One test is that of meaning. You will
 choose *set* when the meaning is _____ and *sit* when the
 meaning is_____.

8 The second test is to note whether the sentence refers to placing a thing. If
 it does, a form of _____ (Which verb?) is required. If it does not, a
 form of _____ is required.

9 Supply the required form of *set* or *sit.*

 A. **I had _____ in the lobby for an hour.**

 B. **Next she _____ her mind to a new task.**

C. Don't _____ on this chair.

D. Where were you _____ when the lights went out?

E. _____ the cans on the floor.

F. The child _____ there sobbing.

10 Raise the lid, please.
The elevator rises swiftly.
I rise each morning at six.

In the first sentence the meaning is "to lift," and the sentence refers to lifting something. In the last two sentences the meaning is "to ascend" or "to get up," and the sentence does not refer to lifting anything.
We may conclude, then, that the verb to use when a sentence refers to lifting something is _____. But when the meaning of the verb is "to ascend" or "to get up," a form of _____ is needed.

11 raise   raises   raised   raising
rise   rises   rose   risen   rising

From the list above, choose the appropriate verb for each sentence.

A. She does not believe in _____ her voice.

B. Does he _____ corn?

C. She _____ as late as she possibly can.

D. The moon had already _____.

E. Two grimy soldiers _____ from the ditch when the captain appeared.

F. I _____ one corner of the box but needed help.

G. They seldom _____ up in anger this year.

H. Lulu _____ a question whenever she can.

I. The wind is _____.

12 In this unit you have reviewed four verbs: set, sit, raise, and rise. Set is similar to (raise/rise) _____. Sit is similar to (raise/rise) _____.

C: ASSIGNMENTS

• Compose two sentences with each of the verb forms listed in exercises 3, 6, and 11.

ANSWERS TO SECTION B

1. "to place"
2. true
3. "to place"   placing something
4. "to take a sitting position"
5. false
6. "to take a sitting position"   placing something
7. "to place"   "to take a sitting position"
8. set   sit
9. A. sat   B. set   C. sit   D. sitting   E. Set   F. sat
10. raise   rise
11. A. raising   B. raise   C. rises   D. risen   E. rose   F. raised   G. rise
    H. raises   I. rising
12. raise   rise

Unit 75—Abbreviations

A: COMMENTARY

The chief purpose of this unit is to point out the relatively small number of abbreviations likely to be found in ordinary formal or semiformal writing. Sentences like the following leave the impression that the writer is hasty and sloppy and that he or she really has little respect for the reader:

The prof. in my lit. course came here from Ga.

Only a few abbreviations are recommended in Section B. Although you may be justified in adding a few other acceptable ones, you will be wise to avoid using many others in your formal and semiformal writing.

B: EXERCISES

1 In reference books, where space-saving is important, numerous abbreviations appear. But in ordinary writing only a small number are customary. Here are some that are readily acceptable in all kinds of writing:

Dr. Graham   **St. Andrew**
Mr. (Mrs., Ms.) Dawson   **Ray Barnes, Jr. (Sr.)**
Mmes. Dot and Gray   **Messrs. Dot and Gray**

Each of the above abbreviations, when correctly used, accompanies a proper name. Is this sentence right? *The Dr. examined Jr. this morning.*

2 Elton Caldwell, D.D.   Samuel Platt, Ph. D.

Abbreviations are used for degrees, when the person's name is used. Would it be correct in formal context to write *He is an M.D.?* _____

3 RIGHT IN FORMAL CONTEXT: She lives in Washington, D.C.

UNDESIRABLE IN FORMAL CONTEXT: She lives in Yuma, Az.

District of Columbia is regularly abbreviated when *Washington* precedes it. Names of states should not be abbreviated in formal writing, although the postal services recommend use of the official two-letter abbreviations in addresses.

What corrections should be made in this sentence? *We moved from*

Ok. to D.C. _____

4 in 420 B.C. (A.D.)   5:20 A.M. (or a.m., P.M., p.m.)
                                        Room No. 211

With numerals or dates the abbreviations above are also regularly acceptable. Which of the following two sentences is correct? _____

A. Early in the A.M. Mike rang the bell on a house with an obliterated No.
B. At 2 A.M. Mike rang the bell on a house with an obliterated number.

5 SATISFACTORY IN MOST CONTEXTS: He started with A, skipped to C, then
                                    to F, etc.
UNSATISFACTORY: Send flour, sheets, mats, etc.

Etc. is overused. It is satisfactory when the reader can readily fill in the unnamed parts. It is unsatisfactory when the reader is left guessing. If you received as a message the sentence labeled UNSATISFACTORY, could you with confidence send any items other than the three named? _____

6 UNSATISFACTORY: They were married on Fri., Dec. 23.

Make up a rule based on the example above.

_____

_____

7 UNSATISFACTORY: King Philip & King George conferred.

The abbreviation for *and* is called *ampersand*. It is sometimes used in official titles of companies, as W. W. Norton & Company, Inc. In ordinary writing, though, it (should/should not) _____ be used.

8 **R.S.V.P.** (sometimes written **RSVP**)

Where would you be most likely to see the above abbreviation?

___

9 **i.e. e.g. cf.** *ca.*

The abbreviations above are rather specialized. All four come from **Latin**. In formal writing the English equivalents, in words, are likely to be used, but in technical and semiformal writing and even in many scholarly books the abbreviations may be found. Consulting your dictionary if necessary, write what each means.

___

10 If you ever do use *i.e.* or *e.g.*, be sure not to confuse them. *I.e.* is short for *id est*, meaning "that is." *E.g.* is short for Latin *exempli gratia*, literally "for the sake of example."

Which might fit in the following sentence, *i.e.* or *e.g.?* _____ Some

metals, _____ aluminum, are very light in weight.

11 In footnotes and bibliographies, but not in regular writing, other special abbreviations are often used, including those below. What does each mean? (Use your dictionary if you need to.)

ibid. op. cit. **ch. vol. p. pp. ll.**

___

___

12 **NBC FBI CIA CORE**

Abbreviations we have considered earlier are punctuated with periods. Most often the periods are omitted in abbreviations written with capital letters, especially those representing governmental agencies. Write two other abbre-

viations of this sort. _____ _____

C: ASSIGNMENTS

• What changes should be made in the following sentences? Assume a semi-formal context for each.
1. The lecturer talked about immigration policies, etc.
2. Mister Cash brought Mrs. to the Dr.
3. We left N.D. on a Thurs.
4. All this started in the B.C. and was continued A.D.
5. I work best and get most done in the P.M.

6. Sometime in Oct. the 1st snowfall came.
7. We got home O.K.; i.e., we were not in any accs.
8. The assignments in both chem. and psych. were heavy.
9. After leaving the U. of Minn. he attended a comm. coll. in LA.
10. The prof who spoke at convo gave some good advice about lab courses for frosh and sophs.

ANSWERS TO SECTION B

1. No
2. No
3. Oklahoma, the District of Columbia
4. B
5. No
6. MODEL   In ordinary writing, names of days and months should not be abbreviated.
7. should not
8. MODEL   In a formal invitation
9. i.e.: "that is"   e.g.: "for example"   cf.: "compare"   *ca.*: "about"
10. e.g.
11. *ibid.*: "from the same source"   *op. cit.*: "from the work cited"   ch.: "chapter"   vol.: "volume"   p.: "page"   pp.: "pages"   ll.: "lines"
12. MODELS   CBS   FFA

MASTERY
TEST

The purpose of this mastery test is to show you the extent to which your study has been profitable. In taking the test and recording the results follow the same procedure as for the diagnostic test. Remember to select well-constructed sentences only. The possible total of correctly encircled items is 117.

The test results may show some groups in which you still make one or more errors. You should review the corresponding units in this book and perhaps (where appropriate) make up some comparable oral or written drills of your own.

Be sure to insert a carbon (shiny side up) behind this page.

Part One—Gaining Respect for Your Ideas

In groups 1 and 2 some statements should be qualified to be really believable. Choose those that seem satisfactory as they are.

1

Vehicle traffic in downtown areas should be banned.   1–1

Use of private automobiles in the twelve square block area of downtown Midvale should be banned.   1–2

The growth of cities, which house most of the American population, has been the greatest curse to befall American civilization.   1–3

Constant competition is the best way to get people to do their best work.   1–4

2

Our dog, Rover, dragged my baby brother from our house when it caught fire.   2–1

Dogs are people's best friends and most valuable allies.   2–2

Full-grown trees are over fifteen feet tall; other woody plants are bushes.   2–3

Permissiveness, which caused the downfall of the Roman civilization, is also ruining the United States.   2–4

In this group choose any statements that are factual or at least possible to check.

3

The area that we call the District of Columbia was once part of Maryland.   3–1

A democratic form of government, as is proved by the success of the United States, is the best form.   3–2

Rowing develops the body better than any other sport does.   3–3

The Great Sphynx of Egypt was not one of the seven wonders of the ancient world.   3–4

1–1

1–2

1–3

1–4

This group tests your ability to distinguish between unwise generalizations and statements that are sufficiently specific. You should have encircled 1–2 but no other number.

_____ Check here if you missed any item.

2–1

2–2

2–3

2–4

This group tests your ability to distinguish satisfactory statements from those that need some qualifying. You should have encircled 2–1 but no other number.

_____ Check here if you missed any item.

3–1

3–2

3–3

3–4

This group tests your ability to distinguish factual or checkable statements from those that represent only opinion. You should have encircled 3–1 and 3–4 but no other number.

_____ Check here if you missed any item.

Be sure to insert a carbon (shiny side up) behind this page.

In groups 4 and 5 select any statements that you believe most thoughtful persons would be willing to accept as true.

4

Some women are more intelligent than some men (and vice versa).   4–1

A large number of students cannot read, write, figure, and reason well enough to be highly successful in college.   4–2

Today's college students are brighter but less hard working than those of a generation ago.   4–3

New Yorkers are more sophisticated than residents of any other American city.   4–4

5

Either the library tax rate will have to be increased or the city's libraries will all have to shut down.   5–1

If the river ever again floods the farms of this prosperous valley, serious property damage is sure to occur.   5–2

If pornographic books and movies are not outlawed, the people of this great land will be inflamed by perversion.   5–3

Either we must strike the enemy first or the enemy will destroy us.   5–4

In this group select statements that seem logical in their wording.

6

Political science courses offer information about local and state governments, as well as a detailed analysis of the national government.   6–1

His purpose in going to technical school is a welder.   6–2

The solution of many murder mysteries is the butler.   6–3

Some politicians preach democracy with one tongue but fear and deny it with the other.   6–4

4–1

4–2

4–3

4–4

This group tests your ability to distinguish stereotypes from statements that are more defensible. You should have encircled 4–1 and 4–2 but no other number.

_____ Check here if you missed any item.

5–1

5–2

5–3

5–4

This group tests your ability to distinguish incorrect *either* . . . *or* statements from those which admit other possibilities. You should have encircled 5–2 but no other number.

_____ Check here if you missed any item.

6–1

6–2

6–3

6–4

This group tests your ability to select statements that are worded in a logical way. You should have encircled 6–1 but no other number.

_____ Check here if you missed any item.

Be sure to insert a carbon (shiny side up) behind this page.

In this group choose the two sentences that would be appropriate in a formal piece of writing.

7

Charlemagne was one of the greatest rulers of all time.	7–1
In a lot of ways he was way ahead of most folks in his day.	7–2
For example, he didn't think it was just the nobles and the rich mucka-mucks that should be protected by the laws.	7–3
Through decrees called *capitularies*, Charlemagne assured fair treatment for the poor and the underprivileged.	7–4

In this group select statements that have no editorial slip-ups or misprints.

8

Although Ralph Welsh scared thirty-six points, our team still lost by twenty-seven.	8–1
The purpose of SIECUS is to do for sex what has already been done for polio, tuberculosis, smallpox, and other human ailments.	8–2
Saratoga firemen responded to a call at 9:50 A.M. The fire is under study.	8–3
The audience began to boo and hiss the tenor gesticulated angrily and left the stage.	8–4

Part Two—The Sentence

In groups 9–15 choose all the sentences that you consider well constructed.

9

Harry S. Truman had no middle name.	9–1
Technically, perhaps, we should write the S. without a period.	9–2
An initial not really an initial unless it stands for something.	9–3
The S actually serves the purpose of a middle name.	9–4

10

Tom and Joe standing under the big umbrella.	10–1
Tom and Joe stood under the big umbrella.	10–2
Tom and Joe under the big umbrella.	10–3
Tom and Joe were standing under the big umbrella.	10–4

7-1
7-2
7-3

7-4

This group tests your ability to select sentences that are written in relatively formal language. You should have encircled 7-1 and 7-4 but no other number.

_____ Check here if you missed any item.

8-1
8-2
8-3

8-4

This group tests your ability to spot careless editing or misprints. You should have encircled no number at all.

_____ Check here if you missed any item.

9-1
9-2
9-3
9-4

This group tests your ability to distinguish a sentence from a fragment. You should have encircled 9-1, 9-2, and 9-4 but not 9-3.

_____ Check here if you missed any item.

10-1
10-2
10-3
10-4

This group tests your ability to recognize sentences containing complete verbs. You should have encircled 10-2 and 10-4 but no other number.

_____ Check here if you missed any item.

11

The morning was cold. It was sunny, though. There was no hint of snow.	11–1
When we had fed the cattle, we started the long ride to Pine Ridge.	11–2
Gray clouds appeared on the horizon. They were in the west. We were still not worried.	11–3
Gradually, however, the clouds got thicker and darker, and the wind strengthened.	11–4

12

Jay was pecking away at the typewriter, and he was writing a play.	12–1
Plays are notoriously difficult to write, and novels are much easier, but Jay wanted to write a play, for he dreamed of Broadway lights.	12–2
A playwright can show only limited action, for the characters are confined in a small physical space.	12–3
A novelist has no such limits for the characters can be moved anywhere and they can fly on planes or they can fight a whole war, but a playwright has no such freedom.	12–4

13

I read in the paper where India's population is up another fifty million.	13–1
An earthquake has rocked northern Japan because I was watching the news on television.	13–2
Although the editor chose only one of my poems, I was jubilant because for the first time I would see my name in print.	13–3
We were strolling down a country road, and a truck went careening into a ditch.	13–4

14

Marie Curie, whose original name was Marya Sklodowska, was born in Warsaw, Poland, in 1867.	14–1
She became a student in Paris. There she lived in a garret. She often had only bread and tea for her meals.	14–2
While still a student, she met and married Pierre Curie, a Frenchman who worked with her until his tragic death twelve years later.	14–3
They were co-discoverers of polonium and of radium, which has saved the lives of countless cancer patients.	14–4

11–1

11–2

This group tests your ability to recognize undesirably short sentences. You should have encircled 11–2 and 11–4 but no other number.

11–3

_____ Check here if you missed any item.

11–4

12–1

This group tests your ability to recognize good compound sentences. You should have encircled 12–3 but no other number.

12–2

_____ Check here if you missed any item.

12–3

12–4

13–1

This group tests your recognition of effective subordination. You should have encircled 13–3 but no other number.

13–2

_____ Check here if you missed any item.

13–3

13–4

14–1

This group tests your ability to recognize other effective methods of subordination. You should have encircled 14–1, 14–3, and 14–4 but not 14–2.

14–2

_____ Check here if you missed any item.

14–3

14–4

15

All people need something that they can believe in so strongly that they are willing to work for it, to live for it, and if need be to die for it.　15–1

The car turned over, having run into a ditch when the driver saw a bee in the car, and he was only slightly injured.　15–2

From the thicket I heard a feeble cry, but previously I had seen leaves moving and had thought that the child might be in that thicket.　15–3

The plane taxied to the main runway, turned, roared away to its graceful takeoff, and, once it had gained altitude, banked sharply.　15–4

In groups 16 and 17 choose the two most emphatic sentences in each group.

16

Around the bend roared a speeding motorcycle.　16–1

A speeding motorcycle roared around the bend.　16–2

Inflation is as bad for poor people as a recession, it seems to me.　16–3

It seems to me that inflation is as bad for poor people as a recession.　16–4

17

A touchdown was scored by Jonas in the last minute.　17–1

Jonas scored a touchdown in the last minute.　17–2

Martha banged out a march on the piano, and Frank blatted a trombone solo.　17–3

A march was banged out on the piano by Martha, and a trombone solo was blatted by Frank.　17–4

Resume choosing all the sentences that you believe are well constructed.

18

The brushes are on the dresser in my bedroom, which is at the north end of the house.　18–1

I want the pencil in the desk in my room that has green lead.　18–2

Students of any teachers who are not passing their courses may get tutorial assistance in Room 426.　18–3

Sir Thomas More, who wrote *Utopia*, refused to endorse the Act of Supremacy and was therefore beheaded.　18–4

15–1

15–2

15–3

15–4

This group tests your knowledge of effective arrangement of sentence parts. You should have encircled 15–1 and 15–4 but no other number.

_____ Check here if you missed any item.

16–1

16–2

16–3

16–4

This group tests your understanding of word order as a factor in emphasis. You should have encircled 16–1 and 16–4 but no other number.

_____ Check here if you missed any item.

17–1

17–2

17–3

17–4

This group tests your knowledge of the relative merits of the active and the passive voice as contributors to emphasis. You should have encircled 17–2 and 17–3 but no other number.

_____ Check here if you missed any item.

18–1

18–2

18–3

18–4

This group tests your recognition of logical placement of adjective clauses to prevent ambiguity. You should have encircled 18–1 and 18–4 but no other number.

_____ Check here if you missed any item.

Be sure to insert a carbon (shiny side up) behind this page.

19

By winning three consecutive championships, the huge trophy became ours to keep.   19—1

Sleeping the sleep of the exhausted, we heard none of the noise from the rooms downstairs.   19—2

Strolling across town occasionally he stops to admire the roses or to watch small children at play.   19—3

To climb to the summit, tons of equipment are needed.   19—4

20

An alert accountant and who knows the tax laws can earn a large income.   20—1

Eva was impressed by the grandeur of the Rockies, the chameleonic coloring of the Grand Canyon, and how ably people had adjusted to life in a terrain quite different from the prairies.   20—2

He is short, modest, and writes fluently.   20—3

Oscar is neither honest nor is he reliable.   20—4

21

I understand punctuation better than any student in my class.   21—1

Mavis likes the teacher better than John.   21—2

Huckleberry Finn, critics say, is better than any of Mark Twain's novels.   21—3

The Wright trial was as sensational, and at times even more dramatic, than the Creagle trial.   21—4

Part Three—Diction

In this group choose the two sentences that are the most concrete.

22

Trucks rumbled across the bridge and labored up the steep hill, holding up a long line of passenger cars.   22—1

Traffic moved along at a very slow pace because of the nature of the terrain.   22—2

Delays in construction occurred because of the weather and also because of labor troubles.   22—3

A wet spring and a plumbers' strike delayed completion of the factory.   22—4

19–1

19–2

19–3

19–4

This group tests your recognition of logical placement of adverbial modifiers, in contrast to "dangling" or "squinting" modifiers. You should have encircled 19–2 but no other number.

_____ Check here if you missed any item.

20–1

20–2

20–3

20–4

This group tests your recognition of parallel structure. You should not have encircled any number.

_____ Check here if you missed any item.

21–1

21–2

21–3

21–4

This group tests your knowledge of accuracy and completeness in the statement of comparisons. You should not have encircled any number.

_____ Check here if you missed any item.

22–1

22–2

22–3

22–4

This group tests your recognition of concrete and abstract words. You should have encircled 22–1 and 22–4 but no other number.

_____ Check here if you missed any item.

Be sure to insert a carbon (shiny side up) behind this page.

In this group choose the two sentences that are least slanted for or against Clancy.

23

Clancy is a crafty politician who is usually able to finagle the legislature into doing whatever he wants.	23–1
Clancy's extraordinary success with legislators is due to his genius in exerting leadership.	23–2
Governor Clancy persuaded the legislature to pass a housing reform bill that two previous legislatures had rejected.	23–3
The legislature, on the recommendation of Governor Clancy, turned down a proposal to legalize parimutuel betting.	23–4

In this group choose the two sentences that make the best use of figurative language.

24

I was hungry as a wolf when I got home, and it made me mad as a hornet to find that dinner was not ready.	24–1
The ski-jumper, his body angled almost like an inverted L, floated over and past us.	24–2
She cried until her eyes were as red as twin rubies set in the white alabaster of her face.	24–3
The furniture was as stark and unadorned as that of a Benedictine monk.	24–4

In groups 25–31 choose the sentences that you believe use all words correctly.

25

I disremember whether Salem or Portland is the capital of Oregon.	25–1
She don't come to class as regularly as she once did.	25–2
He might have earned considerably more money if his personality had been better.	25–3
Irregardless of what the doctor tells him, he still don't watch his diet.	25–4

26

Lot's wife turned into a pillow of salt.	26–1
The soldiers in the calvary units led the attack.	26–2
Lincoln was renowned for telling appropriate antidotes.	26–3
A huge stature of the general stands in the center of town.	26–4

23–1   This group tests your knowledge of connotations. You should have encircled 23–3 and 23–4 but no other number.

23–2   _____ Check here if you missed any item.

23–3

23–4

24–1   This group tests your sensitivity to figures of speech. You should have encircled 24–2 and 24–4 but no other number.

24–2   _____ Check here if you missed any item.

24–3

24–4

25–1   This group tests your recognition of certain nonstandard ex-
25–2   pressions. You should have encircled 25–3 but no other number.

                             _____ Check here if you missed any item.

25–3
25–4

26–1   This group tests your knowledge of certain words sometimes
26–2   confused with other words. You should not have encircled any number.

26–3   _____ Check here if you missed any item.

26–4

Be sure to insert a carbon (shiny side up) behind this page.

27

Altogether he cited over a dozen items of evidence to substantiate his plea.   27–1

As his avocation he is trying to visit all the state capitol cities in the United States.   27–2

The drama coach could never breathe easily until the climatic moments of the play were past.   27–3

I am anxious to except your offer.   27–4

28

A judge should be disinterested and not credulous.   28–1

Do you mean to infer that a little bird was enough to distract your attention?   28–2

The settlement may have been equitable, but it did not seem very humane.   28–3

Since she was only a high school sophomore from a small town, she was understandably ingenious and credible.   28–4

29

Whenever my mother would leave me go to the movies, I considered it a personal triumph.   29–1

Its important to use stationery of good quality.   29–2

Their morale is likely to be high because of praise from such a noted scientist.   29–3

Bryan always speaks respectfully of his high school principal.   29–4

30

The story is not really uninteresting—just difficult to understand.   30–1

An effervescent person on the screen, Judy Garland in private life was often severely depressed.   30–2

We never found any more nuggets of gold nowhere in the siftings.   30–3

Melissa Conklin, the girl who was the valedictorian, she was president of the class.   30–4

27–1

27–2

27–3

27–4

This group tests your knowledge of certain words sometimes confused with other words. You should have encircled 27–1 but no other number.

_____ Check here if you missed any item.

28–1

28–2

28–3

28–4

This group tests your knowledge of certain words sometimes confused with other words. You should have encircled 28–1 and 28–3 but no other item.

_____ Check here if you missed any item.

29–1

29–2

29–3

29–4

This group tests your knowledge of certain words sometimes confused with other words. You should have encircled 29–3 and 29–4 but no other number.

_____ Check here if you missed any item.

30–1

30–2

30–3

30–4

This group tests your recognition of double subjects and double negatives. You should have encircled 30–1 and 30–2 but no other number.

_____ Check here if you missed any item.

31

Where the earthquake was most severe, a huge, enormous crack in the earth's surface is still visible.   31–1

Hartford is in conference and has asked that Plum take all incoming calls.   31–2

The total amounts to the sum of five hundred dollars.   31–3

Today in this modern world we must find ways to feed and house over four billion people.   31–4

In this group choose the two sentences that provide the most specific information.

32

The diameter of Jupiter, the largest planet, is about thirty times that of Mercury, the smallest; Jupiter's gravity is so strong that a body would have to travel 129,000 miles an hour to escape it, compared with 9,600 for Mercury.   32–1

The contrasts between the largest and smallest planets in our solar system are deep and significant, including, for example, considerable differences in diameter, atmospheric conditions, gravitational pull, and escape velocity.   32–2

The installation of a drop ceiling is relatively easy, requiring only simple tools and no great skills in carpentry.   32–3

Anyone who can handle a hammer, snips, and pliers, and who can stand on a stepladder, can install a drop ceiling.   32–4

Part Four—Punctuation and Other Mechanics

In groups 33–56, as you choose the best sentences, pay particular attention to punctuation and other mechanical matters.

33

Oh, no! We can't have a rabbit in the house!!   33–1

Dr. Rogers and Mr. Clare have returned from Washington, DC.   33–2

She asked whether the plane was on time.   33–3

Why did you ask, "What is a ganglion?"?   33–4

31–1

This group tests your alertness to concise expression and your awareness of its opposite—wordiness or redundancy. You should have encircled 31–2 but no other number.

31–2

_____ Check here if you missed any item.

31–3

31–4

32–1

This group tests your ability to distinguish between specific and general statements. You should have encircled 32–1 and 32–4 but no other number.

_____ Check here if you missed any item.

32–2

32–3

32–4

33–1

This group tests your knowledge of terminal punctuation (periods, question marks, and exclamation marks). You should have encircled 33–3 but no other number.

33–2

33–3

_____ Check here if you missed any item.

33–4

34

While Alice called Helen Marion called Faye.	34–1
When we were drinking Caleb Beers, an old friend of mine, saw us.	34–2
To offset this college study is often more intellectually rewarding than that in high school.	34–3
The game over the players returned to their dressing rooms.	34–4

35

Have you seen a yellow, lead pencil?	35–1
A scrawny, sick-looking dog cowered in the doorway.	35–2
The mackerel was a big one, and its scales flashed green and silver in the sunlight.	35–3
The silver green and blue scales flashed in the sunlight.	35–4

36

At Grinnell Iowa we visited friends at the college.	36–1
"Do you know," she asked, "whether pets are allowed?"	36–2
Her reply however it happened was delayed.	36–3
On August 24, 1976, she first met Bob Gaines, a college friend of her brother.	36–4

37

Children who learn to read at an early age generally become very good readers.	37–1
My brother Sam who learned to read when he was four is a much better reader than I am.	37–2
Studying a volume of Western history last night I learned some interesting facts about Pueblo Indians.	37–3
The early history of the Pueblos which was one of invasion and conquest affords a bloody contrast to their later reputation for peacefulness.	37–4

38

My reply was, that the percentage of profit was too low.	38–1
I enjoy reading about British rulers, including, Henry VIII, Queen Elizabeth I, and Oliver Cromwell.	38–2
I enjoy reading, books about Henry VIII, Queen Elizabeth I, and Oliver Cromwell.	38–3
The warriors returned, from the hills, and from the buttes, but not from the valley.	38–4

34–1
34–2

This group tests your knowledge of the use of commas to prevent momentary misreading. You should not have encircled any number.

34–3

_____Check here if you missed any item.

34–4

35–1
35–2

This group tests your knowledge of the use of commas with coordinate elements (similar types of words, phrases, or clauses). You should have encircled 35–2 and 35–3 but no other number.

35–3

_____ Check here if you missed any item.

35–4

36–1
36–2
36–3

This group tests your knowledge of the use of commas with interpolated elements such as dates, places, transitions, appositives, and expressions such as *she said*. You should have encircled 36–2 and 36–4 but no other number.

36–4

_____ Check here if you missed any item.

37–1

This group tests your knowledge of the use of commas with nonessential (nonrestrictive) clauses and phrases. You should have encircled 37–1 but no other number.

37–2

_____ Check here if you missed any item.

37–3

37–4

38–1

This group tests your understanding of the need to avoid unnecessary commas. Since one or more commas should have been left out of each sentence, you should not have encircled any number.

38–2

_____ Check here if you missed any item.

38–3

38–4

39

The Cleopatra we hear so much about was not the only one, the name was a popular one among the Ptolemys.   39–1

The mother of Ptolemy VI, for instance, was called Cleopatra, and so was his sister; who also became his wife.   39–2

Ptolemy VII married his sister-in-law, Cleopatra; later he gave her up and married her daughter, another Cleopatra.   39–3

Ptolemy VIII had a daughter, Cleopatra Berenice, who was the stepmother of Ptolemy X; the Romans pressured Ptolemy X to marry her, but after the marriage he murdered her.   39–4

40

Thomas Carlyle said it this way: "It is unfortunate, though very natural, that the history of this period has so generally been written in hysterics."   40–1

Marie said: "You can't mean it!"   40–2

The team is weak in these respects: bunting, base-running, and out-fielding.   40–3

Dear Madam,
      Your account is now thirty days overdue.   40–4

41

Tom Jone's escapades in Fielding's novel amuse me.   41–1

Fishworm's and minnow's are for sale here.   41–2

Women's clothing and girls' clothing are on different floors.   41–3

Is this Bennett's jacket, or is it your's?   41–4

42

Its too late now, isnt it?   42–1

Did'nt they say what they're trying to find?   42–2

You'd better start, or you'll be late.   42–3

Hasn't the moon risen? I'm sure it's time.   42–4

43

His *as* and *os* are indistinguishable.   43–1

In keeping records, he enjoyed making @s' and florid &s'.   43–2

Dot your *i*'s and cross your *t*'s.   43–3

He constantly connects his explanatory sentences with *now*'s and *then*'s. 43–4

39–1

39–2

39–3

39–4

This group tests your knowledge of the use of semicolons in compound sentences. You should have encircled 39–3 and 39–4 but no other number.

_____ Check here if you missed any item.

40–1

40–2

40–3

40–4

This group tests your knowledge of certain uses of colons. You should have encircled 40–1 and 40–3 but no other number.

_____ Check here if you missed any item.

41–1

41–2

41–3

41–4

This group tests your knowledge of the use of apostrophes with possessives. You should have encircled 41–3 but no other number.

_____ Check here if you missed any item.

42–1

42–2

42–3

42–4

This group tests your knowledge of the use of apostrophes in contractions. You should have encircled 42–3 and 42–4 but no other number.

_____ Check here if you missed any item.

43–1

43–2

43–3

43–4

This group tests your knowledge of the use of apostrophes in certain rather unusual plurals. You should have encircled 43–3 and 43–4 but no other number.

_____ Check here if you missed any item.

44

I first looked up basic information in the encycl-
opedia.

44–1

She tugged at the doorknob with all the strength she had.

44–2

The little girl quickly made friends with the scrawn-
y kitten.

44–3

I was not very greatly impressed by *The Degrada-
tion of the Democratic Dogma.*

44–4

45

My stepfather and my father-in-law had the same great-grandmother.

45–1

With about one half of the season over, three-fourths of the teams had
losing records.

45–2

He made a well-known study of the effects of X-rays on queen bees.

45–3

Forty-six of the nearly one thousand ballots were invalid.

45–4

46

The typewriter—a rusty portable without a cover—was her favorite possession.

46–1

I detest all loud noises, roars -of trucks, screams of children, sonic
booms.

46–2

"Why are," she began.
"I told you to shut up!" he snarled.

46–3

During the war he—or maybe it was just after the war. Anyway, he
thought of his great invention.

46–4

47

The Scottish dialect (a modern form of Northumbrian Old English)
differs from English in pronunciation and vocabulary.

47–1

The Scottish dialect [a modern form of Northumbrian Old English]
differs from English in pronunciation and vocabulary.

47–2

"William Henry Harrison, the tenth President [actually the ninth], died
after a month in office," Mr. Canyon told the class.

47–3

The sales of leather (see Table 8) steadily declined.

47–4

44-1

44-2

44-3

44-4

This group tests your knowledge of the use of hyphens in dividing words at the ends of lines. You should have encircled 44-4 but no other number.

_____ Check here if you missed any item.

45-1

45-2

45-3

45-4

This group tests your knowledge of miscellaneous uses of hyphens. You should have encircled all four numbers.

_____ Check here if you missed any item.

46-1

46-2

46-3

46-4

This group tests your knowledge of some of the uses of dashes. You should have encircled 46-1 and 46-4 but no other number.

_____ Check here if you missed any item.

47-1

47-2

47-3

47-4

This group tests your knowledge of the use of parentheses and brackets. You should have encircled 47-1, 47-3, and 47-4 but not 47-2.

_____ Check here if you missed any item.

Be sure to insert a carbon (shiny side up) behind this page.

48

"Did Burns write "Loch Lomond"?" Jacques asked him.   48–1

His ex-wife declared that the alimony was only a "pitiable pittance."   48–2

"She apparently went down the fire escape," the detective announced.   48–3

The detective said, "that she apparently went down the fire escape."   48–4

49

"American deaths caused by automobiles," the safety expert said, "are
triple the number caused by all our wars."   49–1

Does he ever say, "I beg your pardon?"   49–2

"Please hurry"! she begged.   49–3

The animal was called an "ounce;" it was a member of the cat family.   49–4

50

The magazine *U.S. Camera* published his first article, "Photographing
Mountain Scenery."   50–1

The fourth chapter is called *Fundamental Ethics.*   50–2

We listened to Frost's recording of his poem Death of the Hired Man.   50–3

Did you like the short story *The Great Stone Face?*   50–4

51

"Who was Hannibal?" she asked.
"He was a great Carthaginian general," Roy said.   51–1

"We must act at once. Delay is likely to cost us all chance for
victory.
"As I see it," he went on, "we should move toward the delta."   51–2

"Why hurry?" the captain asked. "They'll group their forces against
us if we don't," the major replied.   51–3

The locker room was a babel of voices. "We did it!" "Great game,
Pete!" "Thanks for that block, Jim." "An undefeated season!"   51–4

52

She reads "Time," "Newsweek," and "U.S. News and World Report."   52–1

Carlyle's most famous book is *Sartor Resartus.*   52–2

Both the *Herald* and the *Star* are delivered to our door.   52–3

The court adjudged him "non compos mentis."   52–4

48–1
48–2
48–3
48–4

This group tests your knowledge of the use of quotation marks with direct quotations. You should have encircled 48–2 and 48–3 but no other number.

_____ Check here if you missed any item.

49–1
49–2
49–3
49–4

This group tests your knowledge of the placement of other punctuation marks with quotation marks. You should have encircled 49–1 but no other number.

_____ Check here if you missed any item.

50–1
50–2
50–3
50–4

This group tests your knowledge of the use of quotation marks with certain kinds of titles. You should have encircled 50–1 but no other number.

_____ Check here if you missed any item.

51–1

51–2

51–3

51–4

This group tests your knowledge of paragraphing of conversation. You should have encircled 51–1, 51–2, and 51–4 but not 51–3.

_____ Check here if you missed any item.

52–1
52–2
52–3
52–4

This group tests your knowledge of the use of italics. You should have encircled 52–2 and 52–3 but no other number.

_____ Check here if you missed any item.

53

He called his creations "plaster forms."	53–1

Dear Mrs. Shaw:

                                        Yours Sincerely,   53–2

"I enjoy poetry," said Marcia, "But I've always considered T. S. Eliot
overrated."   53–3

Norman remarked, "the flags are starting to flutter again."   53–4

54

My Aunt majored in Latin and Philosophy.   54–1

My Uncle Fred majored in Greek and history.   54–2

My mother specialized in German and geography.   54–3

A sergeant approached two lieutenants. "I have a message for lieutenant
Cox. Is that you, lieutenant?"   54–4

55

Professor Lane has edited a book called *Introduction To The Short
Story.*   55–1

In American History I am most interested in the colonial period.   55–2

The Gods of ancient Greece supposedly lived on mount Olympus.   55–3

In the Winter my grandparents always live in the South.   55–4

56

The final score was 14 to 9.   56–1

1776 is a crucial date in American history.   56–2

Ship the package to 1132 East Wayne Place, Dayton, Ohio 45424.   56–3

The detectives counted two hundred thirty-nine paper clips scattered on
the floor in Room seventeen.   56–4

53-1

53-2
               This group tests your knowledge of capitalization in sentences and formal parts of letters. You should have encircled 53–1 but no other number.

53-3
               _____ Check here if you missed any item.

53-4

54-1

54-2
               This group tests your knowledge of capitalization of school subjects, titles of relatives, and other titles. You should have encircled 54–2 and 54–3 but no other number.

54-3
               _____ Check here if you missed any item.

54-4

55-1

55-2
               This group tests your knowledge of capitalization of proper names and miscellaneous items. You should not have encircled any number.

55-3
               _____ Check here if you missed any item.

55-4

56-1

56-2
               This group tests your knowledge of conventional ways of indicating numbers. You should have encircled 56–1 and 56–3 but no other number.

56-3
               _____ Check here if you missed any item.

56-4

Be sure to insert a carbon (shiny side up) behind this page.

Part Five—Usage

In groups 57–75 be sure that the sentences you select have all their words in the proper forms.

57

Just between you and me, the motives are questionable.	57–1
The presents are for neither them nor us.	57–2
Clark and him are the next in line.	57–3
The letter was addressed to my brother and I.	57–4

58

The coach works hard with us linemen.	58–1
Two backs, Cornell and me, were demoted to the third team.	58–2
[*On the telephone*] This is he speaking.	58–3
Do you like him acting so superciliously?	58–4

59

Music has always appealed to me so much that I have thought seriously of becoming one.	59–1
The cold winters that they have in northern Canada must be almost unbearable.	59–2
Jim told his father that he had a rip in his shirt.	59–3
The Presidency is the most demanding office in the world. Day after day he must make vital decisions.	59–4

60

Has everybody remembered to bring their tickets?	60–1
If a person drives carefully, they are less likely to contribute to the fatal statistics.	60–2
An old baseball superstition says that if a pitcher strikes out the first batter, you are liable to lose the game.	60–3
After a person has been in the stadium for a while, the crowd does not seem so huge to them.	60–4

57–1
57–2
57–3
57–4

This group tests your knowledge of the cases of personal pronouns to be used as subjects and objects. You should have encircled 57–1 and 57–2 but no other number.

_____ Check here if you missed any item.

58–1
58–2
58–3
58–4

This group tests your knowledge of the cases of pronouns in predicate nominatives, in appositives, and before gerunds. You should have encircled 58–1 and 58–3 but no other number.

_____ Check here if you missed any item.

59–1

59–2
59–3

59–4

This group tests your knowledge of pronoun reference. You should not have encircled any number.

_____ Check here if you missed any item.

60–1

60–2

60–3

60–4

This group tests your knowledge of consistency in pronoun number and case. You should not have encircled any number.

_____ Check here if you missed any item.

61

Three deers were grazing in the orchard.   61–1

Both my sisters-in-law have several criteria for selecting babysitters.   61–2

Potatos are still reasonable in price, but turkeys cost more than we can
afford.   61–3

The two ladies were O'Learys, we discovered.   61–4

62

Does the melon taste good?   62–1

The tone of the piano sounds unusually well in damp weather.   62–2

The new radio does not work very good.   62–3

The plans seem good, but we shall have to try them to discover how
well they will succeed.   62–4

63

Of the two teams, the Astros have the better record.   63–1

His plans are grandioser than ever.   63–2

The sides of the cliff to the west are more vertical than those on the
other side.   63–3

Although Perkins and Bledsoe have never raced against each other, I am
sure that Perkins is the fastest.   63–4

64

Anderson Motors is one company with which I am always pleased to do
business with.   64–1

The children played all day on the shore and the water.   64–2

He could not remember of ever hearing the name *Gostrewski*.   64–3

Soldiers assembled from the hills and the plains.   64–4

65

Senator Gray was terribly reluctant to debate the issue.   65–1

The stranger talked sort of incoherently.   65–2

They sure have a strong defense.   65–3

Although the weather was somewhat chilly, it was not really cold.   65–4

61–1

61–2

61–3

61–4

This group tests your knowledge of certain plural forms. You should have encircled 61–2 and 61–4 but no other number.

_____ Check here if you missed any item.

62–1

62–2

62–3

62–4

This group tests your knowledge of the use of *good* and *well* and thus indirectly your knowledge of other adjectives and adverbs. You should have encircled 62–1 and 62–4 but no other number.

_____ Check here if you missed any item.

63–1

63–2

63–3

63–4

This group tests your knowledge of comparative and superlative uses of adjectives and adverbs. You should have encircled 63–1 but no other number.

_____ Check here if you missed any item.

64–1

64–2

64–3

64–4

This group tests your awareness of both omitted prepositions and unnecessary prepositions. You should have encircled 64–4 but no other number.

_____ Check here if you missed any item.

65–1

65–2

65–3

65–4

This group tests your knowledge of the use of intensifiers (words such as *very, rather,* and *somewhat*). You should have encircled 65–4 but no other number.

_____ Check here if you missed any item.

Be sure to insert a carbon (shiny side up) behind this page.

66

Is either of the novels worth my time?	66–1
The sugar, as well as the sacks of flour, were thrown away.	66–2
Each of the five brothers were over six feet tall.	66–3
His excuse for his black eyes were that he had bumped into two doors.	66–4

67

Between the houses lie a stretch of level land.	67–1
Here is three copies of the manuscript.	67–2
There was a flurry of excitement in the third inning.	67–3
There was several other flurries of excitement later in the game.	67–4

68

The workers and their supervisor were questioned.	68–1
The supervisor and the workers were questioned.	68–2
Either the workers or their supervisor is likely to be questioned.	68–3
Either the supervisor or the workers is likely to be questioned.	68–4

69

A herd of cows was following a winding path toward the barn.	69–1
A herd of cows were cropping grass, chewing their cuds, or switching their tails at bothersome flies.	69–2
The jury has reached a verdict.	69–3
The jury in groups of two or three has been arguing, playing cards, and debating the significance of parts of the evidence.	69–4

70

We had taken our time and had eaten a late breakfast.	70–1
Although I had never rode a horse, I had often driven a wagon.	70–2
George had shaken hands cordially when he left, but he had never wrote to us afterward.	70–3
I always spoke to him, but he had never spoke to me.	70–4

66–1
66–2
66–3
66–4

This group tests your knowledge of the use of singular and plural verbs when words intervene between subject and verb. You should have encircled 66–1 but no other number.

_____ Check here if you missed any item.

67–1
67–2
67–3
67–4

This group tests your knowledge of the use of singular and plural verbs in sentences where the subject follows the verb. You should have encircled 67–3 but no other number.

_____ Check here if you missed any item.

68–1
68–2
68–3
68–4

This group tests your knowledge of the use of singular and plural verbs with compound subjects. You should have encircled 68–1, 68–2, and 68–3 but not 68–4.

_____ Check here if you missed any item.

69–1

69–2
69–3

69–4

This group tests your knowledge of the use of singular and plural verbs with collective nouns as subjects. You should have encircled 69–1, 69–2, and 69–3 but not 69–4.

_____ Check here if you missed any item.

70–1
70–2

70–3
70–4

This group tests your knowledge of the use of the troublesome verbs *drive, eat, ride, shake, speak, take,* and *write.* You should have encircled 70–1 but no other number.

_____ Check here if you missed any item.

Be sure to insert a carbon (shiny side up) behind this page.

71

We had swum easily across the stream, but Mavis had already begun to worry about the return. 71–1

The soprano sung beautifully, as she had never sang before. 71–2

The waterlogged wood has sank beneath the surface, and snakes and catfish have began to live among the ruins. 71–3

After the bell had rang, Flavin had drunk a quart of beer. 71–4

72

She had come from Red Wing, where she had seen pottery being made. 72–1

My trousers were tore, but at least I had not run away like a coward. 72–2

Had you known that such balloons had never burst? 72–3

She has done her duty but has drawn little applause. 72–4

73

The box is laying where I laid it. 73–1

I'd like to lay down, but my tooth hurts more when I'm lying still. 73–2

Lie on the couch if you like, for I have lain down long enough. 73–3

I laid the little boy on his back, and he lay there sleeping. 73–4

74

Orville raised up to his full height. 74–1

I set the canister on a narrow ledge, but it did not sit firmly. 74–2

Don't set too long in the damp night air. 74–3

Prices have risen steadily, but the administration is unwilling to set any limits. 74–4

75

Umpires call balls, strikes, etc. 75–1

The Rev. went to Redding, Calif., on Thurs., Nov. 2. 75–2

The package came C.O.D. from James Calvin, Sr., of Charleston, West Virginia. 75–3

Mr. and Mrs. Green and Dr. Franks stayed until late in the P.M. 75–4

71–1

71–2

71–3

71–4

This group tests your knowledge of the use of the troublesome verbs *begin, drink, ring, sing, sink,* and *swim.* You should have encircled 71–1 but no other number.

_____ Check here if you missed any item.

72–1

72–2

72–3

72–4

This group tests your knowledge of the use of a number of other troublesome verbs. You should have encircled 72–1, 72–3, and 72–4 but not 72–2.

_____ Check here if you missed any item.

73–1

73–2

73–3

73–4

This group tests your knowledge of the use of *lie* and *lay.* You should have encircled 73–3 and 73–4 but no other number.

_____ Check here if you missed any item.

74–1

74–2

74–3

74–4

This group tests your knowledge of the use of *set, sit, raise,* and *rise.* You should have encircled 74–2 and 74–4 but no other number.

_____ Check here if you missed any item.

75–1

75–2

75–3

75–4

This group tests your knowledge of the correct use of abbreviations. You should have encircled 75–3 but no other number.

_____ Check here if you missed any item.

RECORD SHEET

In each space in the "Error" column place a check if you missed one or more items in a group. The second column is to indicate what you need to study if there is a check mark in the first column. (The numbers in the margin correspond to the numbers of the units in *Competence in English*.) The "Mastered" column may be checked when you have studied the indicated material and believe that you have mastered it.

ERROR	UNITS TO STUDY	MASTERED
1		
2		
3		
4		
5		
6		
7		
8		
9		
10		
11		
12		
13		
14		
15		
16		
17		
18		
19		
20		
21		
22		

ERROR	UNITS TO STUDY	MASTERED
23		
24		
25		
26		
27		
28		
29		
30		
31		
32		
33		
34		
35		
36		
37		
38		
39		
40		
41		
42		
43		
44		
45		
46		
47		
48		
49		
50		

ERROR	UNITS TO STUDY	MASTERED
51		
52		
53		
54		
55		
56		
57		
58		
59		
60		
61		
62		
63		
64		
65		
66		
67		
68		
69		
70		
71		
72		
73		
74		
75		

A 7
B 8
C 9
D 0
E 1
F 2
G 3
H 4
I 5
J 6